Smashing Grammar

Smashing Grammar

A guide to improving your writing skills and avoiding common mistakes

Craig Shrives

KYLE BOOKS

Thanks go to my daughter Jade for helping to find so many of the real-life examples and to Kyle Books for having the balls to publish a grammar book by a guy with zero quals.

An Hachette UK Company
www.hachette.co.uk

First published in Great Britain in 2019 by
Kyle Books, an imprint of Kyle Cathie Ltd
Carmelite House
50 Victoria Embankment
London EC4Y 0DZ
www.kylebooks.co.uk

ISBN: 9780857835888

Publisher: Joanna Copestick
Editorial Director: Judith Hannam
Editor: Sarah Kyle
Design: Peter Ward
Production: Lucy Carter

A Cataloguing in Publication record for this title is available from the British Library.

Printed and bound in the UK

10 9 8 7 6 5 4 3 2 1

CONTENTS

About me

I'm not an academic. I joined the British Army when I was 16. I don't have any English-language qualifications. (Actually, that's not true. I've got an O Level (Grade C) from 1983.)

By the time I left my school in Bletchley, my only language skills were in German. (Before my father started working at Bletchley Park, my family had lived in Germany for a decade, and we are all fluent.) Spotting this, the Army recruiters chucked me on a two-year Russian course, and that's where I first dipped a toe in the grammar pond, quickly discovering that learning a language out of a book is very different to learning one off the streets. After training, I deployed to Germany just in time to catch the end of the Cold War. Pretty soon after that ended, the war in Bosnia started, and my working language became Serbo-Croat. Shortly after that one finished, I completed my scramble up the soldiery ranks and became an officer. For the conflicts that followed in much hotter climes, I was a busy, grown-up intelligence officer, and that's when I first needed some English language skills. Luckily, by then, grammar terms were part of my working vocabulary.

Back in the UK and surrounded by intelligence officers who hadn't cut their teeth as linguists, I noticed that most of them tackled writing intuitively, selecting punctuation and sentence structure 'by feel'. Keen to share my understanding of grammar with them, I produced a 400-slide PowerPoint presentation, which my Commanding Officer allowed me to inflict on some fellow officers. (Sorry, guys.) By 10 a.m., far too many of them were nodding off for the training day to continue. Blaming PowerPoint for failing to impart my grammar knowledge, I learned a bit of HTML and Javascript and converted my 400-slider into www.grammar-monster.com. That was in 1999. I've been fine-tuning it ever since.

In the intelligence game, you read lots of reports – often hundreds a day. When it's time to brief the generals (who are always heart-attack busy), it's not your job to tell them everything you've read but only the bits that matter, and then why. Intelligence officers call this the 'so what?' moment of the intelligence briefing. In this book, each entry ends with a 'so what?' moment, with a heading like 'Why should I care about adverbs?'. The grammar blurb and the examples beforehand are just the intelligence reports.

So, that O Level from 1983, the languages, the website and all the fights with co-authors of countless staff papers and intelligence reports are what make up my experience. I see *Smashing Grammar* as a vocational grammar book, not an academic one. If those incomprehensible grammar entries on Wikipedia, which bear all the signs of linguistics ninjas, are the left of arc, then I wrote this book to be the right of arc. I know there is still a lot I could learn from the academic community, but perhaps this book offers something they could learn from my community: tell all that's needed, not all that's known.

How the entries for this book were chosen

My website has been around for about two decades. It receives more than 500,000 hits a month, and those visitors have raised thousands of questions and observations. Being bit of a data geek, I've been tracking the topics of all that correspondence and who's been sending it. This 'big data' analysis determined the entries for this book. For example, almost no native English speakers asked questions about verb tense, but lots of them asked questions about the subjunctive mood (yeah, really). For that reason, tense is shoehorned into the 'Verb' entry, while the subjunctive mood has its own entry.

My strong sense is that this alignment to the 'big data' has worked. If I were to create, by intuition, a list of the grammar issues that most often affect native English speakers, it would closely match the list generated by the website data. Phew. So, if you expected less or more coverage of a specific topic in a grammar glossary like this one, please be aware that the entries weren't prioritised by a SWAG (Scientific Wild Arse Guess).

Using this book

As this is a reference book about grammar, it's pretty unlikely you'll read it from cover to cover. To help you get the most from it, there are two indexes: a functional index (see page 8) and an alphabetical index (see contents page).

● **The Functional Index**. If you're new to grammar, use this to prioritise your reading.
● **The Alphabetical Index**. Use this to track down a grammar term.

If you were to read this book from cover to cover, you'd notice that some issues were repeated. That's deliberate. The rationale is that someone looking up commas wants to know everything about commas without being sent to all the entries that discuss commas (e.g. adverb, conjunction, clause, vocative case). So please expect some repetition. Rest assured though that every entry uses different examples and presents the grammar points from the perspective of that entry.

✔ = correct or better ✘ = wrong or dodgy

The plan

Lots of people have sound writing skills, but if you talk grammar specifics with them, you'll notice that many are flying by the seat of their pants. It seems their skills have been assimilated osmosis-like over many years. Attaining that level of competence must have been a far tougher process than it needed to be, a lengthy onslaught of unstructured lessons learned. This book aims to capture those lessons learned, order them logically and then present them in a way that is entertaining, succinct and easily searchable. You can get there quicker than we did. That's the plan. There's a plan?

Common Mistakes:
A Functional Index
(In Order Of Severity)

✔ = correct or better   ✘ = wrong or dodgy

MISTAKES THAT COULD DAMAGE YOUR CREDIBILITY

MISTAKES THAT MAKE YOU LOOK CARELESS

MISTAKES YOU'LL BE FORGIVEN FOR

MISTAKES YOU'LL PROBABLY GET AWAY WITH

'MISTAKES' THAT MIGHT ANNOY SOME READERS (THESE AREN'T MISTAKES)

A–Z
of
Punctuation

Apostrophe

An apostrophe (') is a punctuation mark used:

- to show possession (e.g. one **dog's** kennel, two **dogs'** kennel)
- in time expressions (e.g. a **day's** pay, two **weeks'** holiday)
- in contractions (e.g. **can't**, **isn't**, **don't**)
- to show an awkward plural, if it helps your readers (e.g. Hawaii has two **i's**.).

Apostrophes are not used:

- to show normal plurals (e.g. three cat's ✗, two video's ✗)
- randomly before the letter s (e.g. He like's me. ✗).

EXAMPLES USED FOR POSSESSION

- **Wagner's** music is better than it sounds. (Author Mark Twain)
- My reputation as a **ladies'** man led to 10,000 nights alone. (Singer Leonard Cohen)

The big question is whether to put the apostrophe before or after the s.

Basic Rule: The apostrophe goes before the s for a singular possessor (e.g. **one dog's** kennel) and after the s when there are two or more possessors (e.g. **two dogs'** kennel).

In these examples, *dog* and *dogs* are the possessors. The position of the apostrophe has nothing to do with *kennel*. The thing being possessed (let's call it the 'possessee') can be singular or plural. It has no influence on where the apostrophe goes:

- *one dog's* dinner, *one dog's* dinners, *two dogs'* dinner, *two dogs'* dinners. ✔

For the rest of this section, we're going to use the terms 'possessor' (here, *dog* or *dogs*) and 'possessee' (here, *dinner* or *dinners*). These are not common terms for explaining how to use apostrophes for possession, but they should be. ('Possessors' are really called possessive nouns, and 'possessees' are really the complements of possessive nouns.)

The basic rule seems quite straightforward, but there are four quirks.

Quirk 1. A plural possessor that doesn't end in s (e.g. children, women, people, men). In this case, put your apostrophe before the s.

- **children's** toys, **men's** sizes, **people's** poet

    (Possession is sometimes used in the loosest terms. For example, *women's hat* is a hat for women, and *Picasso's painting* is a painting by Picasso.)

Quirk 2. A singular possessor that ends in s. In this case (e.g. *Wales, Moses, Chris Wells*), either add just an apostrophe or an apostrophe and s, depending on how you (yes, you personally) pronounce it.

- **Dr Evans'** report (correct for those who say *Dr Evans report*)
- **Dr Evans's** report (correct for those who say *Dr Evansiz report*)

It's a common convention (by no means a rule) to use just an apostrophe with religious characters and ancient Greek and Roman names.
- **Moses'** tablet was the first to download files from a cloud.
- **Zeus'** thunderbolts didn't always hit their targets.

Quirk 3. A possessor that's a compound noun. With a compound noun like *mother-in-law*, add *'s* to the end, regardless of whether it is singular or plural.

Singular	Plural
sister-in-law's car	sisters-in-law's husbands
maid of honour's bouquet	maids of honour's dresses

Quirk 4. Two possessors. With two possessors, apply the apostrophe ruling to both for individual ownership but just the second for joint ownership.
- **Andrew's and Jacob's** factories (individual ownership)
- **Andrew and Jacob's** factory (joint ownership)
- **India's and Pakistan's** problems (individual ownership, i.e. separate problems)
- **India and Pakistan's** problems (joint ownership, i.e. common to both)

With the individual-ownership construction, it might be unclear whether a plural possessee (*factories* in the first example) means 'one each' or 'more than one each'. Without context, readers will assume that Andrew has one factory and Jacob has one. Another construction is required if this is not the case. (*Andrew's factories and Jacob's factories* is one option.)

EXAMPLES USED IN TIME, VALUE AND DISTANCE EXPRESSIONS

Apostrophes are used in time expressions (also called temporal expressions) such as *a day's pay* and *two weeks' notice*. The big question with these is where to put the apostrophe, and the good news is we've already covered it. The apostrophe goes before the s for a single unit of time (e.g. **one** *day's pay*) and after the s when it's plural (e.g. **two** *days' pay*).
- I never did a **day's** work in my life. It was all fun. (Inventor Thomas Edison)
- Fill the unforgiving minute with sixty **seconds'** worth of distance run. (Poet Rudyard Kipling)

The next examples relate to value and distance.
- Lee has eaten a **pound's** worth of liquorice and two **pounds' worth** of sherbet.
- My neighbour has had 44 concussions. He lives close to me – a **stone's** throw away, in fact. (Anon)

EXAMPLES USED TO REPLACE LETTERS

An apostrophe can be used to replace a letter (or letters) in a word to reflect how we speak. More often than not, this practice will involve merging two words into one. (See Contractions, page 124.)

● When I was born, I was so surprised I **didn't** talk for a year and a half. (Comedian Gracie Allen)
  (Here, *didn't* is a contraction of *did* and *not*. The apostrophe replaces the *o* in *not*.)
● **I'd** agree, but then **we'd** both be wrong. (Anon)
  (Here, *I'd* is a contraction of *I would*, and *we'd* is a contraction of *we would*.)

EXAMPLES IN AWKWARD PLURALS

Apostrophes are not normally used to show plurals, and lots of your readers will hate it if you use an apostrophe for this purpose. However, there are times when it helps.

● There are no **a's** in definite and definitely.
● You use too many **but's** in your writing.
● Your **z's** look like **2's**.

WHY SHOULD I CARE ABOUT APOSTROPHES?

You will notice that the top four 'mistakes that could damage your credibility' on page 8 are all linked to apostrophes. So, it's worth learning about them. You are definitely being judged. Here are the key issues related to apostrophes.

Issue 1. Be accurate when identifying your possessor. Identify the posessor and then put the apostrophe immediately after it. If you do this, you can ignore the first two quirks on page 14.

Category	What are you trying to say?	Write it with no apostrophe	Identify the possessor	Put your apostrophe immediately afterwards
singular noun	ball of the dog	dogs ball	dog	dog's ball ✔
plural noun	kennel of the dogs	dogs kennel	dogs	dogs' kennel ✔
plural noun not ending in s	poet of the people	peoples poet	people	people's poet ✔
singular noun ending in s	emblem of Wales	Wales emblem	Wales	Wales' emblem ✔ (see quirk 2 on pages 14–15)

If you identify the possessor accurately and put your apostrophe next, it will always be correct. Always.

- Charles Dickens' novel
  (His name is Charles Dickens.)
- John Dicken's profile
  (This person is John Dicken.)

Interestingly, possessive apostrophes are linked to those that replace letters. In old English, possession was shown by adding es *(e.g. doges nose, dogses noses)*. The apostrophe later replaced the e or the es to reflect how people spoke, giving us *dog's nose* and *dogs' noses*.

This little history lesson gives us another simple process that works for every type of noun, regardless of its ending or whether it's singular or plural. First, identify the possessor and add es (like they used to). Then replace the e with an apostrophe. If the word now ends s's (which is a bit scruffy), delete the last s.

Category	Word to make possessive	Add es	Replace e with apostrophe	If it ends s's, delete the last
singular noun	man	manes	man's	man's ✔
plural noun	slugs	slugses	slugs's	slugs' ✔
plural noun	women	womenes	women's	women's ✔
not ending s singular noun ending s	species	specieses	species's (see quirk 2 on pages 14–15)	species' ✔

Issue 2. Don't add an apostrophe just because a word ends with an s. This is a common mistake, and it's a credibility-smashing howler.

- I like **pig's**. **Dog's** look up to us. **Cat's** look down on us. **Pig's** treat us as **equal's**. ✗
- **Tomato's** and oregano make it Italian; wine and tarragon, French; garlic, good. ✗
  (Nouns ending in an o or a (video's ✗ banana's ✗) are especially prone to this error.)
- A spoken word is not a sparrow. Once it **fly's** out, you cannot catch it. ✗
  (This mistake occurs with verbs too. This should be *flies*.)

Issue 3. Don't use an apostrophe just because you've written a unit of time in the plural (e.g. seconds, hours, weeks, days, years). Only use an apostrophe where the word *of* could have been used.

- a **year's** insurance (a year of insurance), two **weeks'** holiday (two weeks of holiday) ✔

● Old age is always 15 **years'** older than I am. ✗ (Badly written quotation of painter Francis Bacon)

Issue 4. Be careful with *it's, you're* and *they're.* Don't confuse the contractions *it's, you're* and *they're* with *its, your* and *there/their.* A mistake involving one of these is a howler.

Here's a fool-proof way to avoid a mistake with *it's, you're* or *they're*: never use them. This tip works because you can always expand them to *it is* (or *it has*), *you are* or *they are.* So, you don't need to use them at all. A bit draconian? Okay, let's soften the tip. If you can't expand your *it's, you're* or *they're* to the full version, then you should be using *its, your* or *their/there.* (See also Determiners on page 133.)

Issue 5. The contractions *could've, should've* and *would've* expand to *could have, should have* and *would have.* You won't get away with writing *could of, should of* or *would of.* Not once.

● **Could of** ironed it. ✗

(In March 2018, an internet troll posted a picture of a badly creased International Women's Day banner with the caption above. He was attacked more for writing *could of* than for being sexist.)

Issue 6. Think seriously about avoiding an apostrophe that shows an awkward plural. This is still highly unpopular, so it's worth looking for an alternative.

● There is no A in definite or definitely.
  (Instead of 'There are no a's in definite and definitely.')
● You use 'but' too much in your writing.
  (Instead of 'You use too many but's in your writing.')
● Your Zs look like 2s.
  (Instead of 'Your z's look like 2's.')

If the alternative looks unwieldy, use an apostrophe for your plural – and fight like a dog if challenged.

KEY POINTS
When showing possession, everything to the left of the
apostrophe is the possessor.
If you can't expand your *it's, you're* or *they're* to a
two-word version, then it's wrong.
Don't write *could of, should of* or *would of.* Ever.
Don't shove an apostrophe into a word just because it ends with an *s.*

Brackets (Round)

Round brackets ( ) are used:

- to insert additional information into text (the additional information is usually an expansion or clarification of whatever preceded, or an afterthought)
- to introduce an abbreviation
- to show a plural option alongside a singular one.

EXAMPLES TO INSERT ADDITIONAL INFORMATION INTO TEXT

- The stegosaurus (*a genus of herbivorous thyreophoran dinosaur*) was predated by the allosaurus.
  (The round brackets insert an expansion.)
- The stegosaurus (*the herbivore with scales on its back and a spikey tail*) weighed the same as a car.
  (The round brackets insert a clarification.)
- The plates on a stegosaurus's back were for display. (*It is unlikely they had a thermoregulatory function like an elephant's ears.*)
  (The round brackets insert an afterthought.)

The additional information (italics) is called a parenthesis. A parenthesis can be removed without any loss of meaning.

EXAMPLES TO INTRODUCE AN ABBREVIATION

If there's a chance your readers might not be familiar with an abbreviation, it is standard practice to write it out in full the first time it's used and to put the abbreviation in brackets afterwards.

- The Master of Business Administration **(MBA)** teaches business management.

EXAMPLES TO SHOW A PLURAL OPTION

- Please append the name of your **guest(s)** to the list.
  (This avoids 'your guest or guests'.)

When using brackets to show a plural option, it could start getting complicated if you provided an option with everything that ought to change.

- Ensure the **rod(s) is (are)** aligned with the top section.
  (This is untidy.)
- The routine uses the **output(s)** of that **(those) process(es)**.
  (This is almost unreadable.)

The normal practice is to use (s) or (es) with just the key word and to treat everything else as singular.

- The routine uses the output of that **process(es).**

Using brackets to present two ideas at once is sometimes used for a bit of fun.

● Bring your A game on Monday. We're going to crack Mission **(Im)possible.**
● I'm calling it an **(experi)mental** project.

WHY SHOULD I CARE ABOUT ROUND BRACKETS?

Here are the three most common issues raised regarding round brackets.

Issue 1. Brackets are considered informal. Brackets are a great way to add additional information because they're easy to spot and won't disrupt reading flow. However, lots of businesses and universities do not permit their use in formal documents. Don't worry. You can use commas or dashes instead.

● The stegosaurus, the best-known herbivorous dinosaur, had a brain the size of a ping-pong ball.
● The stegosaurus – the iconic dinosaur that lived 150 million years ago – had a top speed of five miles per hour.

Be aware that brackets trump commas and dashes when used like this:

● A large stegosaurus could be 9 metres (29.5 feet) long and weigh 7 tonnes (15,432 pounds).
  (Everyone permits brackets for this purpose.)

The advantages and disadvantages of brackets, commas and dashes are covered in Parenthetical Punctuation on page 49.

Issue 2. Uncertainty over whether the full stop goes inside or outside the close bracket. The big question with brackets is where to put the end punctuation (usually a full stop). Does it go inside or outside the brackets? When using brackets, the positioning of end punctuation follows logic. Sometimes it goes outside the close bracket, and sometimes it goes inside.

● She will ride a pony. (However, she will not ride a Dartmoor pony.) ✔
  (The full stop belongs to the full sentence in the brackets.)
● She will ride a pony (but not a Dartmoor pony). ✔
  (The full stop belongs to the main sentence, not to the text in the brackets.)
● She will ride a pony (she told me yesterday) but not a Dartmoor pony. ✔
  (The text inside the brackets (i.e. the parenthesis) is a standalone sentence within another sentence. When this happens, you should start the parenthesis with a lowercase letter and omit the full stop.)

Things can get quirky with question marks and exclamation marks because you might need to double up on end punctuation. The principle is the same: end punctuation follows logic.

- The group paid with a stolen credit card (my credit card!). ✔
  (The exclamation mark belongs with *my credit card*, and the full stop ends the whole sentence.)
- The group paid with a stolen credit card (didn't you lose your card?). ✔
  (The question mark belongs with the bracketed question, while the full stop ends the sentence.)

Issue 3. There can be uncertainty with capital letters when expanding an abbreviation. When introducing an abbreviation, there's nothing to think about if the abbreviation represents the name of something (i.e. a proper noun).

- The motto for the Federal Bureau of Investigation (FBI) is 'fidelity, bravery, integrity'.

If your abbreviation does not represent a proper noun, you must decide whether to use capital letters.

- Food crops are the most controversial genetically modified organism (GMO).
  (With this style, the definition of the abbreviation isn't immediately obvious.)
- The term Genetically Modified Organism (GMO) was popularised by the media, not scientists.
  (The capital letters aren't justifiable under capitalisation rules, but the definition of the abbreviation now stands out.)

So, each option has a pro and a con. If the institution you're writing for doesn't offer any guidelines, then pick a method and be consistent. (If you go for the 'non-caps' option, you'll have far fewer pedants on your case.)

KEY POINTS

Brackets are a great way to insert additional information (called a parenthesis).
You can insert additional information using commas or dashes if you think brackets are too clumsy.
The placement of end punctuation with a close bracket follows logic (like this).
(It just follows logic.)

Brackets (Square)

Square brackets [ ] are used in quotations to show that the text within is not the work of the original author. More specifically, they are used in quotations:

- to explain something in the quotation
- to modify the quotation
- to replace unnecessary text with [...] (called an ellipsis).

Conversely, they are used with [sic] to show that the quoted text **is** the work of the original author.

EXAMPLES TO EXPLAIN SOMETHING IN A QUOTATION

In these examples, the original text is intact, but an explanation has been inserted using square brackets. Square brackets tell your readers that the bracketed text did not feature in the original.

- 'Most people save all their lives and leave it **[their money]** to somebody else.' (Actress Hedy Lamarr)
- 'It **[electricity]** is really just organized lightning.' (Comedian George Carlin)

EXAMPLES TO MODIFY A QUOTATION

In the next examples, the original text has been modified. The words that needed explaining have been replaced with the explanations.

- 'Most people save all their lives and leave **[their money]** to somebody else.'
- '**[Electricity]** is really just organized lightning.'

This technique is also used to alter a quotation to ensure it aligns grammatically.

- Angela Merkel believes 'it's **[her]** damn duty and obligation to do everything possible for Europe to find a united path.'
  (The original quotation was 'It's my damn duty ...')
- Quoting author Flannery O'Connor, Jason often reminded his children that '**[t]he** truth **[did]** not change according to **[their]** ability to stomach it.'
  (Original 'The truth does not change according to our ability to stomach it'.)

Typically, aligning a quotation means changing a pronoun (e.g. *my* to *his*) or changing a verb tense (e.g. *does* to *did*). Some people also like to show that a capital letter has been changed to a lowercase letter, as in the second example. (That's a bit much, IMHO.) If you find yourself tweaking other types of words, be careful not to change the intended meaning of the quotation. Also, if you find yourself over-tweaking, try to revert to the original quotation.

- Alice Cooper famously said that 'from the moment **[he]** leave**[s] [his]** house or hotel room, the public owns **[him]**.' ✗ (This is a mess.)
- Alice Cooper famously said: 'From the moment I leave my house or hotel room, the public owns me.' ✔ (This is much tidier.)

EXAMPLES TO REPLACE UNNECESSARY TEXT

Three dots (called an ellipsis) are often used to show that text has been omitted from a quotation. An ellipsis punctuation mark is written '...' or '[...]'.

- Education is the most powerful weapon […] to change the world.
(President Nelson Mandela) (The ellipsis replaces the words 'which you can use'.)
- Andy Warhol is the only genius […] with an IQ of 60. (Author Gore Vidal)
(The ellipsis replaces the words 'I've ever known'.)

EXAMPLES WITH [SIC]

The term '[*sic*]' shows that the preceding text featured in the original quotation. Often, [*sic*] is used to indicate that a writing error was committed by the original author.

- He claimed his statement was 'appropriate and did not undermine the moral [*sic*] of our troops'.
(It should be *morale*, not *moral*.)

[Sic] is the opening word of *sic erat scriptum* (Latin for 'thus was it written'). It is not an acronym meaning 'said in copy' or 'spelling is correct'. Therefore, [s.i.c.] is wrong. *[sic]* is not solely used for highlighting writing errors. It can be used to highlight unusual word usage (e.g. archaisms, dialectic language), surprising facts or facts known to be wrong.

WHY SHOULD I CARE ABOUT SQUARE BRACKETS?

There are two good reasons to care about square brackets.

Reason 1. Square brackets allow you to fit quotations snugly into your work.
Quotations are a great way to incorporate information from other sources into your writing, and they are particularly useful for supporting arguments. Quotations carry a sense of honesty and believability. They're like an impartial vote for your assertion. You can use square brackets to trim quotations to fit into your writing. So, chop and change away, but remember not to change the intended meaning.

Reason 2. Slam someone with [sic]. If you're ever the recipient of antagonistic correspondence that contains a writing error, you could use [*sic*] to slam the sender for their error.

- Antagonist: I am not adverse to change, but I will not be voting for your proposal.
You: I'm pleased you're not adverse [*sic*] to change because my proposal has been approved.
(The antagonist should have used *averse*. Using [*sic*] this way is fairly aggressive. Do it sparingly.)

KEY POINT
Use square brackets to make quotations clearer or a better fit for your work, but take care not to change the original meaning.

Colon

A colon (:) is a punctuation mark used as a separator. Also called a 'full colon', a colon is used:

- at the end of an introduction (e.g. I know this much: he is disappointed.)
- before an end-of-sentence appositive (e.g. He needs just one trait: discipline.)
- before quotations (e.g. Here's my advice: 'Don't jump'.)
- in references, ratios, times and titles (e.g. Read Matthew 2:1 before 11:00.).

EXAMPLES IN INTRODUCTIONS

- I have made an important discovery: alcohol, taken in sufficient quantities, produces all the effects of intoxication. (Playwright Oscar Wilde)
  (Notice how the text on the right of the colon equals *an important discovery* in the introduction.)
- Here's my advice for those who want to receive the Lifetime Achievement Award. Start early! (Actress Shirley Temple)
  (Notice how the text on the right of the colon equals *my advice*. Also, when the text on the right is a sentence, it can be written with a capital letter.)

EXAMPLES WITH APPOSITIVES AT THE END OF A SENTENCE

A colon can be used to introduce an appositive (an 'equal term' that renames something previously mentioned; *see also* Appositive on page 91).

- He blamed his divorce on one thing: beer.
  (The appositive is *beer*. It renames *one thing*.)
- In life, you need three things: a wishbone, a backbone and a funny bone. (Anon)
  (The appositive renames three things.)

You might find it useful to think of a colon as an equals sign (=).

- I would like to change just one aspect of your draft: the words.
  (*one aspect = the words*)
- The Victorian printing set is missing the following characters: Q, R, K and the question mark.
  (*following characters = Q, R, K and the question mark*)

EXAMPLES IN REFERENCES, RATIOS, TIMES AND TITLES

A colon can be used as a separator in references, ratios, times and titles.

- Genesis 1:1 starts 'In the beginning God created the heavens and the earth.' (Reference)
- It's myth that the ratio of women to men in Nottingham is 6:1. (Ratio)
- The happiest hour of the day is between 19:00 and 20:00. (Time)

- The marathon world record is 2:02:57. The 800-metre world record is 1:40.91. (Time)
  (Colons can be used in timings greater than a minute.)
- *Pirates of the Caribbean: Dead Man's Chest* (Title)
  (A comma or the word *or* are also commonly used to separate a title from a subtitle.)

EXAMPLES WITH QUOTATIONS

A quotation can be preceded by a colon, a comma or nothing. You should opt for a colon when the introduction is an independent clause (i.e. when it could stand alone as a sentence). You could also opt for a colon if the quotation itself is an independent clause, especially if you intend to start it with a capital letter.

- The guides in Gibraltar give the same advice: 'Leave the apes alone, and they'll leave you alone.'
- The prisoner muttered: 'Leave me alone.'
  (You could use a comma here. See *also* Quotation Marks on page 52.)

WHY SHOULD I CARE ABOUT COLONS?

There are three noteworthy reasons to care about colons.

Reason 1. Use an end-of-sentence appositive to mix up your writing style, for emphasis and to show off a little. Using a colon to introduce an appositive at the end of a sentence is not common in everyday writing, but it's a good tool to keep in your back pocket for mixing up your sentence structures to keep your writing interesting. Also, an end-of-sentence appositive has the feel of a punchline, so it is an effective way to create emphasis.

- His success is attributed to one thing: determination.
  (Emphasises determination.)

Reason 2. Don't use a colon like a semicolon. A semicolon (;) can be used to merge two closely related sentences into one when a full stop feels like too much of a speed bump between sentences (see page 57). You can't use a colon for this. (Remember that a colon is like an equals sign when it extends a sentence. The text on the right must be a renaming of something on the left.)

- Many receive advice: only the wise profit from it. ✗
  (These are two closely related sentences. A semicolon would have worked here, but a colon doesn't.)
- If stock market experts were so expert, they'd be buying stock: they wouldn't bestselling advice. ✗
  (The text on the right is not renaming anything on the left.)

Similarly, don't use a semicolon like a colon. So, don't use a semicolon to introduce lists (a common mistake), and don't use a semicolon to introduce an appositive.

Reason 3. Avoid a colon to introduce a list if your introduction is not an independent clause. If you're using a colon before a normal list (i.e. not a vertical list like bullet points), to keep things grammatically pure, try to write an independent clause for your introduction.

- The team will be the following: Fred Bloggs, Joe Bloggs and John Doe. ✔
  (The introduction for this list is an independent clause, so the colon is justified.)
- The team will be: Fred Bloggs, Joe Bloggs and John Doe. ✘
  (Strict grammarians would tut at this because the introduction is not an independent clause.)

When introducing a vertical list (e.g. with bullet points or numbers), there's more leniency.
- The team will be:
  (1) Fred Bloggs
  (2) Joe Bloggs
  (3) John Doe. ✔

As some stricter pedants might view even this as sloppy, try to write an introduction that's an independent clause.
- The following points were noted during the fire-safety survey:
  (1) fire exits blocked by empty PC boxes
  (2) batteries dead in smoke detectors
  (3) waste-paper bins used as ashtrays.

Many writers craft their introductions to include '*the following*', which helps to create an independent clause, justifying the colon.
- The winners are: John, Sarah and Simon. ✘
  (Untidy. 'The winners are John, Sarah and Simon' would be safe.)
- The winners are the following: John, Sarah and Simon. ✔
  (An introduction with *the following* might feel incomplete, but from a grammatical perspective, it's good enough to create an independent clause.)

Let's not pretend this isn't pedantry. The example below (which features a colon on each line) is fine, and it has no independent clauses.
- Contact us by:
  (1) Phone: 01908 311267
  (2) Email: colin@lion-tamers.co.uk
  (3) Twitter: @liontamers

KEY POINTS
There are three good reasons to use a colon with an appositive at the end of sentence: to spice up your writing, to emphasise a point and to show off.
When introducing a list, consider using the words *the following* to avoid scrutiny of your colon.

Comma

A comma (,) is a punctuation mark used to mark the divisions in text caused by phrases, clauses or conjunctions. Commas are also used to separate list items and in numbers to aid reading.

EASY EXAMPLES

When to use a comma	Examples
After 'setting the scene' at the start of a sentence	In our solar system, there are eight planets.
After a transitional word like *however* or *therefore*	Venus takes 243 days to rotate and 225 days to orbit the Sun. Therefore, a day is longer than a year on Venus.
After an interjection (e.g. *hey, yes* or *crikey*)	Yes, there is ice in Mercury's permanently shadowed craters.
Before a conjunction (e.g. *and, or, but*) joining two independent clauses	Saturn has over 60 moons, but Venus has none.
To separate list items	The Martian atmosphere is 95 per cent carbon dioxide, 39 per cent nitrogen, 1.6 per cent argon and 0.4 per cent other bits and bobs.
To offset nonessential information	Neptune's winds, according to NASA, blow faster than the speed of sound on Earth.
When addressing someone directly	'Houston, we have a problem.' (Tom Hanks in *Apollo 13*)
Before a quotation	Apollo 13 astronaut Jack Swigert actually said, 'Okay, Houston, we've had a problem here.'
In numbers	The Earth is 149,598,262km from the Sun.

EXAMPLES AFTER 'SETTING THE SCENE'

It is common for a sentence to start with a phrase or clause that 'sets the scene'. Offset by a comma, these scene-setting words usually tell the reader where, when, why or how the action takes place (i.e. they function as adverbs), or they describe something in the main part of the sentence (i.e. they function as adjectives).

27

- **In Nicaragua,** it is common to point with the lips instead of the index finger.
  (This is an adverbial phrase. It sets the place.)
- **In September,** share prices tend to lose one per cent of their value.
  (This is an adverbial phrase. It sets the time.)
- **If you are explaining,** you are losing. (President Ronald Reagan)
  (This is an adverbial clause. It sets a condition.)

These 'fronted' (as they're called) scene-setting words vary hugely.

- **Naughty but nice,** a cream tea is a must when visiting Devon.
- **Tall, solidly built, face adorned by a luxuriant growth of whiskers that swept down from his ears to his clean-shaven chin,** Ambrose E. Burnside was a fine figure of a man – imposing, dapper and conspicuous. (Major John B. Pizer)
  (Each is an adjective phrase describing a noun (underlined). *See also* Adjective, Adverb and Present and Past Participle on pages 67, 77 and 213.)

EXAMPLES AFTER A TRANSITIONAL PHRASE

A transitional phrase (or a conjunctive adverb, as it's also called) is a word or phrase like *however, consequently, therefore* and *as a result.* It sits at the start of sentence and acts like a bridge to an idea in the previous sentence. A transitional phrase is followed by a comma, not preceded by one.

- All progress is initiated by challenging current conceptions. **Consequently,** the first condition of progress is the removal of censorships. (Playwright George Bernard Shaw).

EXAMPLES AFTER AN INTERJECTION

An interjection is usually a short word inserted into a sentence (normally at the start) to express an emotion or feeling. Expressions such as 'yes', 'phew' and 'indeed' are interjections. They are usually offset with commas.

- **Yes**, aphids often give birth to pregnant aphids.
- Thanks for saying '**Wow**, you're photogenic' and not '**Hey**, you're ugly in person'.
  (Comedian Jimmy Fallon)

If the interjection expresses a powerful emotion or feeling (and it's not mid-sentence), then it can be followed by an exclamation mark. (*See* Exclamation Mark on page 40.)

EXAMPLES BEFORE A CONJUNCTION

When a word like *and, or* or *but* (see Conjunctions on page 115) joins two independent clauses (ones that could stand alone as sentences), it is usual to precede the conjunction (bold) with a comma.

- Lee can sing, **and** he can do the robot.
  (The conjunction *and* joins two independent clauses: 'Lee can sing' and 'He can do the robot.')
- Actors are con men, **and** con men are actors. (Actor Edward Burns)

● Our eyes are always the same size from birth, **but** our nose and ears never stop growing.

Here are incorrect examples:
● Lee can sing, **and** do the robot ✗
(Here, *and* is not joining two clauses that could stand alone as sentences. This is just a list of things that Lee can do. This section is not about using commas in lists. That's next.)
● When you have got an elephant by the hind leg, **and** he's trying to run away, let him run. ✗ (President Abraham Lincoln)
(*When you have got an elephant by the hind leg* could not stand alone as a sentence.)

EXAMPLES IN A LIST
When writing a list in sentence form (i.e. not as bullet points), it's normal to separate the list items with commas.
● Fish, chips, peas and scratchings.
● Fish, chips, peas, and scratchings.

The big question is whether to use a comma before the *and* (called a coordinating conjunction). Unfortunately, there's no simple rule for this. In general, when there are just two items in a list, there's no comma.
● Fish and chips ✔
● Fish, and chips ✗

However, you can use a comma if you think it helps your reader.
● The Bakerloo Line runs between Harrow and Wealdstone, and Elephant and Castle ✔.
(A comma is typically used with two list items when one or both of the list items includes an *and*.)

Things get trickier when there are three or more list items. In that case, those following US convention should use a comma before the conjunction (usually *and* or *or*), and those following UK convention shouldn't.
● Fish, chips **and** peas
(No comma is the most common convention in the UK.)
● Hamburger, fries **, and** a shake
(The comma is practically demanded in the US.)

However, it's not that simple. The comma before the conjunction in a list is known as an Oxford comma, because it's used by the Oxford University Press. So, as you might expect, the Oxford comma is used by some individuals and organisations in the UK. (There's more on the Oxford comma to come.)

Commas can also be used to separate a list of adjectives.

● He was a condescending, unfulfilled, nit-picking and tortured man.
(Neither the *and* nor the commas are essential. There's a lot of leniency with a chain of adjectives. See also Adjectives on page 67.)

EXAMPLES TO OFFSET NONESSENTIAL INFORMATION

Commas can be used to offset nonessential information (as can brackets and dashes). Nonessential information (known as a parenthesis) is usually a word, phrase or clause added as an explanation or afterthought. A parenthesis is sometimes called an interrupter, as it interrupts the flow of text. When a parenthesis is removed, the surrounding text is still grammatically sound.

● Cleopatra, who was born in 69 BC and died in 30 BC, lived closer to the release of the first iPhone, which came in 2007, than she did to the building of the Great Pyramid of Giza, which was completed around 2560 BC.

● Actresses fear being disliked. I, on the other hand, revel in it.
(Actor Michael Douglas)

If you deleted the nonessential information in the examples above, there would be no loss of meaning. The only thing missing would be the information deleted. Look at these examples though.

● Alan's sister, who lives in London, has lost her cat. ✔
(This is like the ones above. *Who lives in London* is nonessential information. Reading this, someone would infer that Alan has one sister. The underlined text is called a non-restrictive modifier.)

● Alan's sister who lives in London has lost her cat. ✔
(This is different. Here, *who lives in London* is essential information because it tells us which sister. Reading this, someone would infer that Alan has more than one sister. Removing *who lives in London* would affect the meaning of the sentence. The underlined text is essential information, so it's not offset with commas. It's called a restrictive modifier.) See also Relative Pronoun on page 221.

EXAMPLES AFTER A LONG SUBJECT

Some writers like to show the end of a complicated subject with a comma. This is not a popular practice, but if you think it helps your reader, you can do it.

● Leaving a list of internet passwords, increasing your life insurance and writing a will, will give you peace of mind. ✔
(The writer judges that a comma after *will* helps to group the subject for the reader.)

● He who knows, does not speak. He who speaks, does not know. ✔
(Chinese philosopher Lao Tzu)
(The translator judges that the commas after the subjects are helpful. The commas also add a pause for effect.)

Here's an example without a comma marking the end of the subject.

● He who does not know how to create should not know. (Poet Antonio Porchia)
  Did you identify the subject without backtracking?

EXAMPLES WITH NUMBERS
Commas can be used every three decimal places in large numbers to make them more readable.

● 12,128,153,356   175,757.01

EXAMPLES BEFORE A QUOTATION
When a quotation is preceded by words like 'He said', 'The author stated' or 'Anna wrote' (called words of attribution), a comma can be used afterwards to separate them from the quotation.

● She declared, 'You look better without your glasses.' He whispered to himself, 'So do you.'

You don't have to use a comma here. You could use nothing. You could even consider a colon (:) if either the quotation or the introduction is an independent clause and could stand alone as a sentence. (*See also* Colon and Quotation Marks on pages 24 and 52.)

EXAMPLES WITH THE VOCATIVE CASE
Words used to address somebody or something directly are said to be in the vocative case. (*See also* Vocative Case on pages 97–99.) Words in the vocative case are offset with commas.

● I know your sister, Jason. ✔
● Will I be able to play the piano, Doctor? ✔

WHY SHOULD I CARE ABOUT COMMAS?
Were you told a comma is where you take a breath? This might be useful advice to help a young child with reading aloud, but it's terrible advice for determining when to use commas in writing. Lots of writers fly by the seat of their pants when it comes to commas. More often than not, they get them right. All too often, they don't. Here are six good reasons to think more carefully about commas.

Reason 1. Avoid the most common mistake made by decent writers: the run-on error. A comma is not a baby full stop. Once you've written a sentence, you must end it appropriately, with a full stop, a question mark or an exclamation mark. A comma isn't an option. If you end your sentence with a comma and then write another sentence, it's called a run-on error. It's by far the most common mistake involving commas.

● I like clowns, they can be scary though. ✘
  (This should be two sentences.)

Here are some options for this sentence.

- **Use a full stop:** I like clowns. They can be scary though. ✔
- **Create a compound sentence with a conjunction:** I like clowns, but they can be scary. ✔
- **Use a semicolon:** I like clowns; they can be scary though. ✔
  (Tip: Don't overuse semicolons. They get annoying.)
- **Use a dash:** I like clowns – they can be scary though. ✔
  (Don't overuse dashes. They're even more annoying than semicolons.)

Writers commit the run-on error because they feel that a full stop is too harsh a barrier between their closely linked sentences. It isn't. A full stop is fine. The run-on error is particularly common with the word *however*. When used as a transitional phrase (or *conjunctive adverb* as it's really called), *however* is not preceded by a comma.

- I like clowns, however, they can be scary. ✘

Here are some options for this sentence:

- **Use a full stop:** I like clowns. However, they can be scary. ✔
- **Use a semicolon:** I like clowns; however, they can be scary. ✔
- **Use a dash:** I like clowns – however, they can be scary. ✔

The trick to avoiding a run-on error is being clear on what constitutes a sentence (see page 237).

Reason 2. Be consistent with your style for commas in lists, but remember that clarity trumps style. Should you use the Oxford comma? If those around you use it, then yes. If they don't, then no. If no one around you knows what you're talking about, then adopt whatever style suits you and be consistent. As a general rule, Brits tend not to use it, but Americans do. Advocates of the Oxford comma claim it eliminates ambiguity and cite examples like this:

- **Without an Oxford comma:** I like to have a mug of tea, bacon and eggs and toast.
- **With an Oxford comma:** I like to have a mug of tea, bacon and eggs, and toast.

They correctly claim that it's unclear whether the first list represents:

(1) a mug of tea (2) bacon and eggs (3) toast, or
(1) a mug of tea (2) bacon (3) eggs and toast.

They also correctly claim that there's no ambiguity with an Oxford comma.

Here's a real example:

- Disorderly conduct, armed robbery, assault and battery, and rape increase during a full moon.
  (Without the Oxford comma, readers might think that *battery and rape* is a thing. The Oxford comma removes that ambiguity and aids reading.)

An Oxford comma can actually introduce ambiguity though. Look at these examples:
● Jack left the pub with John Smith (a constable) and Simon Jones.
● Jack left the pub with John Smith, a constable, and Simon Jones.
Both of these are grammatically sound, but with the second one, you cannot be sure whether Jack left the pub with two people (Constable John Smith and Simon Jones) or three people.

Not using an Oxford comma can introduce the same type of ambiguity.
● Jack left the pub with the twins (Sarah and Janet).
● Jack left the pub with the twins, Sarah and Janet.
Both these sentences are grammatically sound, but, with the second one, you cannot be sure whether it's two people (a set of twins called Sarah and Janet) or four people (a set of twins and Sarah and Janet).

So, there are arguments for and against the Oxford comma. In truth, there are more for than against, but there are still those who consider it a waste of ink. Whatever you go for, be consistent … ish. If your local convention means putting ambiguity into your writing, break the convention to eliminate any potential misunderstanding.
● Jack left the pub with the twins, Sarah, and Janet.
   (To make it clear it's four people, the Oxford comma is correct, regardless of the convention.)

Given the issues surrounding the Oxford comma, here's a trick to keep in your back pocket. Put list items containing *and* early in your list to avoid any confusion with the *and* at the end.
● Disorderly conduct, assault **and** battery, armed robbery **and** rape increase during a full moon.

Reason 3. Consider dashes and brackets as an alternative to commas used to offset non-essential words, phrases or clauses. The best way to determine whether a word, phrase or clause is essential or nonessential is to mentally delete it. If you're happy with it gone, it will almost certainly be nonessential and should be offset with commas, brackets or dashes. (The advantages and disadvantages of brackets, commas and dashes are covered in Parenthetical Punctuation on page 49.)
    When the text being offset is an interjection (e.g. *indeed, jeepers*) or an adverb (e.g. *consequently, subsequently*), use commas. You could – at a push – use dashes, but avoid brackets. Brackets say 'this text is not part of my sentence structure' louder than dashes and far louder than commas.

Reason 4. Decide for yourself whether to use a comma after a short 'scene-setting' phrase. Using a comma after a scene-setting text aids reading by showing where the main clause starts. However, when the text is short (e.g. *Nowadays, Now, Yesterday*), the comma can look awkward.

● <u>When I was a boy</u>, I was told that anybody could become President. <u>Now</u> I'm beginning to believe it. (Lawyer Clarence Darrow)
  (Note the comma after the first scene-setting adverb of time but not the second.)

Reason 5. Use a comma after a salutation (e.g. Dear Mike, Hi, Susan) and then start the next line with a capital letter. With letters and emails, there's a quirk. Even though the salutation ends with a comma, the opening sentence (on the line below) starts with a capital letter.

Dear Michael,	Hello, Michael,
Last night went exactly as planned.	Last night went exactly as planned.

For some people, this is too illogical, and they end their salutations with a colon. A comma is fine. (Note that with '*Dear Michael*', both words are in the vocative case. With '*Hello, Michael*', only *Michael* is. That's why there's no comma before *Michael* in *Dear Michael*. See also Vocative Case on pages 97–99.)

Reason 6. Be aware that using a comma after a long subject is unpopular. If you're tempted to use a comma after an awkward or long subject, there will be a good reason. You may be seeking a pause for effect or trying to aid reading. Be aware though that it's a widely disliked practice.

● Whoever is trying to bring you down, is already below you.
  (Most grammarians would tut at this comma, but some would pat you on the back.)

KEY POINTS
Don't write a sentence, use a comma, and then write another sentence.
Use the Oxford comma or don't. Be consistent but not at the expense of clarity.
If you're unsure whether to use commas with an adjective clause (typically starting *which* or *who*), mentally delete it. If you're still happy, offset it with commas (or brackets or dashes).

Dash

A dash (– or —) is typically used to create a break but, occasionally, a connection. For the most part, the dash does not have a unique role but is used as an alternative for another punctuation mark. A dash can be inserted into a sentence as an alternative for:

- a colon (e.g. It depends on one thing – trust.)
- a semicolon (e.g. It depends on trust – it always has.)
- three dots (an ellipsis) used as a pause for effect (e.g. It needed – trust.)
- brackets or commas (e.g. It depends – as my mother used to say – on trust.).

A dash can also be used:
- between dates (e.g. World War II ran 1939–1945.)
- to credit a quotation (e.g. 'Love is a serious mental disease.' – Plato)
- with a compound adjective of two equal parts (e.g. the NATO–Warsaw Pact era).

There are two kinds of dash: the em dash (—) and the en dash (–). The em dash is the same length as an uppercase M, and the en dash is same length as a lowercase n. As dashes do not feature on a standard keyboard, lots of people use hyphens instead. That's not a crime, but it's a missed opportunity to show off. (Some writers use two hyphens (--) to represent a dash.) To get an em dash, press Ctrl + Alt + minus on the numeric pad; for an en dash, it's Ctrl + minus.

When using an en dash mid-sentence, most people like to see a space either side, unless you're writing dates, when the most common convention is no spaces (e.g. 1922–1923). Em dashes are used more commonly by Americans, and most won't use a space either side.

EXAMPLES OF DASHES REPLACING COLONS

An en dash can be used to replace a colon that introduces an appositive at the end of a sentence.
- She demanded just one thing from her students – effort.
  (A colon could have been used here. An appositive renames something. Here, *effort* renames *one thing*. See *also* Colons on page 24.)
- It is by the fortune of God that we have three benefits – freedom of speech, freedom of thought, and the wisdom never to use either. (Mark Twain's original quotation uses a colon.)

EXAMPLES OF DASHES REPLACING SEMICOLONS

An en dash can be used to replace a semicolon between two sentences.
- She demanded effort from her students – that's all she ever asked for.
(A semicolon or a full stop could have been used. Like a semicolon, a dash gives a smoother transition than a full stop. See *also* Semicolons on page 57.)

- It's not the size of the dog in the fight – it's the size of the fight in the dog. (Mark Twain)

  (The original quotation uses a full stop but could have used a semicolon.)

EXAMPLES OF DASHES REPLACING (ELLIPSIS)

A dash (en dash is most popular) can be used to replace three dots (an ellipsis) used as a pause for effect.

- Familiarity breeds contempt – and children. (Mark Twain)

  (The original is written with three dots. See also Ellipsis on page 38.)

EXAMPLES OF DASHES REPLACING PARENTHETICAL PUNCTUATION

Brackets are just one of the choices for inserting extra information into a sentence. You can also use commas or dashes.

- Nigel Richards – who went to my school – is the world Scrabble champion.

  (Brackets or commas could have been used. See Parenthetical Punctuation on page 49.)

- I have never taken any exercise – except sleeping and resting – and I never intend to take any. (Mark Twain's original quotation uses commas.)

EXAMPLES OF DASHES BETWEEN DATES

A dash (en dash is most popular) can be used between times and dates, usually replacing the words *from* and *to* or *between* and *and*.)

- The USSR existed 1922–1991.
- I will visit 0800–0900 to discuss my visit 13 January–15 January.

EXAMPLES OF DASHES WITH QUOTATIONS

A dash (en dash is most popular) can be used to credit a quotation to someone.

- 'Name the greatest of all inventors. Accident.' – Mark Twain (1835–1910)

EXAMPLES OF DASHES WITH COMPOUND ADJECTIVES WITH TWO EQUAL PARTS

A dash (en dash is most popular) can be used in a compound adjective with two equal elements.

- The **West German–Soviet** dialogue thawed the chill in **East–West** relations and led to the **Bonn–Moscow** Treaty of 1970.

WHY SHOULD I CARE ABOUT DASHES?

It's worth learning about dashes to make use of their versatility, but if that's not enough, here are two more good reasons to include a little more 'Ctrl minus' action in your work.

Reason 1. A dash will be safe if you're unsure whether to use a colon or a semicolon.

● Take my advice – I don't use it anyway.

(The dash replaces a semicolon (;). A colon would be wrong because nothing in the second 'sentence' renames anything in the first.)

● Take my advice – stay alive.

(Here, the dash replaces a colon (:). A semicolon would be wrong because 'sentence' 2 renames *my advice* in 'sentence' 1.

Dashes are stark though and a page full of them is not a good look. They're safe, but they're a bit slapdash (pun intended).

Reason 2. Dashes used as parenthetical punctuation are unmistakably clear.

When dashes are used to mark a parenthesis (an explanation or afterthought that you'd happily put between brackets or commas), they demarcate your parenthesis brazenly. That could be a good thing to give your parenthesis some emphasis. Dashes can look a little unwieldy, but they're a good alternative for brackets when brackets might be too clumsy, and for commas when the sentence already has lots of commas.

● Last week, Dr Mark Jones – a resident of Bexley since he graduated from Bexley Secondary School in 1990 – was crowned, for the second year running, the world Cluedo champion.

(The writer decided brackets were too heavy-handed and more commas would've been confusing.)

KEY POINTS

If you're unsure whether to use a colon or a semicolon, use a dash. Easy life.
If you need a parenthesis to stand out – I mean really stand out – replace your clumsy brackets or confusing commas with daring dashes.

Ellipsis

An ellipsis (...) is a punctuation mark made up of three dots. An ellipsis (plural 'ellipses') is used:

- to show an omission of a word or words (including whole sentences) from a text
- to create a pause for effect
- to show an unfinished thought
- to show a trail off into silence.

When using ellipses, be consistent with your formatting. In order of popularity, the formats are as follows:

- A big ... man
- A big...man
- A big [...] man

When an ellipsis is used to indicate a pause or a trailing off into silence at the end of a sentence, your options are as follows:

- Join in or....
- Join in or... .
- Join in or ... .

EXAMPLES THAT INDICATE AN OMISSION OF A WORD OR WORDS FROM A TEXT

- I stopped believing in Santa Claus ... when he asked for my autograph. (Actress Shirley Temple)

  (Original: 'I stopped believing in Santa Claus when my mother took me to see him in a department store and he asked for my autograph.')

Some writers like to place an ellipsis in square brackets to make it clear that the ellipsis did not appear in the original text or to differentiate it from a pause for effect.

- [...] The Eagle has landed. (Astronaut Neil Armstrong)

  (Original: 'Houston, Tranquillity Base here. The Eagle has landed.')

- He would eat [...] jam, ham, spam, lamb and cram ... berries by the tram load.

  (The square brackets around the ellipsis tell us the author has removed some text. They also differentiate the omission from the later pause for effect.)

EXAMPLES THAT CREATE A PAUSE FOR EFFECT

- Jealousy ... is a mental cancer. (Author Bertie Charles Forbes)
- A credit card stolen in London was used five hours later ... in Bangkok.

  (Square brackets are not used with a pause for effect.)

EXAMPLES THAT INDICATE AN UNFINISHED THOUGHT

Here, an ellipsis ends the sentence, leaving readers to fill in the obvious ending.

- Yeah? Well, you can just….
- That is gruesome. Revenge is one thing, but….
  (When an ellipsis ends a sentence, some writers use four dots (three for the ellipsis and one for the full stop).

An ellipsis can also be used to trail off into silence, leaving the reader's imagination to supply the ending.
- With the Lord's Prayer mumbling across our lips, we climbed the ladders….

WHY SHOULD I CARE ABOUT ELLIPSES?

When you need to reduce a word count (e.g. for an academic paper or to fit text into a tight space), ellipses can remove redundant words from a quotation. They are also useful in creative writing to create hesitation, suspense, an interruption or a change of mood. Here are three common issues related to ellipses.

Issue 1. Your readers might want to see the whole quotation. If you use an ellipsis to remove words, you run the risk of annoying your readers. They might have liked to see the whole quotation.
- I could never write *Jaws* today. Sharks […] don't hold grudges. (Author Peter Benchley)
  (If you'd like to know what the rest of that quotation says, you'll have to google it. Yup, that's how annoying an ellipsis can be.)

Issue 2. Your readers don't know why you've trailed off. If you use an ellipsis to show an unfinished thought, ensure the thought is obvious. Often, the reason will be clear to the writer but not the reader.
- I have rejected the offer for good reasons….
  (Does this mean 'I'm not telling you them' or 'I'll tell you them later'?)

Issue 3. Changing the meaning of a quotation with an ellipsis. Be careful not to change the context (or the entire meaning) when removing words from a quotation.
- No country can really develop…. (President Nelson Mandela)
  (Original: 'No country can really develop unless its citizens are educated.')
- I'm a Christian for … my business. (Actor John Schneider)
  (Original: 'I'm a Christian for my benefit, and how I walk my walk is my business.')

KEY POINTS
Use an ellipsis:
- to keep your writing succinct by removing redundant words from a quotation
- to show an unfinished (but obvious) thought
- to create a pause for … effect
- to tail off into silence…. [tumbleweed rolls past].

Exclamation Mark

An exclamation mark (!) is used to indicate a sudden or forceful order, intensity of emotion or volume. An exclamation mark can be used to end:

● An exclamatory sentence (one that conveys excitement or emotion).
● An imperative sentence (one that issues an order).
● An interjection (a term that expresses feeling or sudden emotion).

EXAMPLES WITH EXCLAMATORY SENTENCES

An exclamatory sentence conveys excitement or emotion. All exclamatory sentences end with exclamation marks.

● You're late!
  (This conveys anger.)
● It's a pike!
  (This conveys surprise.)
● If the enemy is in range, so are you! (Infantry Journal)
  (This conveys a stark reality.)

EXAMPLES WITH IMPERATIVE SENTENCES

An imperative sentence issues an order. A lot of imperative sentences end with full stops. An exclamation mark is used to show forcefulness.

● Get out!
● Do not swallow! (sign on a coat hanger)
● Please leave. (This is an imperative sentence, but it's not forceful enough for an exclamation mark.)

EXAMPLES WITH INTERJECTIONS

Typically used at the start of a sentence, an interjection (see page 157) expresses feeling or emotion. It can be followed by a comma, a full stop or an exclamation mark. An exclamation mark intensifies the interjection (bold).

● **Jeepers!** That was close!
● **Yes,** overweight people now outnumber average people in America. Last month you were fat. Now you're average. **Yay!** Let's get a pizza! (Comedian Jay Leno)

WHY SHOULD I CARE ABOUT EXCLAMATION MARKS?

There are two noteworthy points related to exclamation marks.

Point 1. Avoid exclamation marks in formal correspondence. Exclamation marks have their place in creative writing, verse, advertisements, signage, texts and informal emails, but – as a rule – they're not well suited to business correspondence. There are, of course, dozens of business scenarios in which an exclamation mark would be appropriate, but exclamation marks are considered a bit crass.

Another downside of exclamation marks is that without any accompanying explanation of their strength or meaning (e.g. emotion, forcefulness, importance), they're open to misinterpretation.

● Please pay the invoice within 28 days of receipt!
    (That's a pretty risky exclamation mark.)

Point 2. Don't use more than one exclamation mark. If it's appropriate to use one, then go for it, but don't use two (!!) or more (!!!) unless you're texting your mates. It's like laughing at your own jokes. In anything even slightly formal, multiple exclamation marks will be viewed as rudeness or immaturity. ('Five exclamation marks: the sure sign of an insane mind.' – Author Terry Pratchett)

KEY POINTS
Use exclamation marks with caution. They can be
misinterpreted or considered crass.
Don't use more than one exclamation mark.

Full Stop

A full stop (.), called a period in the US, is used:

- at the end of a sentence
- in abbreviations (both initialisms, e.g. B.B.C., and contractions, e.g. Prof. Jones).

EXAMPLES AT THE END OF SENTENCES

Full stops are used at the end of declarative sentences. (A declarative sentence states a fact.)

- Last words are for fools who haven't said enough. (Philosopher Karl Marx)
- Either he's dead or my watch has stopped. (Comedian Groucho Marx)

Full stops are used at the end of imperative sentences that are not forceful enough to warrant an exclamation mark. (An imperative sentence gives a command.)

- Advise no one to go to war or marry. (Spanish proverb)
- Avoid a cure that is worse than the disease. (Greek storyteller Aesop)

EXAMPLES IN ABBREVIATIONS

- B.B.C., a.m., etc., Prof. Munro

WHY SHOULD I CARE ABOUT FULL STOPS?

It's just a small dot, but the full stop is a real grammar villain. Here are six good reasons to think more carefully about full stops.

Reason 1. Once you've written a sentence, put a full stop. Don't put a comma and write a new sentence. The full stop is responsible for the most common mistake corrected by proofreaders: the run-on sentence. A run-on sentence (see page 235) is typically caused by writing a sentence, incorrectly putting a comma and then writing another sentence. In the examples below, the commas should be full stops.

- This suspense is terrible, I hope it will last. ✗ (Playwright Oscar Wilde)
- The answers to life's problems aren't at the bottom of a bottle, they're on TV. ✗ (Homer Simpson)

Reason 2. Use a full stop (not a question mark) to end a declarative sentence containing an indirect question. A declarative sentence can include an indirect question (see Indirect Question on page 151). Resist the temptation to use a question mark.

- She asked if it were true? ✗
- I wonder if a soldier ever does mend a bullet hole in his coat? ✗ (Nurse Clara Barton)

Reason 3. Be confident with full stops in contractions. Writers are often unsure whether to write *Mr Smith* or *Mr. Smith*, or *Dr Jones* or *Dr. Jones*. If you're following US conventions, always put a full stop (*Mr. Smith, Dr. Jones, Prof. Munro*). It's not so simple for Brits. If the last letter of the contraction (e.g. *Mr*) is the same as the last letter of the whole word (e.g. *Mister*), don't use a full stop. If they're different, use one.

- Mister > Mr
- Professor > Prof.
- Read paras 1–9 and para. 23.
  (The last letters of *paras* and *paragraphs* are the same, but those of *para* and *paragraph* aren't.)

Lots of Brits adopt the US method. Nevertheless, knowing the UK rule removes the guesswork. You can now justify the full stop in *Rev. Bloggs* and the lack of one in *Revd Bloggs* (both are acceptable contractions of *Reverend*).

Reason 4. Don't use two full stops at the end of a sentence. If a sentence ends with an abbreviation that includes a full stop, don't use another to mark the end of it.

- The twins compared results from DNA-testing companies like 23andMe, Ancestry, etc.. ✘
- We didn't need a remote control. We only watched B.B.C.. ✘
  (Logically, these are correct, but they're too unwieldy.)

Question marks and exclamation marks are not affected.

- Will the judge support the B.B.C.?
  (This is correct, but it's scruffy. I'd use BBC instead of B.B.C.)
- You were meant to be here at 4 a.m. not p.m.!

The only exception to doubling up end marks with full stops is the ellipsis (...).

- As the galleon shrank out of sight so did his hope….
  (This has three full stops for the ellipsis and one to end the sentence.)

Reason 5. Write uppercase abbreviations without full stops and lowercase ones with. This is not a rule but a common style to achieve consistency. There's just one rule that might trump your striving for consistency: if the abbreviation is a company name, copy the format the company uses.

Reason 6. Be careful not to omit the final full stop of an abbreviation. If you choose to use full stops in your abbreviations, don't forget to give the last letter a full stop too.

- M.O.T While You Wait ✘ (a common sign)

KEY POINTS

If you've still got more to say once you've written a sentence, put a full stop and write another sentence. Don't shove a comma in and carry on writing.
Declarative sentences (i.e. ones that state facts) end with full stops. This includes ones that contain indirect questions.

Hyphen

A hyphen (-) is a punctuation mark used as a joiner. It is typically used to join the separate parts of a compound word (a word made up of more than one word) to make it clear that it's one entity. Hyphens are seen:

- in compound adjectives (e.g. I wrote a **three-page** document.)
- in compound nouns (e.g. I asked a **passer-by**.)
- in compound verbs (e.g. They will **spot-check** the passengers.)
- in prefixed words (e.g. Please **re-enact** the crime.)
- in fractions and numbers written in full (e.g. What's **one-third** of **twenty-one**?)
- with list items that share a common second element (e.g. The **two-** and **three-bedroom** flats will increase in value **four-** or **fivefold**.).

EXAMPLES IN COMPOUND ADJECTIVES

A hyphen joins the words in a compound adjective (one made of more than one word; see page 44).

- **six-foot** table
- There's a difference between a free market and **free-for-all** market.
  (Politician Bob Menendez)

EXAMPLES IN COMPOUND NOUNS

A hyphen can be used to join the words in a compound noun (a single noun made up of more than one word; see page 178).

- a **two-year-old**
- Behind every successful man stands a surprised **mother-in-law**. (French writer Voltaire)

Bear in mind though that lots of compound nouns are unhyphenated, and some are two words. (More on this to come.)

- wheelchair
- hot dog

EXAMPLES IN COMPOUND VERBS

A hyphen can be used to join the words in a compound verb, especially verbs formed from two nouns.

- to **gift-wrap**
- I was **court-martialled** in my absence and sentenced to death in my absence, so I said they could shoot me in my absence. (Playwright Brendan Behan).

Compound verbs are far less common than compound adjectives and compound nouns. They are often invented by the writer to add a bit of flair.

- She will **eyebrow-beat** him into submission.
- He **cold-shouldered** me when I was **fist-pumping** his team mates.

Not all verbs comprising two words are hyphenated. Do not use a hyphen with a phrasal verb (one that comprises a main verb and another word, e.g. *to break out, to drop off; see page 200*).

- Never give in, and never give up. (Politician Hubert Humphrey)

EXAMPLES IN PREFIXES

A hyphen can be used to join a prefix to a word, though most prefixed words are unhyphenated (e.g. *cooperate, defuse*). See *also* Affix, Prefix and Suffix on page 82.

- ultra-expensive
- re-establish

EXAMPLES IN FRACTIONS AND NUMBERS WRITTEN IN FULL

Hyphens are used in fractions written out in full.

- I had **one-third** share.
  (Here, the fraction is a quantifier and is used like a compound adjective. Fractions are always hyphenated when used in this way.)
- She owned **two-thirds** of the business.
  (Here, the fraction is a compound noun. Fractions are commonly, but not always, hyphenated when used as nouns. In both cases, the hyphen aids reading by making it immediately clear that the fraction is one grammatical unit.)

When numbers are written out in full, hyphens are used in all numbers between 21 and 99 (except those divisible by ten).

- **fifty-one**
- two hundred and **thirty-four**
- three thousand, five hundred and **sixty-seven**

EXAMPLES WITH LIST ITEMS SHARING A COMMON SECOND ELEMENT

A hyphen can be used before a common second element in all but the last word in the list.

- You can buy a **two-**, **five-** or **seven-seater** version of this car.
- If our monarchy can show democracy that leads to a **two-**, **three-**, **four-party** system (left, right and centre), then the Brotherhood will no longer be a contender. (Abdullah II of Jordan)

These examples show this technique with compound adjectives that would ordinarily contain hyphens if written out in full. The technique can also be used with compound words that wouldn't ordinarily contain hyphens.

- I don't care if you're **Aqua-**, **Bat-** or **Superman**, Mr Clayderman. You're still late.
- It will increase **two-** or **threefold**.

WHY SHOULD I CARE ABOUT HYPHENS?

A hyphen is typically used to show that the joined words are a single entity (e.g. a single adjective or a single noun). This has the following benefits:

(1) It makes your text easier to read.
(2) It removes the possibility for ambiguity.
(3) It showcases your writing skills a little.

Here are six noteworthy points related to hyphens.

Point 1. Use a hyphen if the unhyphenated version of a compound adjective is ambiguous. Your British readers will expect you to use hyphens with compound adjectives (see *also* page 69), but readers in the US are more lenient. It's common to see compound adjectives without hyphens in both regions, especially with well-established terms that are unlikely to make a reader hesitate (e.g. **ice cream** van, **twentieth century** building). So, it's not a serious error to omit the hyphen from a compound adjective. But, when the unhyphenated version of a compound adjective is ambiguous, you must use a hyphen to link its words.

- a small business grant ✗ (ambiguous)

  (Does this mean a small grant for business purposes or a grant for a small business?)

- a small-business grant ✔

  (With the hyphen, it's clear that it's a grant for a small business. It could be a large grant.)

Point 2. Don't use hyphens with adverbs that end -ly (there are lots) or after the word *very*.

- It is a **wonderfully-decorated** tree. ✗
- Paula is a **very-talented** student. ✗

This applies only to adverbs ending -ly. It does not apply to adjectives ending -ly.

- It's a **friendly-looking**, **family-run** business. ✔

  (*Friendly* and *family* are not adverbs.)

Point 3. Use a hyphen for adverbs that could feasibly be adjectives (e.g. *well*, *fast*, *best*).

- Lee is the **best-known** player on the pitch.

  (Here, Lee is known better than any other player. *Best* is an adverb.)

- Lee is the **best known** player on the pitch.

  (This could feasibly mean that Lee is the best of all the known players, in which case *best* would be an adjective. If you substitute *known* with *chubby*, it will highlight *best* as an adjective.)

This issue commonly crops up with the adverb *well*, which is also an adjective meaning *healthy*.

- We're looking at a **well-developed** fetus. ✔
  (This means the fetus is significantly past the embryonic state.)
- We're looking at a **well developed** fetus. ✘
  (This could mean the same as above or possibly a healthy and developed fetus.)

If you're unsure whether *well* is an adverb or adjective, substitute *healthy* for *well*, and if your sentence makes no sense, put *well* back in and use a hyphen. (See also Adverb on page 77.) This situation can also occur with *fast* and *best* (e.g. *fast-changing wind*, *best-known actor*).

Point 4. Don't join an expression like *three-and-a-half* to your noun with a hyphen. When used like compound adjectives, expressions like *three-and-a-half* and *two-and-a-quarter* (a kind of quantifier) are often hyphenated to make it clear they're one entity. If you decide to use hyphens in such a term, don't join it to your noun with a hyphen.

- He wants **four-and-a-quarter-billion.** ✘
- He wants **four-and-a-quarter billion.** ✔
  (Here, *four-and-a-quarter* is modifying the noun *billion*. Joining them with a hyphen would be as wrong as writing *He wants a nice-car.*)

Be mindful, however, that your quantifier might not end when the expression like *four-and-a-quarter* ends.

- He wants **four-and-a-quarter-billion** pounds. ✔
  (This time, the hyphen between *quarter* and *billion* is correct because *billion* is now part of the quantifier modifying *pounds*.)

On a related point, be particularly careful when writing ages.

- She's a **twenty-four-year-old** woman. ✔
  (All too often, the hyphen after *year* is mistakenly omitted.)

Point 5. Use your spellchecker smartly to spell compound nouns correctly. Some compound nouns (see page 178) are one word (e.g. *snowman*, *aircraft*), and some are two words (e.g. *fish tank*, *cell phone*). Some compound nouns are hyphenated (e.g. *know-how*, *runner-up*), and some have more than one acceptable spelling (e.g. *paper clip*, *paper-clip* and *paperclip*).

Your spellchecker will not test the two-word version or the hyphenated version as a single entity. So, it will not highlight *air craft* or *air-craft* as an error (even though it should be *aircraft*). Therefore, you have to test the one-word version. If your spellchecker doesn't like the one-word version, you have a choice between the two-word version and the hyphenated version. Often, this really is your decision.

Use a hyphen for clarity (i.e. to make it instantly obvious it's a single entity) and to eliminate any ambiguity.

- pen friend / pen-friend
  (The hyphenated version is clearer. It stands out as a single entity, making it easier to read.)
- cooking oil / cooking-oil
  (The hyphenated version makes it clear the oil is not cooking.)

Point 6. Use your spellchecker and your instinct to determine whether to use a hyphen with a prefix. If you're unsure whether to use a hyphen with a prefix, start by not using a hyphen. However, use a hyphen if the unhyphenated version:

- looks too unwieldy for your taste (*antiaircraft* might be an example)
- is highlighted as a spelling mistake by your spellchecker (e.g. *reestablish*)
- is ambiguous (*re-cover the sofa* is not ambiguous, but *recover the sofa* is).

There's more guidance on prefixes in Affix, Prefix and Suffix (see page 82).

KEY POINTS
Use hyphens in compound adjectives to eliminate ambiguity.
Before hyphenating a compound noun, use a spellchecker to ensure it's not acceptable as a single word.

Parentheses

Parentheses (also called parenthetical punctuation) are punctuation marks (commas, dashes or brackets) used in pairs to offset additional information in a sentence. The additional information is called a parenthesis, which is usually inserted as an explanation or afterthought. (NB: In the US, the term *parentheses* is used specifically for round brackets.)

REAL-LIFE EXAMPLES OF PARENTHESES

A parenthesis (i.e. the additional information offset by whatever parenthetical punctuation you choose) can be removed from a sentence without any crucial loss of meaning. All the examples below would still work if every parenthesis (bold) were removed.

Commas as parentheses:

- The Japanese macaques from Minoh**, near Osaka,** have lost the ability to use coins**, which they'd often pickpocket from tourists,** to buy snacks from vending machines because the snacks now cost more than one coin.

Dashes as parentheses:

- A butt of wine **– the equivalent of half a hogshead –** is approximately 477 litres. That's a buttload of wine!

Brackets as parentheses:

- Due to pub quizzes, Buzz Aldrin **(the second man on the Moon)** is now as famous as Neil Armstrong.

It is common to use different parenthetical punctuation in the same sentence:

- If you simply try to tell the truth **(without caring tuppence how often it has been told before)** you will**, nine times out of ten,** become original without ever having noticed it. (Author CS Lewis)
- Barbara's second goat **(called Goat Two)** could **– just like a dog –** sit, shake hands and walk upright on its hind legs.

WHY SHOULD I CARE ABOUT PARENTHESES?

There's one great reason to care about parentheses, and there's one common mistake to avoid.

Great Reason. Control the readability of your sentence. Choosing between commas, brackets and dashes allows you to control how much your parenthesis stands out. Often, it's a trade-off between readability (best achieved with brackets), brashness – best achieved with dashes – and a formal look, best achieved with commas.

Here's a sentence that uses only commas as parentheses. It's not difficult to hack your way through it, but you might find yourself backtracking once or twice.

● In June, the Stoner brothers, Robin, Simon and Jack, who is only 11, and their music teacher, Robert Bobbitt, known locally as Bobby Bobbitt, will attempt, for the second time, to break the record for the Three Peaks Challenge.

Now look at a version with a mix of parentheses (much easier to read).

● In June, the Stoner brothers – Robin, Simon and Jack (who is only 11) – and their music teacher, Robert Bobbitt (known locally as Bobby Bobbitt), will attempt, for the second time, to break the record for the Three Peaks Challenge.

Parenthetical punctuation	Advantage	Disadvantage
Brackets	Easy to spot	Considered clumsy (often to the extent of being banned in formal documents)
Commas	Normal-looking sentence	Easily confused with other commas in the sentence
Dashes	Easy to spot	Look a little stark, so can't be used too often

When the text being offset is an interjection (e.g. *well, crikey*) or an adverb (e.g. *subsequently, consequently*), use commas. You could – at a push – use dashes, but avoid brackets.

● I am, **indeed,** a king because I know how to rule myself. (Author Pietro Aretino)

Common Mistake. Don't forget that parenthetical punctuation marks come in pairs. You would never forget an open or close bracket. Well, omitting the first or second comma or dash is no different.

● My father**, who carries around the picture of the kid who came with his wallet** never calls. ✗
(There should be a comma after *wallet* to end the parenthesis.)

● My father **who has been in a coma for three months,** texted me. ✗
(There should be a comma before *who* to start the parenthesis.)

This mistake is most common with short expressions (e.g. *yes, no, however, consequently*).

● If we extend our senses, then**, consequently** we will extend our knowledge. ✗
(Cyborg artist Neil Harbisson)
(The second parenthetical comma – after *consequently* – was in Neil's original quotation.)

There's a quirk though. When a parenthesis ends a sentence, the second comma or dash isn't used because it would look odd before the end mark, usually a full stop.

● I was texted by my father**, who has been in a coma for three months.** ✔
   (If brackets were used, the end of the parenthesis would be marked, and the full stop would go outside the close bracket.)

Missing out the second punctuation mark of the pairing is also common when a parenthesis is nested within another parenthesis.

● The boys' music teacher**, Robert Bobbitt (known as Bobby Bobbitt)** will accompany them. ✗
   (There should be a comma after the close bracket.)

There's a quirk with this, too. When commas are used, one comma can represent two commas.

● The boys' music teacher, **Robert Bobbitt, known as Bobby Bobbitt,** will accompany them. ✔
   (If you were a logic freak, you might be tempted to use two commas after *Bobbitt*. It'd be indefensibly wrong, but, hey, the logic's sound.)

KEY POINTS
Choose between commas, brackets and dashes to control how much your parenthesis stands out.
Parentheses used mid-sentence come in pairs.

Quotation Marks

Quotation marks (' ' and " "), also known as speech marks, quotes and inverted commas, are punctuation marks used in pairs:

- to identify previously spoken or written words
- to signify irony or indicate *so-called* or *alleged*
- to highlight the names of things like ships, books and plays
- to show that a word refers to the word itself, not the word's meaning (e.g. 'Dogs' is plural.).

EXAMPLES IDENTIFYING PREVIOUSLY SPOKEN OR WRITTEN WORDS

- George Bernard Shaw said: 'When a thing is funny, search it carefully for a hidden truth.'
  (When a quotation is introduced with words like 'He said' (called words of attribution), it's usual to precede the quotation with a comma or a colon. There's more on this coming up, and in Colon on page 24.)
- Your uncle's observation wasn't meant to be just funny. Take Shaw's advice and 'search it carefully for a hidden truth'.
  (When there are no words of attribution, don't use a comma or a colon.)

EXAMPLES SIGNIFYING IRONY OR INDICATING *SO-CALLED* OR *ALLEGED*

- My 'mates' drove off with my clothes.
- Using his father's equipment, Alexander found over 50,000 bacteria on a 'clean' chopping board.
- His 'wife' arrived two hours after Mr Becket checked in.
  (Sometimes, quotation marks perform two roles. Here, they signify *so-called* or *alleged,* but they also suggest that Mr Becket himself described the lady as his wife.)

EXAMPLES HIGHLIGHTING NAMES OF THINGS LIKE SHIPS, BOOKS AND PLAYS

Quotation marks can be used to highlight the names of things like ships, planes, books and plays. However, as quotation marks look a bit untidy, italics are often used instead.

- 'Britannic', which was bigger than its sister ship 'Titanic', sank in 1916 after a mine-strike.
- 'Southern Stars' was Jones's account of the trek.
  (The quotation marks aid reading because *Stars* is a plural word and *was* is singular.)

EXAMPLES SHOWING THAT A WORD REFERS TO THE WORD ITSELF

Quotation marks can be used to show that a word is not being used for its meaning. (This is more commonly done using italics.)

- 'It's' is a contraction of 'it is' or 'it has'. It's got no other uses.

  (In the first sentence, *It's* is not being used for its meaning. We're discussing it. In the second, the *It's* is being used for its meaning as part of the sentence.)

- If you apply the Latin rule for forming a plural, then the plural of 'octopus' is 'octopi'. However, 'octopus' stems from Greek not Latin. If you apply the Greek rule, it's 'octopodes', but a Greek wouldn't use 'octopodes' because the modern Greek word for octopus is 'chtapodi'. The plural of 'octopus' is 'octopuses'.

  (Quotation marks can start to get scruffy. Italics are far neater.)

WHY SHOULD I CARE ABOUT QUOTATION MARKS?

There are four noteworthy issues related to quotation marks.

Issue 1. Being inconsistent with single or double quotation marks. Quotation marks come in two forms: singles ('like these') and doubles ("like these"). Pick either singles or doubles and then be consistent throughout your work. If you opt for singles (and most Brits do), then use doubles to nest a quotation within a quotation.

- She said: 'My dog can say "sausages" more clearly than the one on TV.' ✔
- Homer Simpson said: 'Maybe, just once, someone will call me "Sir" without adding "you're making a scene".' ✔

If you opt for doubles (as Americans tend to), use singles to nest quotations within quotations. There's a lot of leniency on which style to choose. The agreed rule, however, is that singles and doubles should not be mixed at the same level.

- My dog may not be able to add up, spell my name or say "sausages" or 'Esther' like the ones you see on 'That's Life', but he can hold his own in a fight with a badger. ✗

  (Singles and doubles have been mixed at the same level.)

There are two more quirks. If you start with double quotation marks, then it's acceptable to use singles to denote *alleged* or *so-called* to differentiate the word from quoted speech. It's also okay to use singles to highlight individual letters if you think doubles look too stark.

- The 'fresh' scallops ponged a bit and were pretty slimy.
- There's no 'a' in "definite". No, really, there isn't.

Issue 2. Using quotation marks with reported speech. Quotation marks are not used for reported speech (speech usually preceded by the word *that*). Only use quotation marks for actual quotations of speech or writing.

53

- The secretary said that 'the phones were dead.' ✗
  (This is reported speech. The quotation marks do not accurately quote the secretary, who said, 'The phones are dead.')
- The secretary said that the phones were dead. ✔
  (As this is also reported speech, it is correct without quotation marks.)
- The secretary said that the phones were 'dead'. ✔
  (This is also reported speech, but this time the quotation marks are fine because they quote the secretary accurately.)
- The secretary said, 'The phones are dead.' ✔
  (This is not reported speech. The quotation marks show the secretary's actual speech.)

Issue 3. Being unsure whether to use a comma or a colon before a quotation.
When introducing a quotation with words like 'She whispered' or 'It stated' (called words of attribution), you have to decide whether to follow the introduction with a comma, a colon or nothing. In creative writing, writers are free to choose. In more formal writing, punctuation is expected after an introduction for a quotation. The following rules are quite lax, and they overlap, giving you a choice.

Rule A. Use a colon if the introduction is an independent clause.
- New York gang members all advise the following: 'Don't run from fat cops. They shoot earlier.'
  A good tip is to use the words 'the following' to help create an independent clause (i.e. one that could stand alone as a sentence). Using 'the following' will justify using a colon. (Once you've justified a colon, it will be safe to start your quotation with a capital letter.)

Rule B. You can use a colon if the quotation is a complete sentence, especially if you intend to start it with a capital letter.
- The orders state: 'In case of fire, exit the building before tweeting about it.'
  (You could also use a comma here.)

Rule C. Use a comma if the introduction is not an independent clause and the quotation is not a sentence.
- Before each shot, the keeper said aloud, 'bum, belly, beak, bang'.
- Peering over his glasses, he said, 'Never test the depth of a river with both feet.'
  (You could also use a colon here because the quotation is a complete sentence.)

Rule D. You can only use a comma after a quotation.
- 'Always give a hundred per cent, unless you're donating blood', he would always say.
  (A colon is not an option. The question of whether the comma should be inside or outside the quotation mark is covered in Issue 4.)

Rule E. Don't use any punctuation if the quotation is not introduced.

The commas below are wrong.

- I believe there really is, 'no place like home.' ✗
- I would hate to see the worst if this is the, 'best skiing resort in France'. ✗

Issue 4. Being unsure whether to place punctuation inside or outside the quotation. Brits and Americans tend to follow different rules when deciding whether a comma or full stop should live inside or outside a quotation and whether to double up with end punctuation. It's common to find Brits following the US convention.

Punctuation	UK convention	US convention
. and ,	Place your full stops and commas outside (unless they appear in the original). • 'Sick', to today's youth, means 'excellent'. • 'The price of greatness', said Churchill, 'is responsibility.' (The full stop is in the original.)	Place your full stops and commas inside. • "Sick," to today's youth, means "excellent." • "The price of greatness," said Churchill, "is responsibility." (Obviously, don't put your comma inside if it **precedes** the quotation.)

! and ?	Place exclamation marks and question marks inside or outside according to logic.
	• Did he say, 'I love you'?
	  (*I love you* is not a question, but the whole sentence is.)
	• He shouted, 'Do you love me?'
	  (The whole sentence is not a question, but the quotation is.)	

?, ! and .	Don't double up with end marks. But, if you must, you can.
	• Did he ask, 'Do you love me?'?
	  (This is unwieldy but acceptable to some. The sentence is a question, and the quotation is a question.)
	• He shouted, 'Do you love me?'.
	  (Unwieldy but acceptable.)
		Don't double up with end marks.
		• Did she really ask, "Do you love me?"? ✗
		  (This is too unwieldy for US tastes.)
		• Did she really ask, "Do you love me?" ✔

: and ;	Place colons and semicolons outside the quotation. ● Samuel Johnson offered three literal definitions for the word 'slave': someone mancipated to a master, not a free man and a dependant. Johnson offered a fourth definition, 'the lowest form of life'; however, he stated that this definition was only used proverbially.
More on ?, ! and .	Don't end a quotation with full stop when the quotation doesn't end the whole sentence. There's more leniency with question and exclamation marks, but try to avoid that situation too. ● 'I'm free!', he yelled. ✔ (UK) ● 'Am I free?', he asked. ✔ (UK) ● "I'm free!" he yelled. ✔ (US) ● "Am I free?" he asked. ✔ (US) (Americans can't bring themselves to put a comma outside the quotation marks.)

Issue 5. Using quotation marks for emphasis. Don't use quotation marks for emphasis. First, it's not a recognised use for quotation marks, and, second, your readers could interpret them as meaning *alleged* or *so-called*. These are both real examples:
● We sell 'fresh' fish. ✘
● Welcome to a 'clean' Western restaurant. ✘

KEY POINTS
Nest single quotation marks within doubles, or vice-versa (e.g. The instructions say: 'Shout "Yahtzee" loudly.').
Don't put reported speech in quotation marks (e.g. He said that 'he did shout it loudly.' ✘ He said: 'I shouted it clearly.' ✔)

Semicolon

A semicolon (;) is a punctuation mark used:

- in complex lists
- to give a smooth transition into the next 'sentence'
- rarely, before a conjunction (e.g. *and*, *or*, *but*) that joins two 'sentences' with lots of commas.

Once two sentences have been joined using a semicolon, they become independent clauses. Throughout this entry, the word *sentence* has been used because it is helpful to remember them as they were before the semicolon was used.

EXAMPLES IN COMPLEX LISTS

Here's a simple list.

- Lord Loxley
- Lady Loxley
- Master Loxley

When a simple list is written as a sentence, the list items are separated with commas.

- The dinner guests will be Lord Loxley, Lady Loxley and Master Loxley.

Now look at this list.

- Lord Loxley, aged 91
- Lady Loxley, aged 41
- Master Loxley, aged 42

If we used commas to separate these list items, the list could get quite confusing. To avoid this confusion, semicolons can be used to outrank the commas.

- The dinner guests will be Lord Loxley, aged 91; Lady Loxley, aged 41; and Master Loxley, aged 42.

Not all list items have to have commas to justify using semicolons. Only one does.

- The master, aged 81 (82 next week); the servant; and the cook.
  (Note how you can use brackets to add more information to a list item.)

EXAMPLES GIVING A SMOOTH TRANSITION INTO THE NEXT SENTENCE

Most sentences start with a capital letter and end with a full stop. For a smoother transition between your sentences, replace the full stop with a semicolon.

- Never pick a fight with an ugly person. They've got nothing to lose.
- Never pick a fight with an ugly person; they've got nothing to lose.

Often, when merging two sentences into one, the second sentence will start with a bridging phrase (or a conjunctive adverb as it's called). Common ones are *However*,

Consequently and *Therefore*. You can use a semicolon before one of these bridges to create a smoother transition than a full stop.

- Vacation used to be a luxury. However, it has become a necessity.
- Vacation used to be a luxury; however, it has become a necessity.

EXAMPLES USED BEFORE A CONJUNCTION JOINING TWO SENTENCES

Often two sentences are merged into one using a conjunction (e.g. *and*, *or*, *but*)

- Lee loves pies, and he loves cakes.

  (When a conjunction (*here*, *and*) is used to join two sentences, it is preceded by a comma.)

However, when the sentences themselves contain commas, you can outrank those commas by using a semicolon before the conjunction.

- With a fridge full of cheese-and-onion pies, Lee obviously loves pies; but he prefers, from what I have seen, Eccles cakes.

  (These days, this is not a common practice; but, if you think it will help your readers, you can use a semicolon before a conjunction that joins two sentences littered with commas.)

WHY SHOULD I CARE ABOUT SEMICOLONS?

Most proofreaders will tell you that semicolons almost never survive their edit. For the most part, a proofreader will remove a semicolon because it has been used incorrectly, but it's not uncommon for a semicolon to be removed because the alternative is better. For example, the best way to present a complicated list is as bullet points, and the best way to end a sentence is with a full stop. This is food for thought:

- Once you know how to use semicolons, don't.

Now, that advice is a little strong, but if you use too many, you'll probably annoy your readers, and you'll certainly diminish the smoothing effect. Think of the semicolon as an ornament that you show off only on special occasions. Here are three scenarios that could justify a semicolon:

Scenario 1. If your two sentences feel like a cause and effect. If you could merge your two sentences into one with a word like *because* consider a semicolon.

- I am glad that I paid so little attention to good advice; ~~because~~ had I abided by it, I might have been saved from some of my most valuable mistakes. (Playwright Edna St. Vincent Millay)

Scenario 2. If your two sentences are deliberately similar.

- You don't pay taxes; they take taxes. (Comedian Chris Rock)
- Write with the door closed; rewrite with the door open. (Author Stephen King)

Scenario 3. If your two sentences feel closely linked and could be merged with a comma and a conjunction, e.g. *and, or, but, for, so* **(especially the last three).**

- Go not to the elves for counsel; they will say both no and yes.
  (The original by JRR Tolkien is 'for they will say both no and yes.')

Here are three other key issues related to semicolons.

Issue 1. You can merge two sentences into one with a semicolon but not a comma. Beware the comma fault, which is a type of run-on error (see page 237) caused by ending a sentence with a comma and then writing another sentence. It occurs when writers feel a full stop is too much of a speed bump for their closely related sentences.

- The noblest of dogs is the hot dog, it feeds the hand that bites it. ✗
- Don't steal, the government hates competition. ✗
  (Here, the commas should be replaced by full stops or semicolons.)

The run-on error is particularly common with *however*.

- Life isn't always easy, however, it's always simple. ✗
  (The comma before *however* should be replaced by a full stop or a semicolon. See also Run-on Sentence and Conjunctive Adverb on pages 235 and 123.)
- The Arctic is among the least understood places on the planet; however, we do know that its landscape is changing and evolving as quickly as cell phones. (Filmmaker Philippe Cousteau) ✔

Issue 2. If space allows, use bullet points. Lists featuring semicolons are useful for saving space, but they're not as clear as bullet points. (You'll get to showcase your skills with semicolons in lists another time. Clarity trumps showing off.)

Issue 3. Don't confuse a semicolon with a colon. You can't use a semicolon after an introduction. That's what a colon (:) is for.

- I'm going to fester under a quilt and watch the following; (1) *Jaws*, (2) *Avatar*, and (3) *Ted*. ✗
  (This should be a colon. See *also* Colon on page 24.)

KEY POINTS

If you have two sentences that you can't bear to be separated by a full stop, you can unite them using a semicolon.
Using semicolons to separate list items that contain commas is good for saving space and for showing off, but bullet points are far clearer.

A–Z
of
Grammar
Essentials

Acronym

An acronym is an abbreviation spoken like a word. It's not just another word for abbreviation.

EASY EXAMPLES
- NATO (North Atlantic Treaty Organization)
- UNESCO (United Nations Educational, Scientific and Cultural Organization)

MORE EXAMPLES
Some acronyms (e.g. radar: **RA**dio **D**etection **A**nd **R**anging) have turned into common nouns (see page 168) that can now be written with lowercase letters.
- My favourite thing to do on this planet is to *scuba* dive. (Astronaut Buzz Aldrin)
  (scuba: **S**elf **C**ontained **U**nderwater **B**reathing **A**pparatus)
- As an Armenian, I'm obsessed with *laser* hair removal.
  (Reality TV star Kim Kardashian)
  (As *laser* is an acronym of **L**ight **A**mplification by **S**timulated **E**mission of **R**adiation, the word lazer is an incorrect spelling, not the American spelling.)

The acronym NATO, commonly written as Nato, is on the verge of completing its transition from acronym to normal word. In this case, however, it's a proper noun (see page 168), which is why the N is capitalised.

WHY SHOULD I CARE ABOUT ACRONYMS?
Don't use the word *acronym* when you mean *abbreviation*. UNESCO and UNHCR are both abbreviations, but only UNESCO is an acronym. UNCHR is an *initialism* (an abbreviation for which the initial letters are pronounced separately). You will often see something called a 'List of Acronyms' at the end of a formal document. I haven't seen a list of acronyms yet, but I've seen plenty of lists of abbreviations (some of which have been acronyms).

KEY POINT
An acronym is an abbreviation spoken like a word.
It's not a posh word for abbreviation.

Active and Passive Sentences

In an active sentence, the subject performs the action of the main verb. In a passive sentence, the action of the main verb is done to the subject.

EASY EXAMPLES
● The dog ate the biscuits.
  (*The dog* is the subject of the sentence. *The dog* is the subject of the verb *ate*. *The dog* is performing the action of the verb.)
● Hammerhead sharks will pester you as you approach the reef.
  (*Hammerhead sharks* (the subject) is performing the action of *will pester* (the main verb).)
● Some weasel removed the cork from my lunch. (Comedian WC Fields)
  (*Some weasel* (the subject) is performing the action of *removed* (the main verb).)

Here are passive versions:
● The biscuits were eaten by the dog.
  (Here, *the biscuits* is the subject of the sentence. *The biscuits* is the subject of the verb *were eaten*, but the subject is not performing the action of the verb. In fact, the action is being done to the biscuits. Therefore, this is a passive sentence not an active one.)
● You will be pestered by hammerhead sharks as you approach the reef.
  (The action of *will be pestered* (the main verb) is being done to *you* (the subject).)
● The cork was removed from my lunch by some weasel.
  (The action of *was removed* (the main verb) is being done to *the cork* (the subject).)

REAL-LIFE EXAMPLES
In the examples above, the actions of the verbs (*to eat, to pester, to remove*) are easy to envisage. However, the 'actions' of verbs can be mental actions or more subtle actions:
● In 1938, *Time Magazine* chose Adolf Hitler for man of the year.
  (*Time Magazine* (the subject) is performing the verb *chose*.)
● Human birth-control pills work on gorillas.
  (*Human birth-control pills* (the subject) is performing the verb *work*.)

The 'action' of the verb can be very subtle.
● A wise man gets more use from his enemies than a fool from his friends. (Spanish philosopher Baltasar Gracián)
  (*A wise man* (the subject) is performing the verb *gets*.)

Often, the 'action' of the verb is just the act of being.

● A paper cut is a tree's final moment of revenge.

(*A paper cut* (the subject) is performing the verb *is*.)

When the subject is performing the action, the verb is said to be in the active voice. When the action of the verb is being done to the subject, the verb is said to be in the passive voice.

● My house was clean yesterday.

(*My house* (the subject) is 'performing' the verb *was*. Here, *was* is in the active voice.)

● My house was cleaned yesterday.

(Here, *my house* (the subject) is receiving the action, so *was cleaned* is in the passive voice. Get it? *See also* Voice on page 259).

WHY SHOULD I CARE ABOUT ACTIVE AND PASSIVE SENTENCES?

Below are four good reasons to use active sentences and four good reasons to use passive ones.

Reason 1. Active sentences are shorter.

● He ate the pie.

(This active sentence has four words and 12 characters.)

● The pie was eaten by him.

(The passive version has six words and 20 characters.)

Reason 2. Active sentences are more direct. An active sentence ensures the subject takes responsibility for the action.

● I shot the sheriff.

(This active sentence makes it clear who shot the sheriff.)

● The sheriff was shot.

(With this passive sentence, the performer of the action (called the agent) does not have to be named. The sentence could have ended *by me*, but it's grammatically sound without naming the agent.)

Reason 3. Active sentences are more authoritative. As active sentences make it clear who did what to whom and in a succinct manner, they come across as more authoritative.

● We created the law to ensure patient safety.

(In this active sentence, the subject is taking responsibility…and credit.)

● The law was created to ensure patient safety.

(This passive version avoids responsibility… and blame.)

Reason 4. Active sentences are more engaging for the reader. The natural way to make a point is 'A affects B'. With this active-sentence structure, readers absorb information more easily than with the passive-sentence structure ('B was affected by A'). If your readers do not have to expend effort unravelling your meaning, they will apply more effort to absorbing your words.

- The Foreign Office advised me to apply for a work permit.

  (With this active-sentence version, the information is absorbed as you encounter it.)

- I was advised to apply for a work permit by the Foreign Office.

  (This passive-sentence version is pretty clear, but it requires a few more calories to take it in. To reduce your readers' brain-strain, adopt a bias for active sentences over passive ones.)

There are also good reasons to use passive sentences.

Reason 1. Passive sentences can be used to avoid blame.

- The article was released without permission.

  (This passive sentence avoids blame.)

- Jeremy released the article without permission.

  (With the active version, Jeremy is toast.)

Reason 2. Passive sentences can show a neutral or objective tone.

- It is anticipated that concessions will be offered by both parties.

  (This passive sentence expresses a neutral tone.)

Reason 3. Passive sentences are often appropriate when the agent is obvious, unimportant or unknown.

- The burglar was arrested as he left the cottage.

  (The agent is obviously the police.)

- The pigs were last seen on the outskirts of Malmesbury.

  (It's unimportant who saw the pigs.)

- The fire was started in the attic.

  (The perpetrator is unknown.)

Reason 4. Passive sentences allow you to focus on what's important. A passive sentence allows you to shift the focus from the doer of the action to the recipient of the action.

- In 1215, the Magna Carta was signed by King John.

  (This passive sentence focuses on the Magna Carta.)

- King John signed the Magna Carta in 1215.

  (This active sentence focuses on King John.)

Active sentences are considered clear and authoritative while passive sentences are considered indirect and even apologetic. As a result, many companies encourage their staff to avoid passive sentences. This practice is waning, but some grammar checkers still treat a passive sentence as a mistake and suggest an active one. But, if your passive sentence works for you (e.g. if it gives the right emphasis or masks the agent), stick with it. Here's a great example of trying way too hard to avoid a passive sentence:

● An editor who had been trained to avoid passive sentences changed 'The unconscious patient must be placed in the coma position' to 'The unconscious patient must adopt the coma position'. ✗ (grammatically fine but logically not)

Also, if you've trained yourself to use lots of passive sentences because you think they sound more corporate, then swing the needle back towards active sentences. Here's the final advice: use active and passive sentences to control text flow and to stress the important parts of your sentences.

KEY POINTS
Active sentences are shorter, more direct, more informative, more authoritative and easier to absorb.
Passive sentences are useful for avoiding blame, portraying a neutral tone and focusing on the recipient of the verb's action rather than the doer.

Adjective

Adjectives describe nouns and pronouns.

EASY EXAMPLES

An adjective (bold) usually comes directly before the noun or pronoun it describes (or modifies, as they say).

- **old** man
- **grey** coat
- **cheerful** one

(Adjectives that come before nouns are called attributive adjectives.)

An adjective can come after the noun.

- Jack was **old**
- The sky looks **grey**
- He seems **cheerful**

    (These adjectives follow the linking verbs *was*, *looks* and *seems* (see page 160) to describe the noun or pronoun. They're called predicative adjectives.)

Sometimes, an adjective comes immediately after a noun.

- time **immemorial**
- body **beautiful**
- all staff **available**

    (These adjectives are called postpositive adjectives. Postpositive adjectives are most common with pronouns, e.g. *someone interesting, those present, something evil.*)

NOUNS AS ADJECTIVES

Many words that are usually nouns can function as adjectives (e.g. **autumn** colours, **Devon** cream, **fruit** fly).

- Not all **face** masks are created equal. (Entrepreneur Hannah Bronfman)
- You cannot make a revolution with **silk** gloves. (Politician Joseph Stalin)

    (When used like adjectives, nouns are called attributive nouns.)

PARTICIPLES AS ADJECTIVES

Formed from a verb, a participle is a word that can be used as an adjective. It is classified as a verbal (a verb form that functions as a noun or an adjective). There are two types of participle: the present participle (ending *-ing*) and the past participle (usually ending *-ed, -d, -t, -en*, or *-n*). (*See also* Participle and Verb on pages 213 and 253.)

- Be wary of any helpful item that weighs less than its **operating** manual. (Author Terry Pratchett)
- No poet will ever take the **written** word as a substitute for the **spoken** word. (Poet Lascelles Abercrombie)

INFINITIVES AS ADJECTIVES

An infinitive verb (e.g. *to run*, *to jump*) can also function as an adjective. (*See also* Infinitive Verb on page 153.)

● No human creature can give orders **to love**. (Novelist George Sand)

(The infinitive *to love* describes the noun *orders*.)

● Progress is man's ability **to complicate simplicity**. (Norwegian adventurer Thor Heyerdahl)

(An infinitive will often head its own phrase. Here, the infinitive phrase *to complicate simplicity* describes the noun *ability*.)

THE ORDER OF ADJECTIVES

When two or more adjectives are strung together, they should be ordered according to the following list:

Order	Category	Examples
1	determiner (see page 138)	the, my, those
2	number (see page 187)	one, two, ninety-nine
3	opinion	lovely, attractive, rare
4	size	small, medium, large
5	physical quality	thin, lumpy, cluttered
6	shape	round, square, triangular
7	age	young, middle-aged, old
8	colour	red, white, blue
9	origin	British, German, Russian
10	material	wood, metal, plastic
11	type	L-shaped, two-sided, all-purpose
12	purpose	cooking, supporting, tendering
13	attributive noun	service, improvement, head

This 13-adjective string is ordered correctly:

● my two helpful XI thin tubular new white Spanish metallic hinged correcting knee braces

Regardless of how many adjectives are used, the established order is still followed.

- Who's nicked **my two black, wooden** spoons?
  (1: determiner 2: number 3: colour 4: material)
- Give your ticket to **the Italian old waiter.** ✗
  (Age comes before origin. *The old Italian waiter* would have been better.)

This list of precedence is not universally agreed, but all versions are pretty similar. Also the order can change for emphasis. For example, if there were two old waiters, one Italian and one Spanish, then the wrong example above would be correct, and the word *Italian* would be emphasised.

COMPOUND ADJECTIVES

Not all adjectives are single words. Often, a single adjective will comprise two or more words, in which case it is called a compound adjective. Compound adjectives (*see* page 108) are usually grouped with hyphens to show they're one adjective.

- On opening day at the McDonald's in Kuwait City, there was a **seven-mile** queue for the **drive-through** service.
- I like the **busted-nose** look. (Actor Peter Dinklage)

ADJECTIVE PHRASES

An adjective phrase is a group of words headed by an adjective that describes a noun. (*See also* Adjective Phrase on page 75.) In real-life sentences, adjectives are often accompanied by modifiers like adverbs (e.g. *very, extremely*) and prepositional phrases (e.g. *with me, about the man*). In other words, an adjective (bold) will often feature in an adjective phrase (underlined).

- My bankers are <u>very **happy** with me</u>. (The Pop Star Formerly Known as Prince)
  (The adjective phrase describes *bankers.*)
- The dragonfly is an <u>exceptionally **beautiful**</u> insect but a fierce carnivore.
  (Here, the adjective phrase describes *insect.*)

ADJECTIVE CLAUSES

Clauses can also function as adjectives. An adjective clause is a multi-word adjective that includes a subject and a verb. (*See also* Adjective Clause on page 72.) With an adjective clause, the clause is linked to the noun being described by means of a relative pronoun (*who, whom, whose, that* or *which*) or a relative adverb (*when, where* or *why*). Like all clauses, it will have a subject and a verb.

- The people <u>who make history</u> are not the people <u>who make it</u> but the people <u>who make it and then write about it</u>. (Musician Julian Cope)
- I live in that solitude <u>which is painful in youth but delicious in the years of maturity</u>. (Physicist Albert Einstein)
  (It can get complicated. In the adjective clause above, *painful in youth* and *delicious in the years of maturity* are adjective phrases.)

WHY SHOULD I CARE ABOUT ADJECTIVES?

This section covers a lot of adjective-associated terms, many of which have their own entries that highlight their quirks and issues. Below are six key points linked to adjectives.

Point 1. Reduce your word count with the right adjective. Try to avoid using words like *very* and *extremely* to modify adjectives. Pick better adjectives. The best writing is precise and concise.

- very angry > livid
- extremely posh hotel > luxurious hotel

Point 2. Reduce your word count by removing adjectives. Picking the right noun can eliminate the need for an adjective.

- disorderly crowd > mob
- organised political dissenting group > faction

Remove redundant adjectives.

- ~~necessary~~ requirement
- ~~armed~~ gunman

The needless repetition of a single concept is known as tautology.

Point 3. Avoid incomprehensible strings of adjectives. In business writing (especially with technical subjects), it is not unusual to encounter clumsy strings of attributive nouns.

- Factor in the **service level agreement completion** time. ✗
- The system needs a **remote encryption setting** reset. ✗

Noun strings like these are difficult to follow and can bring reading flow to a screeching halt as your readers stop to unpick the meaning (or worse, zone out). To avoid barely intelligible noun strings, completely rearrange the sentence, convert one of the nouns to a verb or use hyphens to highlight the compound adjectives.

- Factor in the time to complete the service-level agreement. ✔
- The system needs a reset of the remote-encryption setting. ✔

Point 4. Punctuate your string of adjectives correctly. With a string of adjectives, it's pretty difficult to mess up the punctuation because the rules are relaxed.

For two adjectives (in order of popularity):
- vast, inhospitable moor (with a comma)
- vast inhospitable moor (with nothing)
- vast and inhospitable moor (with *and*)

For three or more adjectives (in order of popularity):
- vast, inhospitable, windy moor (commas between)

- vast, inhospitable and windy moor (comma(s) between and then *and*)
(Those who use the Oxford comma should stick a comma before *and*.)
- vast inhospitable windy moor (nothing between)
- vast inhospitable and windy moor (nothing and then *and*)

With predicative adjectives, use the normal rules (see Commas in Lists on page 27).
- The moor is vast and inhospitable.
- The moor is vast, inhospitable and windy.

Adjectives that modify the same noun are called coordinate adjectives. Coordinate adjectives should follow the precedence list on page 68. Be careful with the precedence list though because not all adjectives in a string of adjectives are coordinate. It's fairly common for one of the adjectives and the noun to be inseparable because they belong together as a single semantic unit (a recognised thing).
- A Spanish wooden guitar.
  (These are coordinate adjectives.)
- A wooden Spanish guitar.
  (These aren't.)
As a *Spanish guitar* is a single thing, *Spanish* doesn't take its place according to the precedence list. Don't think about it too much. Just follow your instincts. You'll get it right.

Point 5. Don't complete a linking verb with an adverb. For some writers, the linking verb *to feel* (and one or two others) doesn't register as a linking verb, and knowing that adverbs modify verbs, they use an adverb.
- It tastes nice. It smells nice. It seems nice. By Jove, it is nice. ✔
- I feel badly for letting you down. ✘
  (*Badly* is an adverb. It should be *bad*.)
- Bad service and food tasted awfully. ✘
  (This is the title of an online restaurant review. *Awfully* is an adverb. It should be *awful*.)

Point 6. Use postpositive adjectives for emphasis. Putting an adjective immediately after a noun (i.e. using the adjective post-positively) is a technique for creating emphasis. (The deliberate changing of normal word order for emphasis is called *anastrophe*. See page 86.)
- I suppressed my thoughts sinful and revengeful.
- The sea stormy and perilous steadily proceeded.

KEY POINTS
Improve sentence flow by avoiding attributive-noun strings.
Don't say you feel badly unless you're bad at feeling stuff.
Use an adjective postpositively to create a thought everlasting.

Adjective Clause

An adjective clause is a multi-word adjective that includes a subject and a verb. An adjective clause usually follows the noun it modifies.

EASY EXAMPLES

In each example below, the adjective clause is in italics. Within each adjective clause, the subject is bold and the verb is underlined.

- The carpets *which **you** <u>bought</u> last year* have gone mouldy.
- The film *that **she** <u>recommended</u>* scared the kids half to death.

REAL-LIFE EXAMPLES

- The follies *which **a man** <u>regrets</u> most in his life* are those *which **he** <u>didn't commit</u> when he had the opportunity*. (Comedian Helen Rowland)
- Bore: a person *who <u>talks</u> when you wish him to listen*. (Author Ambrose Bierce)

MORE ABOUT ADJECTIVE CLAUSES

An adjective clause has three traits.

Trait 1. It starts with a relative pronoun (*who, whom, whose, that* or *which*) or a relative adverb (*when, where* or *why*). This links the clause to the noun being modified.
Trait 2. It has a subject and a verb. These are what make it a clause.
Trait 3. It tells us something about a noun or a pronoun. This is why it is a kind of adjective.

It is common for the relative pronoun to be omitted.

- The film *~~that~~ **you** <u>recommended</u>* scared the kids half to death.
- The follies *~~which~~ **a man** <u>regrets</u> most in his life* are those *~~which~~ **he** <u>didn't commit</u> when he had the opportunity*.

This is not always possible though.

- Bore: a person ***who** <u>talks</u> when you wish him to listen*. ✘
  (Sometimes, the relative pronoun (here, *who*) is the subject of the clause.)

When the adjective clause starts with a relative adverb (*when, where* or *why*), the relative adverb cannot be omitted.

- I don't remember *a time when **words** <u>were</u> not dangerous*. (Author Hisham Matar)
  (You can often omit a relative pronoun, but you can't omit a relative adverb.)

WHY SHOULD I CARE ABOUT ADJECTIVE CLAUSES?

There are two common questions related to adjective clauses.

Question 1. Should I use a comma before *which*? This is the by far the most common question related to adjective clauses. The answer applies to all adjective clauses, not just those that start with *which*. So, do you offset an adjective clause with commas or not? The answer is sometimes yes and sometimes no.

The rule is this:

Don't use commas if your clause is essential; i.e. it's required to identify its noun. (This is called a restrictive clause.)

Do use commas if your clause is just additional information. (This is called a non-restrictive clause.)

Let's look at some easy examples:

- Mark's dog *which ate the chicken* is looking guilty.
  (Here, the adjective clause identifies Mark's dog. From this, readers would infer that Mark has more than one dog and that we are talking about the one that ate the chicken.)
- Mark's dog, *which ate the chicken*, is looking guilty.
  (Here, the adjective clause does not identify Mark's dog. It's just additional information about his dog. From this, readers would infer that Mark has one dog.)

Let's look at two real-life examples:

- Kindness is the language *which the deaf can hear and the blind can see*.
  (Writer Mark Twain)
  (The adjective clause identifies, i.e. specifies, *the language*. It's not just additional information.)
- True love is like ghosts, *which everyone talks about and few have seen*.
  (Author François de La Rochefoucauld)
  (Here, the adjective clause does not specify ghosts. It's just an observation, i.e. additional nonessential information about ghosts.)

Here's a good tip. If you'd happily put brackets around your clause or delete it, then use commas.

- My brother (*who claimed to have a limp*) sprinted after the bus.
  (As it's just additional information, you can put it in brackets.)
- My brother sprinted after the bus.
  (As it's just additional information, you can delete it.)
- My brother, *who claimed to have a limp*, sprinted after the bus.
  (We have proven that this clause is not required to identify *My brother*. It's just non-restrictive additional information. Therefore, the commas are correct.)

Compare the non-restrictive clause on page 73 to this restrictive clause:

● The tramp *who claimed to have a limp* sprinted after the bus.
   (The clause is required to specify *The tramp*. Without it, we don't know which tramp.)

For completeness, let's look at the non-restrictive version:

● The tramp, *who claimed to have a limp*, sprinted after the bus.
   (Commas are only appropriate if we know which tramp we're talking about.)

Question 2. What's the difference between *that* and *which*? *Which* and *that* are interchangeable, provided we're talking about *which* without a comma. When *which* starts a restrictive clause (one not offset with commas), you can replace it with *that*. In fact, Americans will insist you use *that* instead of *which* for a restrictive clause.

● Mark's dog *which ate the chicken* is looking guilty. ✔ (but ✘ in America)
   (Americans baulk at *which* without a comma. They insist on *that*.)
● Mark's dog *that ate the chicken* is looking guilty. ✔
   (This version will stop you getting hate mail from Americans.)

For many, even Brits, *that* sounds more natural with a restrictive clause. This is something we can use. If all this talk of restrictive and non-restrictive clauses is confusing, try replacing your *which* with *that*. If your sentence still sounds good, you almost certainly want *which* without a comma. This trick works because *that* can only be used with a restrictive clause, and some language-processing area of your brain knows it.

The *that* substitution trick also works with *who*.

● A burglar *who is suing the homeowner* was booed in court.
● A burglar *that is suing the homeowner* was booed in court.
(Substituting *who* for *that* is a good way to test whether an adjective clause needs commas or not, but some of your readers won't like *that* being used for a person, even a burglar. So, if your clause starting *who* sounds okay with *that*, revert to *who* without commas.)

See also Restrictive Clause on page 232.

KEY POINT

If you'd happily delete your clause or put it in brackets, then it's not a restrictive clause, and it should be offset with commas.

Adjective Phrase

An adjective phrase is a group of words headed by an adjective that describes a noun.

EASY EXAMPLES

In the examples below, the adjective phrase is underlined and the head adjective is bold.

- She had <u>extremely **blue**</u> eyes.

  (This adjective phrase describes (or modifies, as they say) the noun *eyes*. The adjective *blue* heads the adjective phrase.)

- Sarah was <u>**hostile** towards me</u>.

  (This adjective phrase modifies the noun *Sarah*. Used after a linking verb (*was*), it's a predicative adjective phrase. There's more on this to come and on page 67.)

REAL-LIFE EXAMPLES

- An <u>overly **sensitive**</u> heart is an unhappy possession on this shaky earth. (German writer Johann Wolfgang von Goethe)

- I'm a <u>fairly **intelligent**</u> person, but I don't think my grades reflected that. (American footballer Barry Sanders)

MORE ABOUT ADJECTIVE PHRASES

In an adjective phrase, the head adjective can be at the start, the middle or the end of the phrase.

- I am **sad** about the result.
- I am <u>awfully **sad** about the result</u>.
- I am <u>very **sad**</u>.

The other words inside the adjective phrase are known as the dependents of the head adjective. They are typically adverbs (here, *awfully*, *very*; see page 77), or prepositional phrases (here, *about the result*; see page 209).

If you ever find yourself discussing *adjective phrases*, it won't be too long before you encounter the terms *attributive adjective* and *predicative adjective*.

- The <u>beautifully **carved**</u> frames are priceless.

  (An attributive adjective typically sits before the noun it is modifying (*frames*).)

- The frames are <u>beautifully **carved**</u> and priceless.

  (A predicative adjective phrase comes after the noun it modifies (*frames*).)

When an adjective phrase (or any adjective, for that matter) appears before its noun, it is highly likely to be an attributive adjective. However, an adjective that appears after its noun can also be attributive.

- The frames <u>beautifully **carved** by monks</u> are priceless.

(The adjective phrase is after the noun it modifies (*frames*), but this time it's an attribute adjective being used postpositively (a posh word for afterwards).)

Let's get technical for a second. Even though most attribute adjectives sit before their nouns, the position of an adjective does not determine whether it is attributive or predicative. An attributive adjective sits inside the noun phrase of the noun it modifies, and a predicative adjective sits outside the noun phrase of the noun it modifies. Typically, a predicative adjective is linked to its noun with a linking verb (e.g. *to be, to look, to smell, to taste*).

● The dog **covered** in mud looks **pleased** with himself.
   (The first adjective phrase – even though it's positioned after its noun (*The dog*) – is attributive because it appears inside the noun phrase *The dog covered in mud*. The second is predicative because it appears outside. Note that it is linked to its noun with a linking verb (*looks*). See also Linking Verb and Noun Phrase on pages 160 and 171.)

Also of note, the term *adjectival phrase* is often used interchangeably with *adjective phrase*, but lots of grammarians reserve *adjectival phrase* for a multi-word adjective that is not headed by an adjective.

● My uncle dated the girl **with the tattoos**.
   (The phrase *with the tattoos* is a multi-word adjective describing *the girl*, but it's not headed by an adjective. Headed by the preposition *with*, this is a prepositional adjectival phrase.)

WHY SHOULD I CARE ABOUT ADJECTIVE PHRASES?

Native English speakers are good at using adjective phrases. They cause few mistakes. By far the most commonly discussed topic related to adjective phrases is whether to use a hyphen to join an adverb to the head adjective. For example, some writers are unsure whether to write *professionally qualified editor* or *professionally-qualified editor*. Here's the quick answer: don't use a hyphen.

When an adverb ending *-ly* (and lots do) is modifying an adjective, don't use a hyphen to join it to the adjective. However, if your adverb is one like *well, fast* or *best* (i.e. one that could feasibly be mistaken for another adjective), then use a hyphen to eliminate the ambiguity.

● She has <u>beautifully-**formed**</u> feet. ✗
   (The hyphen is unjustified when the adverb ends *-ly*.)
● She has <u>well-**formed**</u> feet. ✔
   (The hyphen is justified to make it clear you mean the adverb *well*, i.e. *healthily*, and not the adjective *well*, i.e. *healthy*.)

Most would agree that there's no real ambiguity here, but using a hyphen with *well, best* and *fast* has become a point of style, which is justified with the it-eliminates-ambiguity argument.

KEY POINT
Use a hyphen with *well, best* or *fast* when it modifies an adjective.

Adverb

An adverb is a word that modifies a verb, an adjective or another adverb.

EASY EXAMPLES
- She swims **quickly.**
  (The adverb *quickly* modifies the verb *swims*.)
- She is an **extremely** quick swimmer.
  (The adverb *extremely* modifies the adjective *quick*.)
- She swims **extremely quickly.**
  (The adverb *extremely* modifies the adverb *quickly*.)

ADVERBS THAT MODIFY VERBS
When an adverb modifies a verb, it can usually be categorised as one of the following:

Adverbs of manner tell us how an action occurs. Lots of adverbs of manner end -*ly*.
- The lion crawled **stealthily**.
- Will you come **quietly**, or do I have to use earplugs? (Comedian Spike Milligan)

Adverbs of time tell us when an action occurs.
- I tell him **daily**.
- What you plant **now**, you will harvest **later**. (Author Og Mandino)

Adverbs of place tell us where an action occurs.
- I live **there**.
- Culture resides **in the hearts** and **in the soul of its people**.
  (Indian activist Mahatma Gandhi)

Adverbs of degree tell us to what degree an action occurs.
- He plays **smarter**.
- Doubters make me work **harder** to prove them wrong. (Businessman Derek Jeter)

ADVERBS THAT MODIFY ADJECTIVES AND OTHER ADVERBS
- To expect the unexpected shows a **thoroughly** modern intellect. (Playwright Playwright Oscar Wilde)
  (The adverb *thoroughly* modifies the adjective *modern*.)
- If a thing is worth doing, it is worth doing **very slowly.** (Burlesque entertainer Gypsy Rose Lee)
  (The adverb *very* modifies the adverb *slowly*.)

77

MULTI-WORD ADVERBS

Most of the adverbs in the previous examples are single words, but multi-word adverbs are common too. Adverbs commonly come as phrases (i.e. two or more words) or clauses (i.e. two or more words containing a subject and a verb).

Adverbs of manner often start with a preposition (e.g. *in*, *with*) or one of the following: *as*, *like* or *the way*. These are called subordinating conjunctions.

- Money speaks, but it speaks **with a male voice.** (Author Andrea Dworkin)
  (This is called a prepositional phrase. It's also an adverbial phrase.)
- People who say they sleep **like a baby does** usually don't have one. (Psychologist Leo J Burke)

Adverbs of time often start with a preposition or a subordinating conjunction such as *after*, *as*, *as long as*, *as soon as*, *before*, *no sooner than*, *since*, *until*, *when* or *while*.

- A company like Gucci can lose millions **in a second**. (Gucci CEO Marco Bizzarri)
- **After the game has finished**, the king and pawn go into the same box. (Italian proverb)

Adverbs of place often start with a preposition or one of the following subordinating conjunctions: *anywhere*, *everywhere*, *where* or *wherever*.

- Opera is when a guy gets stabbed **in the back** and, instead of bleeding, he sings. (Conductor Ed Gardner)
- Some cause happiness **wherever they go**; others whenever they go. (Playwright Oscar Wilde)
  (*Wherever they go* is an adverb of place; *whenever they go* is an adverb of time.)

Adverbs of degree (AKA adverbs of comparison) often start with one of the following subordinating conjunctions: *than*, *as ... as*, *so ... as*, or *the ... the*.

- Nothing is **so** contagious **as enthusiasm**. (Poet Samuel Taylor Coleridge)
- **The faster** you go, **the** shorter you are (Physicist Albert Einstein)

Adverbs of condition tell us the condition needed before the main idea comes into effect. An adverb of condition often starts with *if* or *unless*.

- **If the facts don't fit the theory**, change the facts. (Theoretical physicist Albert Einstein)
- Age doesn't matter, **unless you're a cheese**. (Filmmaker Luis Bunuel)

Adverbs of concession contrast with the main idea. They often start with a subordinating conjunction like *though*, *although*, *even though*, *while*, *whereas* and *even if*.

- **Although golf was originally restricted to wealthy, overweight Protestants**, today it's open to anybody who owns hideous clothing. (Comedian Dave Barry)

- A loud voice cannot compete with a clear voice, **even if it's a whisper.**
  (Writer Barry Neil Kaufman)

Adverbs of reason give reason for the main idea. They usually start with a subordinating conjunction like *as*, *because*, *given* or *since*.

- I don't have a bank account **because I don't know my mother's maiden name.**
  (Comedian Paula Poundstone)
- **As we can't change reality**, let's change the eyes which see reality. (Author Nikos Kazantzakis)

WHY SHOULD I CARE ABOUT ADVERBS?

Here are the six most common issues related to adverbs.

Issue 1. Use adverbs ending -ly sparingly. Professional writers often consider adverbs that end -ly unnecessary clutter. If you were to attend a creative writing course, you would be taught to select words that render -ly adverbs redundant. You would also be shown this quote by author Stephen King: 'The road to hell is paved with adverbs.'

As King advocates, if you choose the right verb or the right dialogue, you don't need an adverb. Compare these two examples:

- **Extremely** annoyed, she stared **menacingly** at her rival.
  (Critics would trash this.)
- Infuriated, she glared at her rival.
  (It's sharper with no adverbs.)

Here are three good reasons to kill a -ly adverb:

- She smiled **happily**.
  (The adverb is a tautology, i.e. needless repetition of an idea.)
- 'Ow, pack that in,' Rachel shrieked **angrily**.
  (Scrap the adverb if it's implicit in the dialogue or context. The adverb here is spoon-feeding the reader. This happens most commonly with verbs like *said*, *stated* and *shouted* (known as verbs of attribution).
- Sitting **dejectedly** in its cage, the parrot looked **utterly** unhappy.
  (Sharper would be '*Looking miserable, the parrot lay on the floor of its cage*'. Your readers will know that parrots don't ordinarily lie on the floor. Using 'lay on the floor' as opposed to 'sitting' allows you to delete the adverbs.)

However, if your adverb is part of the story, keep it.

- Your son is **surprisingly** handsome, Lee.

Issue 2. Professional writers hate adverbs such as *extremely*, *really* and *very*. (See Intensifiers on page 151.) For them, using an intensifier demonstrates a limited vocabulary. It's a fair point. If you choose the right words, you can avoid intensifiers.

Don't write ...	Go for something like ...
very bad	atrocious
extremely hungry	ravenous
incredibly tired	exhausted

Many writers assert that intensifiers are so useless, you should delete them even if you can't find a more descriptive word. In this example, the deletion kills a word but not the meaning.
- Ireland is great for the spirit but **very** bad for the body. (Actor Hugh Dancy)

Mark Twain shared this view: 'Substitute "damn" every time you're inclined to write "very". Your editor will delete it, and the writing will be just as it should be.'

Issue 3. When an adverb modifies an adjective, don't join them with a hyphen. This no-hyphen rule applies only to adverbs that are obviously adverbs (e.g. ones that end -*ly*).
- I don't sleep with **happily** married men. (Actress Britt Ekland) ✔
- He described himself as 'a **professionally**-qualified grammarian'. ✗

Issue 4. A few adverbs (e.g. *well* and *fast*) look like adjectives. To make it clear such an adverb is not being used as an adjective, link it to the adjective it's modifying with a hyphen. The hyphen says 'these two words are one entity', making it clear they're not two adjectives.
- She's a **well**-known dog.
  (With the hyphen, it's clear the dog is famous as opposed to well (healthy) and known.)
- He sold me six **fast**-growing carp.
  (With the hyphen, it's clear that the carp grow quickly and are not growing ones that can swim quickly.)

This issue crops up occasionally with *well*, which is almost never used as an adjective in a chain of other adjectives. Therefore, the following rule will cover 99 per cent of situations: use a hyphen with *well* when it precedes an adjective.
- It's a **well**-known tactic.
  (The hyphen really just avoids a reading-flow stutter caused by the possibility of ambiguity.)
- It's a **widely** known tactic.
  (Don't use a hyphen with normal adverbs. They don't cause reading-flow stutters.)

Issue 5. Make it clear what your adverb is modifying. Whenever you use an adverb (a single word or a multi-word one), do a quick check to ensure it's obvious what it refers to. (See *also* Squinting Modifier, Misplaced Modifier and Limiting Modifiers on pages 242, 162 and 159.) Here are some examples of badly placed adverbs.

- Singing **quickly** improved his stammer. ✘
  (Ambiguous. It's unclear whether *quickly* modifies *singing* or *improved*.)
- In November, Peter told us **after Christmas** that he plans to diet. ✘
  (Here, *after Christmas* modifies *told*, but the author's intention was for it to modify *to diet*.)

Usually, a badly placed modifier can be fixed by putting it nearer to the verb it's modifying. (The two previous examples can be amended by moving the bold text to the end.)

Be especially wary with limiting modifiers (e.g. *hardly*, *only*) because they can create logic flaws or ambiguity. As a rule, a limiting modifier should go immediately to the left of what it modifies.

- I **only** eat candy on Halloween. No lie. (Actor Michael Trevino) ✘
  (Potentially ambiguous. Logically, this means all he does on Halloween is eat candy, i.e. he doesn't work or sleep. In everyday speech, it's okay to 'misplace' *only*, but when writing there's time to be more precise.)
- I eat candy **only** on Halloween. ✔
  (Sharper. As a rule of thumb, the best place for *only* is never to the left of a verb.)

Issue 6. Use a comma after a fronted adverbial. When an adverbial phrase or clause is at the start of a sentence, it is usual to follow it with a comma.

- **In colonial America,** lobster was often served to prisoners because it was so cheap and plentiful.
- **If you're called Brad Thor,** people expect you to be 6 foot 4 with muscles. (Author Brad Thor)

When the adverbial phrase or clause is at the back, the comma can be left out. Each of these examples could be re-written without the comma and with the bold text at the end. (There is more about this under Comma and Restrictive Clause on pages 27 and 232.) When the adverbial is at the front, it's not a serious crime to omit the comma, but you should use one because it aids reading. When the adverbial is short (one or two words), you're safe to scrap the comma if you think it looks unwieldy.

- **Yesterday** I was a dog. **Today** I'm a dog. **Tomorrow** I'll probably still be a dog. Sigh! There's so little hope for advancement. (Cartoonist Charles M. Schulz via Snoopy)

KEY POINTS
Render adverbs ending *-ly* redundant with better word choice.
Have you used *very*? Delete it.
Put your adverbs close to what they're modifying and far from what they're not.

Affixes, Prefixes and Suffixes

An affix is letter or group of letters added to a word to change its meaning. An affix added to the front of a word is called a prefix. One added to the back is called a suffix. Prefixes (e.g. *anti-*, *ex-*, *pre-*) modify a word's meaning. Suffixes (e.g. *-ing*, *-ed*, *-s*) alter a word's meaning or ensure it fits grammatically into a sentence.

EASY EXAMPLES OF PREFIXES

- <u>Micro</u>scope
- <u>Tri</u>pod
- <u>Re-</u>establish

(Sometimes, a prefix is written with a hyphen. More on this to come.)

EASY EXAMPLES OF SUFFIXES

Often, a suffix that alters a word's meaning changes it from one part of speech to another (e.g. from a noun to an adjective).

- Joy<u>ous</u>
  (The suffix has changed the noun *joy* into an adjective.)
- Tender<u>ness</u>
  (The suffix has changed the adjective *tender* into a noun.)
- She run<u>s</u> a bar.
  (The suffix makes the verb fit. '*She run a bar*' would be wrong.)

REAL-LIFE EXAMPLES OF AFFIXES AND SUFFIXES

The four most common prefixes are *dis-*, *in-*, *re-* and *un-*. (These account for over 95 per cent of prefixed words.) Here they are in some short quotations.

- He has all of the virtues I <u>dis</u>like and none of the vices I admire.
  (Prime Minister Winston Churchill)
- How <u>in</u>appropriate to call this planet Earth when it's quite clearly Ocean.
  (Writer Arthur C Clarke)
- I <u>re</u>present all the sins you never had the courage to commit.
  (Playwright Oscar Wilde)
- What consumes your mind controls your life. (<u>Un</u>known philosopher)

The four most common suffixes are *-ed*, *-ing*, *-ly* and *-es*. (These account for over 95 per cent of suffixed words.) Here they are in some short quotations.

- If God want<u>ed</u> us to bend over, he'd put diamonds on the floor. (Comedian Joan Rivers)
- Want<u>ing</u> to be someone else is a waste of who you are. (Singer Kurt Cobain)
- The wise decide slow<u>ly</u> but abide by their decisions. (Tennis player Arthur Ashe)
- Many fox<u>es</u> grow gray, but few grow good. (American founding father Benjamin Franklin)

WHY SHOULD I CARE ABOUT AFFIXES?

Here are three good reasons to care about affixes. (Prefixes and suffixes are dealt with separately after this section.)

Reason 1. Using an affix to reduce the word count in your sentence. A word's meaning is changed when an affix is added. Sometimes, you can exploit this to reduce your word count by one or two words and to create a more flowing text.

- not aware > unaware
- not sure > unsure
- check again > recheck
- a comparison of the data shows > comparing the data shows

(The suffix -ing has been used to create a gerund, a type of noun that can take an object (see Gerund on page 185). Gerunds are great for creating succinct sentences.)

Reason 2. Breaking down long words to help with spelling. *Antidisestablishmentarianism* (a 19th-century move to remove the Anglican Church as the state church of England, Ireland and Wales) is best known not for what it represents but for its length (28 letters and 12 syllables). In the 1980s, schoolchildren often challenged each other to spell *antidisestablishmentarianism* (due to its use in the TV series *The Young Ones*). This was an impossible task, surely? Well, no. If you break it down into affixes, it's pretty simple.

- Anti-dis-establ-ish-ment-arian-ism
  (This is a well-used technique to help with spelling.)

Reason 3. Breaking down long words to help with decoding their meaning. Studying affixes in a word (especially if you know its root) can help with understanding its meaning.

- *disrespectfully* breaks down to *dis-respect-ful-ly*
  (Dissecting *disrespectfully* gets you to something like 'not-respect-full of-adverb', which would lead to 'done in a manner that is full of no respect'. That's a pretty good clue to its meaning.)

Not useful? Well, try understanding these without dissecting them:
- *lonelinesslessness*
  (With three suffixes, this is the concept of no loneliness.)
- *semihemidemisemiquaver*
  (With four prefixes, this a hundred-twenty-eighth note.)
  Inspecting a word's affixes to unpick its meaning is useful for non-native speakers.

WHY SHOULD I CARE ABOUT PREFIXES?

By far the most common question with prefixes is whether to use a hyphen or not. In other words, should you write *re-consider* or *reconsider*, or *anti-aircraft* or *antiaircraft*? As a general guideline, avoid a hyphen, but if the unhyphenated version is a spelling mistake or looks too unwieldy for you, then use one.

● proactive, prehistoric, ultraviolet
   (These words can be written with or without a hyphen, i.e. the hyphenated versions are not spelling mistakes. The guiding principle is to avoid the hyphen if your spellchecker lets you.)
● co-opt
   (Your spellchecker will bleat at *coopt*. You must use a hyphen.)
● Antiaircraft
   (*Antiaircraft* is not wrong, but it looks a little unwieldy. If you feel the same way, go for *anti-aircraft*.)

This guidance will help with most situations, but here are six extra points to consider.

Point 1. Use a hyphen with a proper noun (see page 168).
● un-British, pro-Nazi

Point 2. Do not allow the same vowel to double up (unless it's an o).
● semi-industrious, re-enter, ultra-argumentative

If the vowel is 'o', you can bear 'oo' and your spellchecker allows it, omit the hyphen.
● coordinate, cooperate
● coowner ✗
   (Your spellchecker will not allow *coowner*.)

Point 3. You can let different vowels double up.
● proactive, reactivate, semiautonomous
   If your spellchecker doesn't like it or you cannot bear how it looks, go for a hyphen. For many, *semiautonomous* looks too unwieldy.

Point 4. Use a hyphen with *ex* and *self*.
● ex-husband, self-aware

Point 5. Eliminate ambiguity every time. If the unhyphenated version could be confused with a different word, add a hyphen. (This is most common with the prefix *re*.)
● re-cover / recover
   (re-cover = to cover again / recover = to return to a normal state)
● pre-date / predate
   (pre-date = to come before / predate = to prey on)

Point 6. Enjoy the leniency. Most prefixed words exist in both forms. It's often down to how the writer feels about the word.

● The *anti-government* troops did not possess *infrared* goggles.
   (The writer didn't like the look of *antigovernment* or *infra-red*. That's fine. There's leniency)

● Why is <u>non</u>-*hyphenated* hyphenated? The irony!
   (*Nonhyphenated* doesn't need a hyphen, but this popular meme fails without it. Enjoy the leniency.)

WHY SHOULD I CARE ABOUT SUFFIXES?

The *-ing* suffix accounts for two of the three good reasons to care about suffixes.

Reason 1. Using present participles to say two (or more) things at once. Derived from verbs and ending *-ing*, present participles (bolded below) can be used to create a sentence structure that allows you to convey two or more ideas succinctly. (See also Participle on page 213.)

● **Believing** he'd been spotted, Jack raised his arms, **exposing** the explosive belt.
   (Jack did three things (*believed*, *raised* and *exposed*), and we've covered all three in a single sentence. This efficiency with present participles is possible when the actions are simultaneous.)

● **Knowing** trees, I understand patience. **Knowing** grass, I appreciate persistence. (Author Hal Borland)

Reason 2. Using gerunds to create more succinct texts. Derived from verbs and ending *-ing*, gerunds (bolded below) are a great way to reduce your word count and to create flowing text. (See *also* Gerund on page 185.)

● **Knowing** others is wisdom. **Knowing** yourself is enlightenment.
   (Chinese philosopher Lao Tzu)
   (The gerund *Knowing* is a more succinct way of saying 'To know' or 'Knowledge of'.)

● He wants to discuss **developing** the plan.
   (*Developing the plan* is a more succinct way of saying 'the development of the plan'. Using *developing* saves us two words and creates better-flowing text.)

Reason 3. Get 'free' vocab. Learning suffixes is a good way to expand your vocabulary. For example, once you know the root word *pay*, then *pay<u>able</u>, pay<u>ee</u>, pay<u>er</u>, pay<u>ing</u>* and *pay<u>ment</u>* all come 'free'. (This works in other languages too.)

KEY POINTS

Check if you can kill a word or two by adding an affix to a nearby word.
If you or your spellchecker can't bear the unhyphenated version, use a hyphen.
Creating a present participle or gerund by appending
-ing can improve writing efficiency.

Anastrophe

Anastrophe is the deliberate changing of normal word order for emphasis.

EASY EXAMPLES

- She stared into the dog's eyes deep and menacing.
  (Normal order: She stared into the dog's deep and menacing eyes.)
- On a black cloak sparkle the stars.
  (Normal order: The stars sparkle on a black cloak.)
- Bright he was not.
  (Normal order: He was not bright.)
- Powerful you have become. The dark side I sense in you. (Yoda)
  (Yoda's speech is anastrophic.)

WHY SHOULD I CARE ABOUT ANASTROPHE?

Breaking the expected word order places emphasis on the misplaced words. Anastrophe is commonly used in poetry, but it has utility outside poetry. If you're analysing someone else's writing and they've used anastrophe, you ought to recognise it and the impact it has.

- *City Beautiful* was a movement in 1890s to introduce beautification and monumental grandeur in US cities.
  (The expected word order is *Beautiful City*. The 'wrong' order gives the phrase more emphasis. See also postpositive adjectives on point 6, page 71.)

KEY POINT
Emphatic are misplaced words.

Antecedent

An antecedent is the thing (usually a noun) represented by a pronoun. (Note: This entry covers different types of pronoun, all of which have their own entries.)

EASY EXAMPLES

In each example, the pronoun is in bold and its antecedent is underlined.

- Gail said **she** would be late.

  (*Gail* is the antecedent of the pronoun *she*.)
- Tell the professor I'll see **him** tonight.

  (*The professor* is the antecedent of the pronoun *him*.)

In the examples above, the pronouns (*she* and *him*) are both personal pronouns. Spotting an antecedent gets a little trickier with the other types of pronoun. (*See also* Pronoun on page 218.)

- Let Mark do the work **himself**.

  (*Mark* is the antecedent of the emphatic pronoun *himself*.)
- Where's the whelk **which** Lee caught?

  (*The whelk* is the antecedent of the relative pronoun *which*.)
- Jack and Jill love **each other**.

  (*Jack and Jill* is the antecedent of the reciprocal pronoun *each other*.)

If there's a pronoun, then there's an antecedent somewhere (usually nearby and to the left). Sometimes though, the antecedent is not specifically mentioned.

- Please hide **these** from Lee.

  (The antecedent is not mentioned, but it will be understood from context, e.g. the talker might be pointing at some pies.)
- Make sure Mark has **some** before Lee arrives.

  (The antecedent is not mentioned, but it will be understood from context, e.g. the talker might be pointing at a cake.)

Sometimes, the antecedent is a concept.

- The clown was riding a bull, juggling five knives and singing 'Nessun Dorma'.

  That is talent.

An antecedent can come *after* the pronoun. (It's then sometimes called *postcedent*.)

- When **he** is nervous, the professor develops a stammer.
- Did **they** preach one thing and practise another, these men of God?

  (Author Roald Dahl)

It's common for pronouns to share an antecedent.

● I take <u>my wife </u>everywhere, but **she** keeps finding **her** way back.
  (Comedian Henny Youngman)

(It's not unusual for different types of pronoun to share an antecedent. Note that a possessive determiner (here, *her*) is a type of possessive pronoun.)

REAL-LIFE EXAMPLES

Antecedents of personal pronouns *(e.g. he, they)*

● If <u>a man</u> has not discovered something that **he** will die for, **he** isn't fit to live.
  (Civil-rights leader Martin Luther King)

Antecedents of possessive pronouns *(e.g. mine, yours)* and *possessive determiners* *(e.g. my, your)*

● <u>Fear</u> has **its** use, but cowardice has none. (Indian activist Mahatma Gandhi)
● Help <u>others</u> achieve **their** dreams, and <u>you</u> will achieve **yours**. (Author Les Brown)

Antecedents of indefinite pronouns *(e.g. none, several)*

● Fear has its <u>use</u>, but cowardice has **none**. (Gandhi)
  (This example is also used above. Sentences often feature multiple pronouns and antecedents.)

Antecedents of reciprocal pronouns *(e.g. each other, one another)*

● Let <u>my enemies</u> devour **each other.** (Surrealist artist Salvador Dali)

Antecedents of relative pronouns *(e.g. which, who, where)*

● A meeting is <u>an event</u> **where** minutes are kept but hours are lost. (Anon)

Antecedents of reflexive pronouns *(e.g. himself, itself)*

● <u>A fool</u> thinks **himself** to be wise, but <u>a wise man</u> knows **himself** to be a fool.
  (William Shakespeare)

Antecedents of emphatic pronouns *(e.g. himself, itself)*

● Nothing is impossible. <u>The word</u> **itself** says, 'I'm possible'! (Actress Audrey Hepburn)

Antecedents of demonstrative pronouns *(including demonstrative determiners)* *(e.g. this, these)*

● **This** <u>land</u>, **this** <u>water</u>, **this** <u>air</u>, **this** <u>planet</u> – **this** is our legacy to our young.
  (US politician Paul Tsongas)

(The first four *this's* [excuse the apostrophe] are demonstrative determiners, which are a type of pronoun. The antecedents of the first four *this's* [hey, get over it] are not present, but they are understood from context. The antecedent of the fifth *this* (a demonstrative pronoun) is the list of everything that went before.)

Antecedents of interrogative pronouns *(e.g. which, who)*

● **Who** wants to live forever? (Singer Freddie Mercury)

(The antecedent of an interrogative pronoun is something not yet expressed. That's the point. You're asking for the full antecedent. When the interrogative pronoun is *who*, 'an unknown person' is about as much of the antecedent as you can muster before the question is answered.)

WHY SHOULD I CARE ABOUT ANTECEDENTS?

Make your antecedents clear. If the link between your pronoun and its antecedent is unclear, you will – at best – cause your readers to stall. Worse than that, they might misinterpret your text. To portray yourself as a clear thinker, you must ensure the antecedents of your pronouns are obvious. Here are the two most common ways for the link between a pronoun to its antecedent to fail. (This is sometimes called a 'faulty pronoun reference'.)

Issue 1. There is no link.

● I want a job in journalism because **they** make democracy work. ✗

(The antecedent of *they* is meant to be *journalists*, but the word *journalists* isn't present. This error occurs when writers' fingers work faster than their brains. Usually, the meaning is clear, but such an error will do little to portray you as a clear thinker. A fix? Replace *they* with *journalists*.)

● The pie tin was empty because Lee had eaten **it**. ✗

(This is untidy because the intended antecedent (*pie*) is functioning as an adjective. Antecedents are meant to be nouns or pronouns, not adjectives. It's worth a rewrite. 'The tin was empty because Lee had eaten the pie' is one option.)

● The journalist's article reflects **his** experience. ✗

(This is untidy because the intended antecedent (*the journalist*) is in the possessive case and therefore functioning as an adjective. Some grammarians are okay with this. Some aren't. It's worth a rewrite. '<u>The journalist</u> reflects **his** experience in the article' is an option.)

● To deliver oxygen fast to **its** hard-working muscles, the cheetah's respiratory tract is enlarged. ✗

(This is untidy because the intended antecedent of *its* (*the cheetah*) is functioning as an adjective. Of course, the writer could claim the antecedent is in a previous sentence. That's acceptable, but it's good practice to keep each of your sentences tidy.)

Issue 2. The link is ambiguous.

● Jack told John **he** was depressed. ✗

(This is ambiguous. The antecedent of *he* could be *Jack* or *John*. Note that neither '<u>Jack</u> told Jill **he** was depressed' nor 'Jack told <u>Jill</u> **she** was depressed' is ambiguous'.)

89

- The letter from the bosses to the employees gave details of **their** annual bonuses. ✗
  (This is ambiguous. Is the antecedent *the bosses* or *the employees*? Fix? Spell it out. Replace *their* with *the bosses'* or *the employees'*.)
- The villagers pour any leftover mouldy grapes into a horse trough and crush the grapes with unwashed feet. The sludge is then mixed with the local sulphur-rich water. **That** is why their wine is unpalatable. ✗ (too ambiguous)
  (Most people would take the antecedent of *That* to be the whole process described, but the antecedent could feasibly be *the use of sulphur-rich water, mouldy grapes, the horse trough* or *unwashed feet*. If there's doubt, spell it out. 'This whole process is why their wine is unpalatable' is one option.)
- **It** isn't what **they** say about **you**...**it**'s what **they** whisper. (Actor Errol Flynn)
  (This example is included to highlight that the pronouns *it, they* and *you* are often used with deliberately vague antecedents. Here, the antecedents could be as follows: **it** (*what matters* or *what matters to me*), **they** (*the media, cinemagoers, people* or *my peers*) and **you** (*you, the reader, others* or *me*). This could have been rewritten as 'What matters to me isn't what my peers say about me...it's what they whisper.')

Using pronouns like *it, they* or *you* with a deliberately vague antecedent is common in speech, and it's an efficient way of making a point. It's particularly useful when some plausible deniability over the brashness of your message might be appropriate. In formal writing though, use more direct words.

- **It** said in the newspaper that a great white shark had been spotted off Cornwall. ✗
  (This is sloppy. A possible fix: 'According to the newspaper, a great white shark has been spotted off Cornwall.')
- **They** reckon it's going to rain all week. ✗
  (Sloppy. A possible fix: 'The BBC weather forecast said it was going to rain all week.')

KEY POINT
Whenever you use a pronoun (especially *this* or *that*), check its antecedent is present and obvious.

Appositive

An appositive is a noun or a noun phrase that sits next to another noun to rename it or to describe it in another way.

In the examples below, the appositive is underlined and the noun being renamed or described in another way is in bold. Appositives are usually offset with commas.

EASY EXAMPLES
- **Dr Pat**, <u>the creator of the turnip brew</u>, sold eight barrels on the first day.
- **The beast**, <u>a large lion with a mane like a bonfire</u>, was showing interest in our party.

Appositives can also be offset with brackets or dashes.
- **Peter** (<u>my mate from school</u>) won the lottery.
- Prices in **Alton** – <u>a small town only 25 minutes from London</u> – have been soaring.

Often an appositive will just provide bonus information that could be removed without destroying the meaning. Sometimes, however, removing an appositive will leave you with a question.
- **Dr Pat** sold eight barrels on the first day. (Which Dr Pat? Eight barrels of what?)

When an appositive is essential for understanding, it is called a restrictive appositive. When it's just removable bonus information, it's called a non-restrictive appositive. Non-restrictive appositives are always offset with commas, dashes or brackets. Restrictive appositives are usually offset with commas, dashes or brackets but not always.
- If **my dog** <u>Dexter</u> doesn't steal your sarnie, **my army mate** <u>Lee</u> will.

When a restrictive appositive is not offset with punctuation (as above), the structure will be [generic term + specific term], as opposed to [specific term + generic term].
- **My sister** <u>Dawn</u> might actually be an angel.
  (The structure is generic term + specific term.)
- **Dawn**, <u>my sister</u>, might actually be an angel.
  (The structure is specific term + generic term.)

When an appositive appears at the end of sentence, it can be introduced with a colon.
- He demanded just **one thing**: <u>loyalty</u>.
  (A comma or a dash would also be fine.)

REAL-LIFE EXAMPLES
- It is the **perpetual dread of fear,** <u>the fear of fear</u>, that shapes the face of a brave man. (Author Georges Bernanos)

● **Lou Epstein**, <u>the oldest, shortest, and baldest of the three Epstein brothers</u>, barely looked up from the cash register when Alfred entered the store. (extract from *The Contender* by Robert Lipsyte)

It's not uncommon for appositives to be introduced with terms like *i.e.*, *namely* and *in other words.*

● A clairvoyant is a woman who has the power of seeing **that which is invisible to her patron** – namely, <u>that he is a blockhead</u>. (Author Ambrose Bierce)

● There is but **one law for all,** namely, <u>that law which governs all law, the law of our Creator, the law of humanity, justice and equity</u> – <u>the law of nature and of nations.</u> (Statesman Edmund Burke)

(It's rare, but appositives can be lined up. It's called commoratio, deliberate repetition for effect.)

● Is it really fair for the **government** – i.e. <u>the taxpayers</u> – to provide people with cell phones?

(Using an introduction for an appositive (here, *i.e.*) is useful if it's not obviously an appositive.)

The word *appositive* comes from the Latin *ad* and *positio* meaning 'near' and 'placement'. Appositives will nearly always be to the immediate right of the noun they are renaming or describing in another way. However, they do occasionally appear farther away.

● **Panic** sprouted again, <u>desperate fleeing panic</u>, but there was nowhere to flee to. (extract from *The Hitchhiker's Guide to the Galaxy* by Douglas Adams)

This happens most commonly when the appositive follows a colon.

● He knew what **his wish** would be: <u>the ability to turn stones into gold.</u>

WHY SHOULD I CARE ABOUT APPOSITIVES?

You'll naturally be good at creating restrictive appositives (i.e. ones essential for meaning), but non-restrictive ones (i.e. ones that just add bonus information) may come less naturally because it's a more deliberate act to insert them. If that's true for you, it's worth overcoming because appositives are useful for providing detail mid-sentence in a way that doesn't wreck your sentence structure, and they can be good for emphasis. So, there are two good reasons to care about appositives.

Reason 1. Appositives are an efficient way to add information. An appositive can be used to shoehorn interesting information or detail into your sentence without destroying the sentence structure.

● **Alexander Graham Bell,** <u>the man credited with inventing the first telephone</u>, was declared one of the country's greatest inventors in 1936.

● In his 1835 paper published in the *Magazine of Natural History*, **Edward Blyth**, an acquaintance of Charles Darwin's, had documented all the leading tenets of Darwin's work 24 years ahead of **Darwin's 1859 paper** On the Origin of Species.
(Notice how the first appositive is offset with commas, but the second, which appears in the [generic + specific] structure, isn't.)

Reason 2. An appositive can be a way of creating emphasis. When used for this purpose, the appositive is often a near-repeat of the initial noun.

● **This tale**, this tragic tale, was full of cruel wars, savage devastation, unnecessary deaths and the inevitable search for bloody vengeance.

Another great way to create emphasis with an appositive is to put it at the end of the sentence after a colon. To do this, you'll need to deliberately structure your sentence to set the stage for the appositive (like a punchline).

● To pass this course, you need just **one trait**: determination.
(When an appositive is presented in this form, it's called an *emphatic appositive*.)

● Western philosophies are based on the teachings of **the big three**: Socrates, Plato and Aristotle.

KEY POINTS

Use an appositive, i.e. a renaming or new description of your noun,
to shoehorn extra information into your sentence without destroying
your sentence structure.
Use an appositive to generate a near-repeat, a close copy, of your idea
to give it emphasis.
There's a great literary device for generating emphasis:
the emphatic appositive.

Auxiliary Verb

An auxiliary verb (or a helping verb as it's also called) is used with a main verb to help express the main verb's tense, voice or mood.

The main auxiliary verbs are *to be* (which appears in the forms *am, is, are, was, were, will be, being, been*), *to have* (which appears as *has, have, had, will have, having*) and *to do* (which appears as *does, do, did, will do*).

EXAMPLES EXPRESSING TENSE
In these examples, the various forms of the main verbs are bold and the auxiliary verbs are underlined.

- She <u>was</u> **waiting** for an hour.
  (The auxiliary verb *be* helps to form the past progressive tense.)
- History <u>has</u> **done** a great disservice to Anne Boleyn. (Actress Claire Foy)
  (The auxiliary verb *have* helps to form the present perfect tense.)
- She <u>will have been</u> **studying** for a month at that point.
  (The auxiliary verbs *will, have* and *been* help to form the future perfect progressive tense.)

EXAMPLES EXPRESSING VOICE
- The Afghan rug <u>will be</u> **destroyed** by the dog if it's left on the floor.
- Laughing owls <u>were</u> **eaten** to extinction by predators.
  (In these examples, the auxiliary verb *be* helps to form the passive voice. A verb is in the passive voice when its subject does not perform the action of the verb but has the action done to it. *See also* Voice on page 259.)

EXAMPLES EXPRESSING MOOD
- Why <u>do</u> they **call** it rush hour when nothing moves? (Actor Robin Williams)
  (The auxiliary verb *do* is used to form the interrogative mood, i.e. to ask a question.)
- <u>Don't</u> **sweat** the petty things, and <u>don't</u> **pet** the sweaty things. (Comedian George Carlin)
  (The auxiliary verb *do* (here in its negative form) is used to form the imperative mood, i.e. to give an order. *See also* Mood on page 163.)

MODAL AUXILIARY VERBS
There is another kind of auxiliary verb called a modal auxiliary verb (or modal verb). These combine with other verbs to express ideas such as necessity, possibility, intention and ability. The modal auxiliary verbs are *can, could, may, might, must, ought to, shall, should, will* and *would*. These auxiliary verbs never change their forms. In each example opposite, the verb phrase is bold and the modal auxiliary verb is underlined.

Modal auxiliary verbs expressing necessity:
- It is during our darkest moments that we **must focus** to see the light. (Philosopher Aristotle)
- I don't say we all **ought to misbehave**, but we **ought to look** as if we could. (Actor Orson Welles)

Modal auxiliary verbs expressing possibility:
- It is never too late to be what you **might have been**. (Author George Eliot)
- If there were no bad people, there **would be** no good lawyers. (Author Charles Dickens)

Modal auxiliary verbs expressing intention:
- We **shall heal** our wounds, **collect** our dead and **continue** fighting. (Founding father of the People's Republic of China Mao Zedong)

Modal auxiliary verbs expressing ability:
- No one **can feel** as helpless as the owner of a sick goldfish. (Cartoonist Kin Hubbard)
- Well, either side **could win** it, or it **could be** a draw. (Football manager Ron Atkinson)
  (Sometimes, two senses are expressed. Here, *could* expresses ability and possibility.)

Be, have and *do* are not always auxiliary verbs. Here they are as the main verbs (in bold) being supported by modal auxiliary verbs (underlined).
- I have inspiration. If I was educated, I would **be** a damn fool. (Musician Bob Marley)
  (Some might have preferred 'If I were educated', Bob. But, yeah, that's your point!)
- I really like vampire books. I might **have** a problem. (Writer Sarah Rees Brennan)

EXAMPLES OF A VERB PHRASE

There's another related term we should cover: verb phrase. A verb phrase is made up of the main verb and any auxiliary verbs. Any adverbs that appear alongside or inside a verb phrase are not part of the phrase. In each example below, the verb phrase is bold and the auxiliary verbs are underlined.
- Professor McGraw **has been** rigorously **testing** jokes to ascertain what makes them funny.
  (The adverb *rigorously* is not part of the verb phrase.)
- The 1989 film *Pet Sematary* [*sic*] **is** still **scaring** the life out of its viewers.
  (The adverb *still* is not part of the verb phrase.)

WHY SHOULD I CARE ABOUT AUXILIARY VERBS?

I'd wager that you use auxiliary verbs and modal auxiliary verbs without giving them a second thought, so I'm mindful that this entry has covered a lot of gumpf that you don't really need. Well, that's true if we're talking about working in English. If you start learning a foreign language though, it won't be too long before you'll be unpicking how they express tense, voice and mood. A good starting point for that is understanding how we do it. That said, here are three noteworthy points related to auxiliary verbs.

Point 1. Don't write *could of, should of* **or** *would of*...**ever.** These are number one on the Mistakes that Could Damage Your Credibility on page 8. *Could've* is a contraction of *could have*; *should've*, *should have*; and *would've*, *would have*.

Point 2. To be grammatically pure, use *can* **for ability and** *may* **for permission.** *Can* is a modal auxiliary verb meaning *to be able to*. *May* is a modal auxiliary meaning *to be permitted to*.
● I can whistle.
    (I have the ability to whistle.)
● May I have a biscuit?
    (Am I permitted to have a biscuit?)
● 'Can I go outside, grandma?' 'You can, dear. You're just not allowed.'
    This is full-on pedantry. Nowadays, *can* is routinely used for permission.

Point 3. Expand *can't* **to** *cannot* **not** *can not*. *Cannot* (one word) is the most common expansion of the contraction *can't*.
● There cannot be a crisis next week. My schedule is already full.
    (US statesman Henry Kissinger)

Can't can also be expanded to *can not* (i.e. two words), but this is less common and usually reserved for emphasis.
● I can not do it!
    (The two-word version provides emphasis.)

KEY POINT
Don't write *could of, should of* or *would of*. Just don't.

Case

Case shows a noun's or a pronoun's relationship with the other words in a sentence. The main cases you will encounter are the subjective case, the objective case, the possessive case and the vocative case.

EASY EXAMPLES

In English, nouns do not change their forms in any of the cases other than the possessive case (e.g. *Lee* becomes *Lee's*). Pronouns, however, change their forms in the possessive case (e.g. *he* becomes *his*) and the objective case (e.g. *he* becomes *him*). The table below shows how nouns and pronouns change (or don't change) in the main cases.

Subjective Case	Objective Case	Possessive Case		Vocative Case
		Possessive Determiner	Possessive Pronoun	
I	me	my	mine	
you (singular)	you	your	yours	Get off, **you.**
he/she/it	him/her/it	his/her/its	his/hers/its	
we	us	our	ours	
you (plural)	you	your	yours	**You,** scram!
they	them	their	theirs	
dog	dog	dog's		Hands up, **dog.**
dogs	dogs	dogs'		Run away, **dogs.**

MORE EXAMPLES OF THE SUBJECTIVE CASE

The subjective case (bold) is used for a noun or pronoun that is the subject of a verb, i.e. the person or thing carrying out the action or being described. (*See* Subject on page 243.)

- **Lee** went to Greggs.
- **He** supports Greggs.

The subjective case is also used for a subject complement (underlined). A subject complement completes a linking verb, e.g. *to be*, *to seem*, *to smell*. (*See* Linking Verb on page 160.)

- **Almonds** are <u>a member of the peach family.</u>
  (*Are* is a linking verb.)
- **It** was <u>he</u>.
  (Through common usage, *him* is also acceptable.)

MORE EXAMPLES OF THE OBJECTIVE CASE

The objective case (bold) is for a noun or pronoun that is either the direct object or indirect object of a verb or the object of a preposition. (*See* Object on page 191.)

Direct Object. You can find the direct object (bold) by finding the verb (underlined) and asking 'what?' or 'whom?' (i.e. by finding what the verb is acting upon).

- Frogs <u>don't drink</u> **water**. They <u>absorb</u> **it**.
- If you <u>wish to make</u> **an apple pie** from scratch, you first <u>must invent</u> **the universe.** (Astronomer Carl Sagan)

Indirect Object. You can find the indirect object (bold) by finding the recipient of the direct object (underlined). (The indirect object is usually the beneficiary of the action.)

- Give **her** <u>this message</u>.
  (Here, *this message* is the direct object. *Her* is the indirect object, i.e. the recipient of *this message*.)
- Computers are useless. They can only give **you** <u>answers</u>. (Painter Pablo Picasso)
  (The direct object is *answers*. *You* is the indirect object, i.e. the recipient of *answers*.)

Object of a Preposition. The object of a preposition (bold) is the noun or pronoun governed by a preposition (e.g. *around, against, with, in, on, by, of*). The prepositions are underlined.

- Jules Verne's Phileas Fogg travelled <u>around</u> **the world** <u>in</u> **80 days**.
- Kites rise highest <u>against</u> **the wind** not <u>with</u> **it**. (Prime Minister Winston Churchill)

MORE EXAMPLES OF THE POSSESSIVE CASE

The possessive case (bold) shows possession. With nouns, it is shown with an apostrophe. Pronouns in the possessive case come in two forms: possessive determiners (e.g. *my, your*) and possessive pronouns (e.g. *mine, yours*).

- An **ostrich's** eye is bigger than **its** brain.
- **Bader's** philosophy was **my** philosophy. **His** whole attitude to life was **mine.**
  (Actor Kenneth More, who played RAF fighter ace Douglas Bader in *Reach for the Sky*)

(*See also* Apostrophe on page 14, Possessive Determiner on page 139 and Possessive Pronoun on page 220.)

MORE EXAMPLES OF THE VOCATIVE CASE

The vocative case (bold) shows when someone (usually a person, but it can also be an animal or object) is being addressed directly. Words in the vocative case are offset with comma(s). (See Vocative Case on page 97.)

- **Ladies and gentleman**, please take your seats.
- Come here, **you big lump**. Take your noogie like a man.
- I know your auntie, **David**.

WHY SHOULD I CARE ABOUT CASE?

As a rule, Brits are awesome at the cases in English, even if they've never heard of them. You will most likely encounter the term *case* if you decide to study a foreign language, and this is the main reason for including an introduction to grammatical case in this book. That said though, here are three noteworthy points:

Point 1. Don't get possessive apostrophes wrong. The rules for placing apostrophes in possessive-case nouns cause a headache for some writers, and grammar checkers usually don't help because a wrongly placed apostrophe often creates a feasibly correct phrase from the grammar checker's perspective.

- I have one dog, not two dogs. My **dogs' kennel** is green. ✗

(This is wrong (it should be *dog's*), but a grammar checker wouldn't spot it because *dogs' kennel* (meaning the *kennel of more than one dog*) is a grammatically sound phrase. The grammar checker ignored the sentence before. It just checked *dogs' kennel*.)

The rules for creating possessive-case nouns are covered in Apostrophe on page 14.
If you're planning on going to that entry, take this golden rule with you: everything to the left of the apostrophe is the possessor. (If you remember that, you'll **never** misplace the possessive apostrophe.)

Point 2. Don't forget to use a comma for the vocative case. You might not have heard of the *vocative-case comma*, but there are plenty of times when you should use one.

- Hi, **John**.
  (When addressing someone directly, offset the term of address (usually their name) with a comma.)
- **Mark**, clean your room.
- Hey, **little darling**, look over there.
  (Use two commas if the term of address is mid-sentence. It's quite rare.)

Also, keep an eye out for this. When your sentence ends with a word in the vocative case, be sure to finish your sentence properly before starting a new one. For example:

● Take it from me, **dear**, it's not true. ✗

(This is called a run-on error (see page 235). You can't end a sentence with a comma and then write another sentence.)

● Take it from me, **dear**. It's not true. ✔

Point 3. Don't put apostrophes in possessive-case pronouns. Apostrophes are used with possessive-case nouns (e.g. *parson's nose*), but they're not used with possessive-case pronouns. So, there are no apostrophes in the possessive pronouns *yours, hers, its, ours* or *theirs*.

● Bull reindeer lose their antlers in winter. The cows lose **their's** in the summer. ✗

In particular, remember that there's no apostrophe in the possessive-case pronoun *its*. *It's* (with an apostrophe) has nothing to do with the possessive case. It is always (100 per cent of the time) a contraction of *it is* or *it has*.

● A cat always lands on **it's** feet. ✗

Actually, there is a pronoun that takes an apostrophe in the possessive case: *one*.

● One faces the future with **one's** past. (Author Pearl Buck)

KEY POINTS

Here's a really short explanation of apostrophe placement in possessive nouns:
Identify the possessor. Add 's. Delete the last s if it now ends s's. Sorted.
Oi, you, don't forget the commas if you address someone directly.
There are no apostrophes in any possessive-case pronouns (except *one's*, but these days only royalty and the super posh need worry about that).

Clause

A clause is a group of words that includes a subject and a verb.

A clause contrasts with a phrase, which does not contain a subject and a verb, e.g. *in the morning, dancing in the moonlight.* A clause can act as a noun, an adjective or an adverb.

EASY EXAMPLES
In each example, the clause is italic, the subject is bold and the verb is underlined.

- During the day, **Vlad** <u>slept</u> *in a coffin.*
  ('During the day' is a phrase. There's no verb.)
- When **the Moon** <u>shone</u>, **he** <u>lurked</u> *in the shadows.*
- **He** <u>stalked</u> *a pretty milkmaid,* **who** <u>lived</u> *in the neighbouring village.*

REAL-LIFE EXAMPLES
There are two types of clause:

- an independent clause (one that can stand alone as a sentence)
- a dependent clause (one that is usually a supporting part of a sentence).

In these quotations, the independent clauses are shown in bold and the dependent clauses aren't.

- Even though I made $800 million, **I am still grounded**. (Boxer Floyd Mayweather)
  (The independent clause could be a standalone sentence, but the dependent clause couldn't.)
- **A computer once beat me at chess** but was no match for me at kickboxing. (Comedian Emo Philips)
- After I die, **I'll be forgotten**. (Anon)

The opening words of the dependent clauses (*Even though*, *but* and *After*) are all subordinating conjunctions (see page 121). Their job is to link a dependent clause to an independent clause.

EXAMPLES OF NOUN CLAUSES
- She cannot remember <u>what she said last night</u>.
  (The clause functions as a noun. It could be replaced with a noun, e.g. *her rant.*)
- Now I know <u>why tigers eat their young</u>. (Mobster Al Capone)
  (This clause could be replaced with a noun, e.g. *the reason.*)

EXAMPLES OF ADJECTIVE CLAUSES
- My friend <u>who lives in London</u> looks like Homer Simpson.
  (The clause could be replaced with an adjective, e.g. *my London-based friend.*)
- Never make fun of something <u>that a person can't change about themselves</u>. (YouTuber Phil Lester)
  (This clause could be replaced with an adjective, e.g. *unchangeable.*)

EXAMPLES OF ADVERBIAL CLAUSES

- He lost his double chin <u>after he gave up chocolate</u>.
  (The clause could be replaced with an adverb, e.g. *recently*.)
- I am not afraid of the pen, the scaffold or the sword. I will tell the truth <u>wherever I please</u>. (Labour rights campaigner 'Mother Jones')
  (This clause could be replaced with an adverb, e.g. *here*.)

WHY SHOULD I CARE ABOUT CLAUSES?

Native English speakers can create and combine clauses and phrases without stumbling into too many snags. However, there are two great reasons to care about clauses.

Reason 1. Understanding when to offset an adjective clause with commas.

The adjective clauses in these two sentences are identical, except that one is offset with commas and one isn't. They are both punctuated correctly. So, what's going on?

- A boy <u>who went to my school</u> won the lottery.
- Michael Carroll, <u>who went to my school</u>, won the lottery.

When an adjective clause is required to identify its noun (*boy* in the first example), then it's not offset with commas. (In other words, the subject of the sentence is *A boy who went to my school*.)

When an adjective clause is just additional information, it is offset with commas. In the second example, the subject of the sentence is *Michael Carroll*. If you'd happily put brackets around the clause or delete it, then it should be offset with commas. Let's look at this in more detail:

- You went through a phase <u>when you dyed your hair purple</u>.
  (There is no comma because the clause is needed to identify *a phase*. A clause necessary for identification is called a *restrictive clause*.)
- You went through a punk phase, <u>when you dyed your hair purple</u>.
  (There is a comma because *the phase* has already been identified as the punk phase. The clause is just additional information, called a *non-restrictive clause*.)
- You went through a mod phase, <u>when you started school</u>, a punk phase when <u>you dyed your hair purple</u> and a punk phase <u>when you dyed your hair green</u>.
  (The first adjective clause is just additional information (note the commas), but the other two are required to identify the punk phases (note no commas).)

This subject is covered again from slightly different perspectives in other entries, including Relative Pronoun and Restrictive Clause (on pages 221 and 232). Don't worry. It's the same idea every time: if you'd happily put the phrase or clause in brackets or delete it (i.e. it's nonessential information), offset it with commas.

Reason 2. Understanding when to offset an adverbial clause with commas.
The adverbial clauses in these two sentences are identical, except that one is offset with a comma and one isn't. They are both punctuated correctly. So now what's going on?

- <u>When the game has finished</u>, the king and pawn go in the same box. (Italian proverb)
- The king and pawn go in the same box <u>when the game has finished</u>.

When an adverbial clause (or phrase) is at the front of a sentence (often called a fronted adverbial), it is followed by a comma (as in the first sentence above). When it's at the back, it is not offset with a comma (as in the second sentence). This "rule" works well with most adverbial clauses (which tend to be adverbs of time, place or condition). Check out the commas below after the fronted adverbials:

Adverbial Clauses of Time
- <u>When you win</u>, say nothing. <u>When you lose</u>, say less. (NFL coach Paul Brown)
- Say nothing <u>when you win</u>. Say less <u>when you lose</u>.

Adverbial Clauses of Place
- <u>Where there are too many soldiers</u>, there is no peace. <u>Where there are too many lawyers</u>, there is no justice. (Chinese philosopher Lin Yutang)
- There is no peace <u>where there are too many soldiers</u>. There is no justice <u>where there are too many lawyers</u>.

Adverbial Clauses of Condition
- <u>If you think you can</u>, you can. <u>If you think you can't</u>, you're right. (Businesswoman Mary Kay Ash)
- You can <u>if you think you can</u>. You're right <u>if you think you can't</u>.

This rule will see you through, but there's a little more to it. See Point 4 in Clauses, Dependent and Independent on page 107.

KEY POINTS
If your clause identifies your noun, don't offset it with commas.
If your clause is additional information, offset it with commas.
If your adverbial clause is fronted, use a comma. Don't use a comma if it's not.

Clause, Dependent and Independent

An independent clause is a clause that can stand alone as a sentence; i.e. it expresses a complete thought. A dependent clause (or subordinate clause) is one that cannot stand alone as a complete sentence; i.e. it does not express a complete thought.

EASY EXAMPLES

In all examples, the independent clauses are italic, and the dependent clauses aren't. (Notice how italic clauses could stand alone as sentences). Over the next two pages, the subject of each clause is bold and the verb of each clause is underlined.

- When **it** <u>rains</u>, *the **daffodils** <u>bow</u> their heads.*
- *The **patrol** <u>had spotted</u> the sniper,* **who** <u>was hiding</u> in an attic.

REAL-LIFE EXAMPLES

- *The **secret of life** <u>is</u> honesty.* If **you** <u>can fake</u> that, *you<u>'ve got</u> it made.*
  (Comedian Groucho Marx)
- If **you**<u>'ve heard</u> this story before, *<u>don't stop</u> me,* because **I**<u>'d like to hear</u> it again.
  (Comedian Groucho Marx)
  (Notice there is no subject in the independent clause. *Don't stop me* is an order (i.e. an imperative sentence), and the subject *you* is implied. We'll discuss the comma before *because* later.)
- *<u>Go</u>, and never <u>darken</u> my towels again.* (Comedian Groucho Marx)
  (These are both imperatives. The subject *you* is implied in both.)

Do not confuse clauses and phrases. The non-italic texts in the example below are not dependent clauses. With no subjects or verbs, they're not clauses at all. They're adverbial phrases.

- Outside of a dog, ***a book*** *<u>is</u> a man's best friend.* Inside of a dog, *<u>it's</u> too dark to read.*
  (Comedian Groucho Marx)

Adverbial and adjective clauses are often linked to an independent clause with a subordinating conjunction, e.g. *after, although, because, if, since, unless, until* (see page 121) or a relative pronoun, e.g. *which, who, whose* (see page 221).

- If **I** <u>held</u> you any closer, *I <u>would be</u> on the other side of you.* (Comedian Groucho Marx)
  (The dependent clause is linked to the independent one with the subordinating conjunction *if.*)
- ***Wives*** *<u>are</u> people* **who** <u>feel</u> they don't dance enough. (Comedian Groucho Marx)
  (The dependent clause is linked to the independent one with the relative pronoun *who*. A dependent adjective clause headed by a relative pronoun (e.g. *which, who, that*) is also known as a *relative clause.*)

Dependent clauses usually function as adjectives or adverbs.

Type	Example
Adjective clause	*I <u>refuse</u> to join any club* **that** <u>would have</u> *me as a member.* (The dependent clause '*that would have me as a member*' describes the *club*.)
Adverbial clause	*I <u>find</u> television very educating.* When **it'<u>s</u>** on, *I <u>go</u> into the other room and <u>read</u> a book.* (Comedian Groucho Marx) (The dependent clause '*When it's on*' modifies the verb *go*.)

The number of independent clauses and dependent clauses in a sentence determines the sentence-structure type. There are four.

Type	Structure	Example
Simple sentence	one independent clause only	**Humour** <u>is</u> *reason gone mad.* (Comedian Groucho Marx)
Complex sentence	one independent clause and at least one dependent clause	**No man** <u>goes</u> *before his time,* unless **the boss** <u>leaves</u> *early.* (Comedian Groucho Marx)
Compound sentence	two independent clauses	*I <u>have had</u> a perfectly wonderful evening, but* **this** <u>wasn't</u> *it.* (Comedian Groucho Marx)
Compound-complex sentence	at least two independent clauses and at least one dependent clause	**Those** <u>are</u> *my principles,* and if **you** <u>don't like</u> *them, I <u>have</u> others.* (Comedian Groucho Marx)

WHY SHOULD I CARE ABOUT DEPENDENT AND INDEPENDENT CLAUSES?

There's a great reason to care about independent and dependent clauses: comma placement. Here are four noteworthy points linked to comma placement.

Point 1. Use a comma before 'and' that links two independent clauses. This rule does not apply only to '*and*'. It applies to any coordinating conjunction, e.g. *but*, *or*, *yet* (see page 115).

- Yesterday is dead, **and** tomorrow hasn't arrived yet. I have just today, **and** I'm going to be happy in it. (Groucho Marx) ✔
  (In each compound sentence, there are two independent clauses linked by *and* with a comma.)

● I never forget a face, **but** in your case I will be glad to make an exception. (Groucho Marx) ✔

(This rule applies to all coordinating conjunctions not just '*and*'.)

● In Hollywood, brides keep the bouquets **and** throw away the groom. (Groucho Marx) ✔

(There is no comma before *and* because '*throw away the groom*' is not an independent clause. This is a simple sentence not a compound one.)

Point 2. Use commas with nonessential dependent clauses that start with *who* or *which* (or any relative pronoun for that matter). If a dependent clause functioning as an adjective is essential to specify its noun, it's not offset with commas. The dependent clauses below are italic.

● Tim's sister *who lives in London* was arrested.

(The clause is essential to identify Tim's sister. Readers would infer that Tim has more than one sister.)

● Tim's sister, *who lives in London*, was arrested.

(The clause is nonessential. It does not identify *Tim's sister*. Without more context, readers would infer that Tim has one sister. The clause is just additional information. It could be deleted.)

● The first thing *which I can record concerning myself* is that I was born. This life, *which neither time nor eternity can bring diminution to,* began. My mind loses itself in these depths. (Groucho Marx) ✔

(The first dependent clause specifies *thing*. The second one is nonessential. It's just additional information, so it's offset with commas. It could also have been offset with brackets or deleted, and that's a good test to spot nonessential clauses.)

● Anyone *who says he can see through women* is missing a lot. (Groucho Marx) ✔

(The dependent clause is essential to specify *anyone*.)

Point 3. Use a comma after a dependent clause that sits before an independent clause. Don't use a comma if it follows the independent clause. Using a comma after a fronted adverbial dependent clause is such a common style, it's becoming increasingly safe to call it a rule. The purpose of the comma is to show your readers where the clause ends. Omitting a comma isn't a hideous crime, but it can cause your readers to stumble as they try to find the end of the dependent clause. Can you read these two without stumbling?

● When the witch cooked her cat lurked by her feet.

● While you're cleaning the water can steam.

Here are some examples with commas. The independent clause is italic, the dependent clause isn't. As the adverbial dependent clause is at the front, it is offset with a comma

● Whenever I see you next, *remind me not to talk to you.* ✔ (Groucho Marx)

● Before I speak, *I have something important to say.* ✔ (Groucho Marx)

With the clause at the back, there's no comma.

- *Remind me not to talk to you* whenever I see you next. ✔
- *I have something important to say* before I speak. ✔

Point 4. There's more to Point 3. The rule that states 'do not use a comma when the adverbial clause follows the independent clause' is not actually all of the rule. In fact, post-positioned adverbial clauses are treated the same as post-positioned adjective clauses (see Point 2). So, use a comma if the adverbial clause is nonessential. The problem is that it's difficult to decide whether an adverbial clause is essential or nonessential. As the vast majority of adverbial clauses are essential, it's pretty safe, but not entirely safe, to assume that a post-positioned adverbial clause isn't preceded by a comma. This issue typically crops up with a *because* that explains a negative.

- Joe didn't win because he was the best player. He won because he paid the referee.
  (In this example, Joe actually won. The dependent clause '*because he was the best player*' is deemed essential to distinguish it from the situation below.)
- Joe didn't win, because he was the worst player.
  (In this example, Joe lost, as you'd expect the worst player to.)

The comma distances the dependent clause from *didn't win*. In the two examples above, the contexts make the meaning clear, but look at this:

- Joe didn't win because he was rich.
  (Now we're unsure whether Joe won. The absence of a comma tells us he did win, but, really, who'd read this sentence and deduce that Joe won?)

The take-away point here is that a comma before a post-positioned adverbial clause distances it from the verb in the independent clause. It makes the clause nonessential.

- He died as you'd expect a young officer to.
  (He died with honour.)
- He died, as you'd expect a young officer to.
  (This could mean he died because he was useless or because it was statistically likely.)

If you ever find yourself relying on the comma before a post-positioned adverbial clause for clarity, don't. Reword.

KEY POINTS

When a conjunction like *and*, *but* or *or* joins two independent clauses,
put a comma before it.
If you'd happily put your relative clause, which will usually start with *which* or *who*,
in brackets or delete it, then it's nonessential and should be offset with commas.

Compound Adjective

A compound adjective is a single adjective made up of more than one word.

The words in a compound adjective are usually grouped together using hyphens to show they are a single adjective.

EASY EXAMPLES
- **four-foot** table, **12-page** magazine, **free-range** eggs, **never-to-be-forgotten** experience, **well-deserved** award

REAL-LIFE EXAMPLES
- Internet memes are **modern-day** propaganda.
- Why does Macbeth go from being a seemingly reasonable man to a **cold-blooded** killer?
- As a **five-year-old** boy, I survived being dropped from a **fifth-storey** window.

It's not all about hyphens. Compound adjectives can also be grouped using italics, quotation marks and title case.
- In 1998, Jackie Chan became a ***bona fide*** star after starring in Rush Hour.
  (It's a common convention to write foreign words in italics.)
- With transgenderism, most agree that a **'live and let live'** philosophy is best.
  (Quotation marks can group the words in a compound adjective.)
- The ***Harry Potter*** author shares her birthday with the titular character.
  (Title case (see page 251) can group the words in a compound adjective. As a title is a proper noun, the compound adjective is an attributive noun. See page 67.)

WHY SHOULD I CARE ABOUT COMPOUND ADJECTIVES?
Grouping your compound adjectives (typically with hyphens) will not only showcase your writing skills but also help your readers. When a compound adjective is not grouped, your readers' reading flow will stutter as they group the words into one grammatical unit themselves. (In the UK, readers expect hyphens in their compound adjectives. In the US, they are more lenient.)

- Women in mystery fiction were largely confined to **little old lady** snoops.
  (US author Marcia Muller)
  (Brits would have preferred *little-old-lady snoops*.)

Showing off and maintaining reading flow are the best two reasons to care about compound adjectives. Here are four others (slightly more technical).

Reason 1. The hyphen might be essential to eliminate ambiguity. Sometimes, a hyphen is essential to avoid ambiguity. Look at the two examples below:
- a **heavy-metal** detector
- a **heavy metal** detector

Both versions are correct, but they mean different things. The first device detects heavy metal (e.g. mercury, cadmium). The second is heavy and detects metal. For a device that detects heavy metal, *heavy metal detector* (no hyphen) is wrong in both the UK and the US.

The following examples highlight why hyphens might be essential. If you wrote '*twenty four hour shifts*' (i.e. without hyphens), you'd be relying on your readers knowing the context to guess the right version, and you'd have done little to portray yourself as a clear thinker.
- Twenty-four hour shifts.
  (These shifts last an hour. There are 24 of them.)
- Twenty four-hour shifts.
  (These shifts last four hours. There are 20 of them.)
- Twenty-four-hour shifts.
  (These shifts last 24 hours. The number is unspecified.)

Here's an oft-cited, but probably apocryphal, headline in a local newspaper:
- Doctor helps dog bite child.
  (Clearly, *dog-bite child* would have been clearer.)

The next one is not apocryphal. In August 2018, the grammar world was set alight by this headline in the *The Pratt Tribune* (from Pratt, Kansas):
- Students get first hand job experience.
  (*Students get first-hand job experience* would have avoided the Twitter spike of the hashtag #hyphensmatter. *Firsthand* as one word would also have been acceptable.)

Reason 2. Sometimes there's a hyphen. Sometimes there isn't. Writers often ask questions like 'Is there a hyphen in tax avoidance?' or 'Is airport parking hyphenated?'. Well, the answer to those questions is sometimes yes and sometimes no. If those terms are being used as adjectives, then yes. If they're not, then no.
- He is a specialist in tax avoidance. ✔
- He is a **tax-avoidance** specialist. ✔
  (Both are correct. In the second version, *tax-avoidance* is a compound adjective modifying *specialist*.)
- How much is airport parking? ✔
- What are the **airport-parking** fees? ✔

There's a trap though. It's not uncommon for your adjective to be a compound noun as well (see page 178), which gets hyphens in its own right.

● He attended a course on self-awareness. ✔

● He attended a **self-awareness** course. ✔

    (Both are correct. In the first example, *self-awareness* is a hyphenated compound noun (see page 178).)

Reason 3. Sometimes it's one word not two, so you don't need any hyphens. Before you ask yourself a question like '*Is counter intelligence hyphenated?*', just check it's not acceptable as one word. (NB: *Counterintelligence* is acceptable as one word.) The quickest way is to test whether your spellchecker likes the one-word version. If it does, use it. If it doesn't, it's worth checking in a recent dictionary because spellcheckers take time to catch up with the latest trends.

● Students get **firsthand** job experience.

    (Writing *firsthand* as one word would have saved *The Pratt Tribune* its embarrassment. Most spellcheckers show *firsthand* as an error, but all the big dictionaries allow it.)

Reason 4. Only the words in the same adjective are joined by hyphens. Don't be tempted to string all adjectives together with hyphens. It's common to use more than one adjective to describe something (called *enumeration of adjectives*).

● She's an intelligent articulate lady.

    (*Intelligent* and *articulate* are standalone adjectives. They're called *coordinate adjectives* (see page 71). Rightly, there are no hyphens in this example.)

If you're unsure whether you're dealing with one compound adjective or two coordinate adjectives, put the word 'and' between the two words. If there's no loss of meaning, you're dealing with two adjectives, and you don't need a hyphen.

● large proud rooster > large and proud rooster ✔

    (This still makes sense. It's two adjectives. No hyphen is required.)

● first aid post > first and aid post ✗

    (This is nonsense. It's not two adjectives but a compound adjective. It should be *first-aid post*.)

KEY POINT

Group your compound adjectives to showcase your writing skills,
to avoid reading stutter and to eliminate ambiguity.

Conditional Sentence

A conditional sentence is a sentence that gives a condition (e.g. *If it snows*) and the outcome of the condition occurring (e.g. *the game* will be cancelled).

EASY EXAMPLES

There are four types of conditional sentences (the condition clauses are bold):

Type	Function	Example
Zero conditional	Expresses something as a fact	● **If you sleep,** you dream.
First conditional	States the result of a possible future event occurring	● **If you get some sleep,** you will feel better.
Second conditional	States the result of an unlikely event occurring or an untruth being true	● **If you became an insomniac,** you would understand.(unlikely event occurring) ● **If you were an insomniac,** you would understand. (untruth being true)
Third conditional	States how the situation would be different with a different past	● **If you had slept last night,** you would have beaten your record.

REAL-LIFE EXAMPLES

A zero-conditional sentence expresses a general fact (i.e. a situation where one thing always causes another). The simple present tense is used in both clauses. Also, the words *if* and *when* are interchangeable.

- **If you rest,** you rust. (Actress Helen Hayes)
- **If you sneeze,** you lose. (A bloke I overhead in a pub – yup, he actually said sneeze.)
- **If I make money,** I'm happy. **When I lose money,** I'm happy. (Gambling magnate Lui Che Woo)

A first-conditional sentence states the result of a hypothetical, but possible, future event occurring. The simple present tense is used in the if-clause, and the simple future tense used in the main clause.

- **If one swain [young lover] scorns you,** you will soon find another. (Roman poet Virgil)
- **If I like a food, even if it's bad for me,** I will eat it. (Reality TV star Kim Kardashian)

A second-conditional sentence states the result of an unlikely event occurring (e.g. *If the boat sank*) or an untruth being truth (e.g. *If they were on time*). The simple past tense is used in the if-clause, and *would* (rarely *should* or *could*) with the base form of a verb is used in the main clause.

- **If I had any humility,** I would be perfect. (Media mogul Ted Turner)
- **If you set out to be liked,** you would compromise on everything and achieve nothing. (Margaret Thatcher)

Nowadays, it's safe to say that the simple past tense is used in the if-clause, but in fact it's the past subjunctive (see page 163), which is like the simple past tense except when *I* and *he/she/it* are used with the verb *to be* (e.g. *If I were a millionaire, If she were to try*).

- Life would be tragic **if it weren't funny.** (Theoretical physicist Stephen Hawking)
- **If I were a rich man**, all day long I'd biddy-biddy-bum. (Extract from *Fiddler on the Roof*)

That said, the subjunctive mood is dying out, so the actual simple past tense has become acceptable.

- **If I was a man,** I would not settle down before I was 50.
  (Journalist Mariella Frostrup)

Third-conditional sentences express how the situation would be different if the past had been different. The past perfect tense is used in the if-clause, and *would have* (rarely *could have*) with a past participle is used in the main clause.

- **If my lawyer and I had communicated properly in January 1958,** this whole history would have been entirely different. (Inventor of the laser Gordon Gould, who fought unsuccessfully to patent it)
- **If I had known how hard it would be to do something new in the payments industry,** I would never have started PayPal. (Co-founder of PayPal Peter Thiel)

MORE ABOUT CONDITIONAL SENTENCES

An if-clause can be introduced with other terms such as *when, unless, provided that* and *as long as* or by using inversion (e.g. 'Were he available, he would be selected.').

- I will swim **unless the water is too cold.**
- I will swim **as long as the water is not too cold.**
  ('When', 'provided that' and 'as long as' can usually be replaced with 'If'. 'Unless' can usually be replaced with an 'if … not' construction. So, despite being disliked by some grammarians, the term *if-clause* is pretty accurate. It's certainly convenient.)

Occasionally, a conditional sentence will 'steal' the structures from two different types of conditional sentences. This most commonly occurs with a conditional sentence that uses the structure of a second-conditional sentence for one clause and the structure of a third-conditional sentence for the other. These are called *mixed conditionals*.

Mixed conditionals are typically used to express regret for past action or past inaction.
- **If we were smarter,** we wouldn't have set off in this weather.
  (The if-clause is second-conditional structure. The main clause is third-conditional structure.)
- **If you had checked the weather,** we wouldn't be stranded now.
  (The if-clause is third-conditional structure. The main clause is second-conditional structure.)

WHY SHOULD I CARE ABOUT CONDITIONAL SENTENCES?

Fortunately, the vast majority of native English speakers can create conditional sentences of all 4 'flavours' and the mixed 'flavours' without tripping themselves up. It's because native English speakers are naturally great at tenses. That said, there are some fairly common hiccups related to tense worth covering and also a point on using commas.

Point 1. Using a comma with an if-clause. When the if-clause precedes the main clause, use a comma after the if-clause.
- **If I were white**, I could capture the world. (African-American actress Dorothy Dandridge)
- **If you steal from one author,** it's plagiarism; **if you steal from many**, it's research. (Playwright Wilson Mizner)

If the main clause precedes the if-clause, don't use a comma before the if-clause.
- Dreams grow **if you grow.** (Author Zig Ziglar)
- There are consequences **if you act militarily,** and there are big consequences **if you don't act**. (US Diplomat Dennis Ross)

You can use a comma before the if-clause, particularly if you want to weaken the condition (i.e. make it non-restrictive). This is covered more in Dependent and Independent Clauses on page 104.

Point 2. Using the wrong tense in one of your clauses. Tense errors can creep in. Below are the most common ones with each structure.

Zero-conditional Structure. To express something as a fact, you should use the zero-conditional structure (*if* + simple present tense, simple present tense). However, writers sometimes incorrectly use the first-conditional structure (*if* + simple present tense, simple future tense), which states the result of a possible future event occurring.
- When dogs die, they **will** go to doggy heaven. ✗
  (The *will* should be deleted.)

First-conditional Structure. With the first-conditional structure, writers sometimes use the simple future tense (instead of the simple present tense) in the if-clause.

- You can have everything in life you want if you **will** help others get what they want. (Author Zig Ziglar)
  (The *will* should possibly be deleted. This hasn't been marked as wrong because *will* can be used for emphasis.)

Second-conditional Structure. With the second-conditional structure, writers sometimes use the simple present tense (instead of the simple past tense) in the if-clause.

- If you **become** an insomniac, you would understand. ✗
  ('*If you became an insomniac*' would be correct.)

The next most common mistake is to use *will* (instead of *would*) in the main clause.

- If you became an insomniac, you **will** understand. ✗
  ('*You would understand*' would be correct.)

Third-conditional Structure. With the third-conditional structure, writers sometimes use *would have* (instead of the past perfect tense) in the if-clause.

- If you **would have** slept last night, you would have beaten your record. ✗
  ('*If you had slept last night*' would be correct.)

KEY POINTS
When the if-clause is before the main clause, use a comma.
Do not use a comma when the if-clause is after the main clause.

Conjunction

A conjunction is a word used to connect words, phrases or clauses.

There are three types of conjunction:
- coordinating conjunctions (e.g. *and*, *or*, *but*).
- correlative conjunctions (e.g. *either/or*, *neither/nor*, *not only/but also*).
- subordinating (or subordinate) conjunctions (e.g. *although*, *because*, *until*).

Conjunction, Coordinating

Coordinating conjunctions join like with like. For example, a coordinating conjunction can be used to join an adjective with another adjective, a noun with another noun, or a clause with another clause. The three most common coordinating conjunctions are *and*, *or* and *but*. There are seven in total: *for*, *and*, *nor*, *but*, *or*, *yet* and *so*. You can remember them using the mnemonic FANBOYS.

EASY EXAMPLES
- Lee likes sandwiches **and** cakes.
  (*and* joins two nouns)
- She will sing **and** dance.
  (*and* joins two verbs)
- He's a small **but** aggressive little rascal.
  (*but* joins two adjectives)
- He typed the letter quickly **but** accurately.
  (*but* joins two adverbs)
- John, his deputy **or** his secretary will see you.
  (*or* joins three nouns)
- She sings like an angel **but** dances like a statue.
  (*but* joins two phrases)
- She must be able to sing like an angel, **and** she must be able to dance like Michael Jackson.
  (Here, *and* joins two sentences. As they're now in the same sentence, they've become independent clauses, i.e. clauses that could stand alone as sentences. Note the comma before *and*. This is a key point, which we'll cover later.)

REAL-LIFE EXAMPLES
- The best solutions are often simple **yet** unexpected. (Rock musician Julian Casablancas)
- He is richest who is content with the least, **for** content is the wealth of nature. (Greek philosopher Socrates)

WHY SHOULD I CARE ABOUT COORDINATING CONJUNCTIONS?

There are two common questions related to coordinating conjunctions.

Question 1. Do you put a comma before *and*? Mostly no but sometimes yes. Unfortunately, the answer to this question isn't short. Here's a summary of the rules.

The Rule for Two Items. When *and* (or any coordinating conjunction) joins two items, don't use a comma.

● Lee has eaten all the cheese **and** biscuits.

The whole world agrees on this point, but if you think it helps your reader, you can use a comma.

● I used to watch *Columbo*, **and** *Cagney and Lacey*.
(This example has two list items: '*Columbo*' and '*Cagney and Lacey*'. Without the comma the list items could feasibly be '*Columbo and Cagney*' and '*Lacey*'.)

So, unless it helps your readers, don't use a comma when 'and' (or any member of FANBOYS) joins two items. There's an important exception to this rule though. It's important because it's common.

The Exception to the Rule for Two Items. When your coordinating conjunction joins two (or more) independent clauses (i.e. ones that could stand alone as sentences), then use a comma. In these examples, the independent clauses are underlined and the conjunction is bold.

● <u>I like sweet things</u>, **but** <u>I prefer savoury dishes</u>. ✔
(If the clauses being joined by the conjunction could stand alone as sentences, use a comma.)
● <u>I like sweet things</u> **but** prefer savoury dishes. ✔
('*Prefer savoury dishes*' isn't an independent clause, so there's no comma before *but*.)

Here are two quotations by film director Woody Allen that cover this point:
● <u>The lion **and** the calf shall lie down together</u>, **but** <u>the calf won't get much sleep</u>. (Film director Woody Allen) ✔
(The *and* joins two nouns (no comma). The *but* joins two independent clauses (comma).)

● <u>My wife was immature.</u> <u>I'd be at home in my bath</u>, **and** <u>she'd come in **and** sink my boats.</u> ✔
(The first *and* joins two independent clauses (comma). The second joins two verbs (no comma).)

Hopefully, that's clear. But, there's a quirk: If the two independent clauses are short, it's acceptable – for style purposes – to omit the comma.

● <u>Craig caught a bass</u> **and** <u>Lee caught a cold</u>. ✔

Look at this though:

● The man caught the boy and the girl caught the dog.
  (For a fleeting moment, readers will think that the man caught *the boy* and *the girl*. You should write in a way that doesn't cause a reading stutter. A comma before the *and* would prevent that. This example shows why there's a comma before a coordinating conjunction joining two independent clauses.)

The Rule for Three or More Items. When there are three or more list items, life gets a little more complicated because there are two conventions.

Some people will write this:

● Bacon, eggs, **and** tomatoes
  (The comma before the *and* is called an Oxford comma. This is the convention followed by most (but not all) Americans.

Others will write:

● Bacon, eggs **and** tomatoes
  (This is the convention followed by most (but not all) Brits. The most notable exception is the Oxford University Press, after which the Oxford comma is named.)

There are plenty of people out there who would happily start a fight with you for not using an Oxford comma, but there are also plenty of others who consider the Oxford comma a waste of ink. In essence, it's a battle of clarity versus economy. The arguments for and against the Oxford comma are covered in Commas on page 29.

Question 2. Can you start a sentence with *And* or *But*? Despite what you may have been told at school, you can start a sentence with a conjunction like *And*, *Or* and *But*. Bear in mind though that a conjunction at the start of a sentence looks quite striking, so don't do it too often (it gets annoying quickly). Nevertheless, keep this practice in your back pocket to create an impactful start to a sentence. Think of it like this:

And is an impactful way of saying *In addition*
But is an impactful way of saying *However*
Or is an impactful way of saying *Put another way*

Here are some real-life examples:

● I'm selfish, impatient and a little insecure. I'm hard to handle. **But** if you can't handle me at my worst, you don't deserve me at my best. (Actress Marilyn Monroe)

● **And** let every other power know that this hemisphere intends to remain the master of its own house. (President John F Kennedy)

When a conjunction starts a sentence, you could argue it's not being used to join like terms but rather as a link between two sentences (i.e. like a conjunctive adverb such as *however, consequently* and *therefore*). So, the real question is not whether you can use a coordinating conjunction to start a sentence but whether *and, but* and *or* are conjunctive adverbs as well as coordinating conjunctions. And, it seems they are.

That raises a different question. Should you now put a comma *after* your conjunction like with a conjunctive adverb? Well, that's up to you. If you want a pause, go for it. If you don't, don't.

● It is better to be beautiful than to be good. **But**, it is better to be good than to be ugly. (Playwright Oscar Wilde)
(The comma provides a pause. It's not a grammar thing. It's a controlling-the-flow of-text thing.)

KEY POINTS
Use a comma before 'and' (or any FANBOYS conjunction)
joining two independent clauses.
Don't use a comma before 'and' joining two things.
Don't use a comma before 'and' in a list of three or more things
unless you're an Oxford commarist.
(But, break the last two rules if doing so provides clarity.)

Conjunction, Correlative

Correlative conjunctions are used in pairs to link equivalent elements in a sentence.

The most common correlative conjunctions are 'either/or', 'neither/nor', 'not only/but also', 'as/so' and 'not/but.'

EASY EXAMPLES

Just like coordinating conjunctions, correlative conjunctions link like with like.

- It was **neither** big **nor** clever. (linking adjectives)
- **Either** go big **or** go home. (linking verbs)
- He stole **not only** the TV **but also** the laptop. (linking nouns)

REAL-LIFE EXAMPLES

- It is **not** death **but** dying which is terrible. (Author Henry Fielding)
- Flowers are restful to view. They have **neither** emotions **nor** conflicts. (Neurologist Sigmund Freud)
- Education is **not only** the filling of a pail **but also** the lighting of a fire. (Poet William Butler Yeats)

WHY SHOULD I CARE ABOUT CORRELATIVE CONJUNCTIONS?

Correlative conjunctions not only provide a succinct structure in which to say two things but also express how those two things are related. Generally, they don't create any serious snags, but here are four noteworthy issues.

Issue 1. Keep a parallel structure. Correlative conjunctions come in pairs. Strive to use the same type of word after each one of the pair.

- He should **either** sell his watch **or** his car. ✗
  (This is untidy. 'Either' is before a verb (sell), but 'or' is before a noun (his car).)
- He should sell **either** his watch **or** his car. ✔
  (Both now sit before nouns.)
- He should **either** pawn his watch **or** sell his car. ✔
  (Both now sit before verbs.)

Issue 2. Don't use commas with correlative conjunctions. Some writers are unsure whether to use a comma with correlative conjunctions. This problem arises most often with the pairing *not only* or *but also*.

Here's the rule: Don't use commas with correlative conjunctions.

- Lee likes **not only** pies, **but also** cakes. ✗

Unfortunately, it's a little bit more complicated than that. Here's the exception: If the second conjunction sits before an independent clause (i.e. words that could be a standalone sentence), then use a comma.

● **As** a father has compassion on his children, **so** God has compassion on those who fear him. (Psalm 103:13)

It is rare for an independent clause to follow a correlative conjunction, but it does happen, especially with the pairing 'not only/but also'.
● **Not only** does Lee like pies, **but** he **also** likes cakes.

Issue 3. Be careful with subject–verb agreement. When the pairing 'either/or' or 'neither/nor' features in the subject of a verb, the verb is singular if both elements are singular.
● **Neither** the inspector **nor** the constable <u>was</u> available for comment.
  (Both elements (*the inspector* and *the constable*) are singular, so the verb (*was*) is singular; i.e. using *were* would be wrong.)

However, things get complicated if one of the elements is plural. There are two conventions.
Rule A. The Proximity Rule. Under this convention, the element next to the verb determines whether it's singular or plural.
● **Neither** the inspector **nor** the constables <u>were</u> available for comment.
  (The element nearest the verb (*constables*) is plural, so the verb (*were*) is plural.)

Rule B. The Logic Rule. Here, if either of the elements is plural, the verb is plural.
● **Neither** the inspectors **nor** the constable <u>were</u> available for comment.
  (The first element (*inspectors*) is plural, so the verb is plural. This would be wrong under The Proximity Rule.)

So, should you use the Proximity Rule or the Logic Rule? Well, both are common, so the quick answer is pick one and be consistent. But, there's a better answer: satisfy both. If one of your elements is plural, deliberately put it next to the verb.
● **Either** the cat **or** the budgies <u>have</u> to go.

Issue 4. Be aware that 'neither/nor' plays a negative role in your sentence. Be careful not to use a double negative.
● We did not discuss **neither** the flooding **nor** the landslide. ✗ (double negative)
● We discussed **neither** the flooding **nor** the landslide. ✔

Of course, two positives don't make a negative, but it can happen. Yeah, right.

KEY POINT
Position your correlative conjunctions so the same type of word follows each one. That's a parallel structure.

Conjunction, Subordinating

A subordinating conjunction links a dependent clause (also called a subordinate clause) to the main clause.

Here is a list of common subordinating conjunctions: *although, as soon as, because, before, even though, if, in order that, once, only if, provided that, rather than, since, than, that, though, until, when, whenever, where, wherever, whether, while, why.*

EASY EXAMPLES

A subordinating conjunction provides a bridge between the main clause and the dependent clause. In each example below, the subordinating conjunction is underlined, and the dependent clause is bold. (The normal text is the main clause.)

- Keep your hand on the wound <u>**until**</u> **the bleeding stops**.
- She left <u>**because**</u> **Mike arrived.**
- <u>**If**</u> **it rains**, the bet is off.
- <u>**Even though**</u> **she's skint**, she'll still look a million dollars.

REAL-LIFE EXAMPLES

The role of the subordinating conjunction and dependent clause is usually to establish a time, a place, a reason, a condition or a concession for the main clause.

- I find television very educating. <u>**Every time**</u> **somebody turns on the set**, I go into the other room and read a book. (Comedian Groucho Marx)
  (The dependent clause establishes a time for the main clause.)
- <u>**Wherever**</u> **the art of medicine is loved**, there is also a love of humanity. (Greek physician Hippocrates)
  (The dependent clause establishes a place.)
- People are more violently opposed to fur than leather <u>**because**</u> **it's safer to harass rich women than motorcycle gangs.**
  (The dependent clause establishes a reason.)
- Man is ready to die for an idea <u>**provided**</u> **that idea is not quite clear to him**. (Author Paul Eldridge)
  (The dependent clause establishes a condition.)
- I'm always ready to learn <u>**although**</u> **I do not always like being taught.** (Sir Winston Churchill)
  (The dependent clause establishes a concession.)

When a sentence has a main clause (also called an independent clause) and at least one dependent clause (also called a subordinate clause), it is known as a complex sentence.

WHY SHOULD I CARE ABOUT SUBORDINATING CONJUNCTIONS?

As a native English speaker, you don't need to worry about whether your subordinating conjunction is heading up a clause that establishes a time, a place, a reason, a condition or a concession. You'll do that bit naturally. The most common question related to subordinating conjunctions is whether to offset the dependent clause with a comma or not. Here's the rule: When a dependent clause starts a sentence, separate it from the main clause with a comma. These are often called *fronted dependent* clauses. The comma makes it clear where the main clause starts.

- **If you shoot at mimes**, should you use a silencer? (Comedian Steven Wright)
- **Now that I'm over sixty**, I'm veering toward respectability. (Actress Shelley Winters)

When a dependent clause ends a sentence, you can drop the comma.
- Should you use a silencer **if you shoot at mimes**?
- I'm veering toward respectability **now that I'm over sixty**.

There's a quirk though: You can use a comma before a subordinating conjunction for a deliberate pause or break. As a rule though, try to resist (more on this below).
- Money is better than poverty, **if only for financial reasons**.
  (Film director Woody Allen)

If you were told at school that a comma represents a pause, then your teacher was giving you reading advice not writing advice. There are specific rules on using commas, and 'to create a pause' isn't one of them, even though you'd probably get a few right if you adopted it. However, this is a time when a comma can be used for a pause or a break, but the role of a comma before a dependent clause isn't really to create a timing pause. It's to mark the clause as non-restrictive (see page 232). This is a difficult concept to nail with adverbial clauses (it's much easier with adjective clauses). Don't worry, though. The 'don't use a comma unless you want a pause' rule (which is simple) will see you right.

KEY POINTS
If your subordinate conjunction heads a clause at the start of your sentence, offset the clause with a comma.
Don't use a comma if your subordinate conjunction heads a clause at the back of your sentence, unless you want a pause.

Conjunctive Adverb

A conjunctive adverb links the ideas in two sentences or two independent clauses.

The following words are conjunctive adverbs: *also, consequently, furthermore, however, incidentally, likewise, meanwhile, nevertheless, nonetheless, therefore.* Conjunctive adverbs can also be phrases: *as a result, as a consequence, for example, on the contrary.*

REAL-LIFE EXAMPLES

● God could not be everywhere. **Therefore,** he made mothers.
   (Author Rudyard Kipling)

A conjunctive adverb typically starts a new sentence, but, if you want a smooth transition between your ideas, it is possible to use a semicolon before a conjunctive adverb.

● Orthodox medicine has not found an answer to your complaint; **however**, luckily for you, I happen to be a quack. (Cartoonist Mischa Richter)
● Not all chemicals are bad. **For example,** without hydrogen and oxygen, there'd be no way to make water, a vital ingredient in beer. (Author Dave Barry)
● I think; **therefore**, I am. (French philosopher René Descartes)

WHY SHOULD I CARE ABOUT CONJUNCTIVE ADVERBS?

Using a conjunctive adverb is a great way to keep your readers on track because it prepares them for the impending information by contextualising it with the story so far. (As conjunctive adverbs provide the logic for the transition between your ideas, they are also known as *transitional phrases.*) There's a common mistake related to conjunctive adverbs though: Don't use a comma before one. No, really, don't. No, really.

● The food is good, **however**, the management is horrible. ✗
   (TripAdvisor critic 'Shannon')

Preceding *however* (or any conjunctive adverb) with a comma and writing a new sentence is known as a run-on error or a comma-fault error (see page 59). A conjunctive adverb is typically written with a capital letter and is preceded by the end punctuation (usually a full stop) of the last sentence. It is possible to use a lowercase letter for your conjunctive adverb and precede it with a semicolon (see page 57), but don't do it too often. It quickly gets annoying.

KEY POINTS

For a smooth transition, use a semicolon before your conjunctive adverb.
Don't precede a conjunctive adverb (including *however*) with a comma.

Contraction

A contraction is an abbreviated version of a word or words.

EASY EXAMPLES

Contractions can be formed by replacing missing letters with an apostrophe. (Note how two words can be merged into one.)

- **can't** (contraction of *cannot*)
- **don't** (contraction of *do not*)
- **could've** (contraction of *could have*)
- **he's** (contraction of *he is*)

Contractions can be formed by compressing a word.

- **Mr** (contraction of Mister)
- **Dr** (contraction of Doctor)
- **Prof.** (contraction of Professor)

REAL-LIFE EXAMPLES

- If **you're** hotter than me, then **I'm** cooler than you.
- If we **shouldn't** eat at night, **why's** there a light in the fridge?

WHY SHOULD I CARE ABOUT CONTRACTIONS?

There are four common issues involving contractions.

Issue 1. Putting a full stop at the end of a contraction. Writers are often unsure whether contractions like *Mr* and *Dr* should be written with full stops (i.e. *Mr.* and *Dr.*). There are two conventions:

Rule A. Use a full stop every time.

- **Dr.** Smith asked **Prof.** Bloggs to remove **para.** 7 and **paras.** 18 to 22.

Rule B. Use a full stop only if the last letter of the contraction and the full word are different.

- **Dr** Smith asked **Prof.** Bloggs to remove **para.** 7 and **paras** 18 to 22.
  (Just like *Dr* and *doctor*, *paras* and *paragraphs* share the same last letter, so there's no full stop.)

Rule A dominates in the US. Rule B is most popular in the UK, but Rule A is not uncommon. Pick a rule, and then be consistent.

Issue 2. Confusing contractions with other words. The following contractions are often confused with other words:

- **It's** gets confused with *its*.

- **You're** gets confused with *your.*
- **They're** gets confused with *there* and *their.*
- **Who's** gets confused with *whose.*

A mistake involving *it's, you're, they're* or *who's* is a howler, and if you make too many, your readers will think you're a bit dim.

Here's a top tip: Expand your contraction. If your sentence still makes sense, then you're safe to put your contraction back in. If your sentence doesn't make sense with the contraction expanded, then the contraction is wrong. Let's try one:

- Time is a great teacher, but unfortunately it kills all **it's** pupils.
  (We need to check if *it's* is correct.)

Let's apply the tip:

- Time is a great teacher, but unfortunately it kills all **it is** pupils. ✗
  (We've expanded the contraction, and our sentence makes no sense. Therefore, we shouldn't be using a contraction.)
- Time is a great teacher, but unfortunately it kills all **its** pupils. ✔

This tip works every time. (See *also* Possessive Determiners on page 139.)

Issue 3. Expanding a contraction like should've to *should of.* Contractions that shorten the word *have* (e.g. *should've, could've, must've*) sound as if they end with the word *of.* They don't. Writing *should of, could of* or *must of* is a serious howler.

Issue 4. Using contractions in business writing As many people still consider contractions to be informal, they are best avoided in business documentation, especially if you're writing about something serious and you're unsure of your readership. However, this is far from a ruling. Contractions can make text less stuffy and more enjoyable to read. If you're a cool or casual company and the subject is appropriate, whack those contractions in.

KEY POINTS
If you can't expand a contraction to its full version, then it's wrong.
Don't write *could of, should of* or *would of.* Ever.

Dangling Modifier

A modifier describes a word or makes its meaning more specific. A dangling modifier is a modifier that has nothing to modify.

EASY EXAMPLES

Dangling modifiers (shown in bold) usually occur because writers get ahead of themselves. They assume the thing they're talking about is so obvious from the context that they forget to mention it.

- **Upon entering the room,** a skeleton caught my eye. ✗
  (Nothing in this sentence entered the room. The skeleton didn't. My eye didn't.)
- **Having followed a strict diet,** her weight dropped rapidly. ✗
  (Nothing in this sentence followed a strict diet. Her weight didn't.)

REAL-LIFE EXAMPLES

- **Having read your letter,** my cat will stay indoors until the ducklings fly off. ✗
  (It's pretty clear that the cat's owner read the letter, but the owner is not mentioned.)

In a way, the owner is mentioned because *my* represents the cat's owner, i.e. the cat's owner is the antecedent (see page 87) of *my*. However, it's good practice to keep a modifier and whatever noun or pronoun it's modifying in the same sentence – even next to each other. In the next examples, the modifiers (including the dangling ones) are bold. The noun being modified is underlined.

- **Having read your letter,** <u>we</u> will keep our cat indoors until the ducklings fly off. ✔
  ('*Having read your letter*' now modifies *we*.)
- **Packing my kit into three huge holdalls,** the dog could tell a long trip was coming. ✗
  (Nothing in this sentence packed the kit.)
- **Packing my kit into three huge holdalls,** <u>I</u> knew the dog could tell a long trip was coming. ✔
  (Now, *Packing my kit* modifies *I*, which makes sense.)

It can get a little trickier.

- **Meticulous and punctual,** David's work <u>ethic</u> is admirable. ✗
  (This is untidy because *David* is not the head noun in the phrase *David's work ethic*. *Meticulous and punctual* is modifying the head noun *ethic*, which is illogical.)
- **Meticulous and punctual,** <u>David</u> has an admirable work ethic. ✔
  (*Meticulous and punctual* is now modifying *David* as it should, not *David's work ethic*.)

Sometimes, a modifier can dangle a bit. This happens when the word being modified is present but not next to its modifier.

● **Vicious smelly creatures with huge tusks**, the ship's crew found it difficult to drive <u>the male walruses</u> from the beach.

(This is called a misplaced modifier. See page 162.)

WHY SHOULD I CARE ABOUT DANGLING MODIFIERS?

Dangling modifiers don't usually lead to ambiguity because the missing term is nearly always implicit. However, using a dangling modifier will tell your grammar-savvy readers that you're not a clear thinker. (Also, knowing about dangling modifiers allows you to tell your boss or your mates that they've used a dangling modifier, which is a win in anyone's book.)

To ensure you don't use a dangling modifier yourself, assume any modifier you use is dangling until you've nailed it to the term it's modifying.

● **Walking through the cemetery,** the trees became long-fingered ghouls. ✗
(If you were writing this, alarm bells should be sounding before you reached the end of *the trees*.)

● **Walking through the cemetery,** I saw the trees become long-fingered ghouls. ✔

Often, it's best to sidestep the modifier by rewording.

● As I walked through the cemetery, the trees became long-fingered ghouls. ✔

To avoid a misplaced modifier, put your modifier next to (typically to the left of) the term it's modifying.

● **While crossing the road,** the bus hit <u>Janet</u>. ✗
(Janet is present, so this is a misplaced modifier, i.e. it's not fully dangling.)

● **While crossing the road,** <u>Janet</u> was hit by the bus. ✔

KEY POINTS
Assume your modifier is dangling until you're sure it isn't.
Put your modifier next to whatever it's modifying (usually to the left).

Degree

The term degree (often called the degree of comparison) relates to adjectives and adverbs. Every adjective and adverb can be written in one of three degrees:

- **The Positive Degree.** This offers no comparison. It just tells us about the existence of a quality (e.g. *slow, slowly*).
- **The Comparative Degree.** This compares two things to show which has the lesser or greater degree of the quality (e.g. *slower, more slowly*).
- **The Superlative Degree.** This compares **more than two** things to show which has the least or greatest degree of the quality (e.g. *slowest, most slowly*).

EASY EXAMPLES
Here is the adjective *hungry* in all three degrees of comparison:

- Lee is <u>hungry</u>. (positive degree)
- Lee is <u>hungrier</u> than Mark. (comparative degree)
- Lee is the <u>hungriest</u> of all. (superlative degree)

Here is the adverb *dangerously* in all three degrees of comparison:

- Lee played <u>dangerously</u> today. (positive degree)
- Lee played <u>more dangerously</u> than Mark. (comparative degree)
- Lee played <u>most dangerously</u>. (superlative degree)

REAL-LIFE EXAMPLES
Here's the adjective *ugly* in all three degrees of comparison.:

- I may be drunk, Miss, but in the morning, I will be sober and you will still be <u>ugly</u>. (Prime Minister Winston Churchill)
  (*Ugly* is in the positive degree. It offers no comparison.)
- At the age of 18, children are thrust into the real world and shown its <u>uglier</u> side, but not before. (Australian author Margo Lanagan)
  (*Uglier* is in the comparative degree, describing adulthood as having the trait *ugly* to a greater degree than childhood.)
- Last week, I stated that this woman was the <u>ugliest</u> woman I had ever seen. I have since been visited by her sister and now wish to withdraw that statement. (Writer Mark Twain)
  (*Ugliest* is in the superlative degree, describing the woman as having the trait *ugly* to the greatest degree of all.)

Here is the adverb *beautifully* in all three degrees of comparison:

- Making money is a hobby that will complement any other hobbies you have <u>beautifully</u>. (Businessman Scott Alexander)
  (*Beautifully* is the positive degree. It offers no comparison)
- This will be our reply to violence: to make music more intensely, <u>more beautifully</u>, more devotedly than ever before. (Composer Leonard Bernstein)
  (*More beautifully* (the comparative degree) tells us how music will be made in the future compared to the past; i.e. it's a comparison of **two** things.)
- Palermo is the <u>most beautifully</u> situated town in the world – it dreams away its life in the Conca d'Oro, the exquisite valley that lies between two seas. (Playwright Oscar Wilde)
  (*Most beautifully* (the superlative degree) tells us that Palermo trumps every other town for its location; i.e. it's a comparison of **more than two** things.)

Forming the Comparative and Superlative Degrees

Here are the rules for forming the comparative and superlative degrees of adjectives:

Type of Adjective	Example in the Positive Degree	How to form the Comparative Degree	How to form the Superlative Degree
one syllable	strong	**add er** stronger	**add est** strongest
one syllable ending vowel consonant	thin	**double consonant and add er** thinner	**double consonant and add est** thinnest
more than one syllable	famous	**add less or more** more famous	**add most or least** least famous
more than one syllable ending y	silly	**remove y add ier** sillier **for less** less silly	**remove y add iest** silliest **for least** least silly
irregular	bad good many	**no rules** worse better more	**no rules** worst best most

Here are the rules for forming the comparative and superlative degrees of adverbs:

Type of Adverb	Example in the Positive Degree	How to form the Comparative Degree	How to form the Superlative Degree
one syllable	fast	**add _er_** faster	**add _est_** fastest
more than one syllable	carefully	**add _less_ or _more_** more carefully	**add _most_ or _least_** most carefully
irregular	badly well	**no rules** worse better	**no rules** worst best

WHY SHOULD I CARE ABOUT DEGREE?

If you're planning on learning a foreign language, then knowing the terms _comparative_ and _superlative_ is a useful starting point for learning their rules for forming them. That aside, here are five noteworthy issues related to degree.

Issue 1. Double comparatives and double superlatives are serious grammar mistakes. Don't apply two rules for forming a comparative or a superlative.

● You get <u>more sillier</u> as the night goes on. ✗
● She can run <u>most fastest</u>. ✗

These grammar errors are called _double comparatives_ or _double superlatives_. They are more common in speech than in writing. When spoken, they can be dismissed as a slip of the tongue. However, if you use one in writing, you're toast. Credibility shot.

Issue 2. Use the comparative degree when comparing two things. A common mistake is using the superlative degree when comparing just two things. (That's when you should use the comparative degree.)

● Of the two, she is the <u>most suitable</u> candidate. ✗
  (_More suitable candidate_ would be correct.)

Often, the number of things being compared isn't known.
● She is the <u>most suitable</u> candidate.
  (Reading this, we'd assume there were more than two candidates. If there were just two, it should say _more suitable_.)

Issue 3. 'Dead' means dead. You can't be more dead...or can you? Arguably, there are adjectives that should not have comparative or superlative forms because their meanings already express the qualities to the highest possible degree. Here are four adjectives that could attract criticism if you used them in the comparative or superlative degree. (They're ordered by their ability to annoy.)

- Dead (Can something be deader or deadest?)
- Single (Can something be more or most single?)
- Unique (Can something be more or most unique?)
- Instantaneous (Can something be more or most instantaneous?)

Issue 4. You can use 'quicker' or 'more quickly' as an adverb. 'Quicker' and 'more quickly' are both acceptable comparative forms of the adverb 'quickly'. It's a common misconception that 'quicker' has only recently passed into English as an adverb through common usage and ignorance of the difference between adverbs and adjectives. In fact, throughout most of the 19th and 20th centuries, 'quicker' was far more common than 'more quickly'. Only since the 1970s has 'more quickly' overtaken 'quicker' as an adverb.

The other quirky comparative is 'stupider', which is an acceptable alternative to 'more stupid'.

- Think how stupid the average person is – half of us are stupider than that. ✔
  (Comedian George Carlin)

Issue 5. 'Taller than me' and 'Taller than I' are both acceptable. When using the comparative degree, many writers are unsure whether to use a construction like 'taller than me' or 'taller than I'. The quick answer is both are correct, but not everyone agrees that both are correct, and that's the problem. Here's the root of the debate: the word *than* can be a conjunction or a preposition.

When *than* is used as a conjunction (remember that a conjunction joins like terms), it looks like this:
- John is taller than I am

or
- John is taller than I. (This is just a more succinct version.)

When *than* is used as a preposition (a preposition shows the relationship between words), it looks like this:
- John is taller than me.

For most people, the 'than me' version sounds the more natural, but this is the version that runs the higher risk of being attacked because the 'than I' version has been around longer and, for many, seems more grammatically correct. For others, however, the 'than I' version sounds pretentious. So, there's a lot to weigh up without any definitive guidelines. There's another issue to consider – sometimes, the 'than me' version introduces ambiguity. Look at this example:

● John likes Peter more than me.

This could mean:

● John likes Peter more than I like Peter.
or
● John prefers Peter to me.

A good way to remove this ambiguity is to use the 'than I' version and to expand the sentence (which means adding at least the verb).

● John likes Peter more than I do.
or
● John likes Peter more than he likes me.

This construction will also protect you from accusations of pretentiousness.

KEY POINTS
Don't apply two rules for forming a comparative (e.g. *more prettier*) or a superlative (*most best*). That's a serious mistake.
Use the comparative degree (not the superlative) when comparing just two things.

Determiner

A determiner is a word placed in front of a noun to specify quantity (e.g. one dog, many dogs) or to clarify what the noun refers to (e.g. my dog, that dog, the dog).

TYPES OF DETERMINER

Most determiners can be classified as one of the following:

- articles (*a*, *an*, *the*)
- demonstratives (*this*, *that*, *these*, *those*)
- possessives (e.g. *my*, *your*, *his*, *her*, *its*, *our*, *their*)
- quantifiers (e.g. *many*, *much*, *more*, *most*, *some*)

(Each type is covered in detail on the pages that follow.)

MORE ABOUT DETERMINERS

In traditional grammar, determiners are classified as adjectives, but many contemporary grammarians insist they aren't. This situation is unhelpful because terms like 'possessive adjective' are still commonly used, particularly on foreign-language courses. Whatever side of that debate you're on, this much is true: there are big differences between normal adjectives and determiners.

Difference 1. Unlike a normal adjective, a determiner cannot have a comparative form. *Happy otters* in its comparative degree would be *happier otters*. With a demonstrative determiner (e.g. *those otters*), there is no comparative form.

Difference 2. Unlike a normal adjective, a determiner often cannot be removed from the sentence.

- **The** <u>hungry</u> herons visited **our** <u>fishing</u> lake.
  (This sentence has adjectives (underlined) and determiners (bold).)
- **The** herons visited **our** lake.
  (Here, the adjectives have been removed. It still makes sense.)
- <u>Hungry</u> herons visited <u>fishing</u> lake. ✗
  (The determiners have been removed and it doesn't work.)

Difference 3. Unlike a normal adjective, a determiner can have an antecedent (i.e. something it refers back to).

- **The** <u>hungry</u> herons visited **our** <u>fishing</u> lake.
  (In this example, *the herons* tells us we're talking about herons that we've already discussed. Similarly, *our* refers back to some people. Normal adjectives don't refer back to things; i.e. they don't have antecedents.)

WHY SHOULD I CARE ABOUT DETERMINERS?

We will cover the issues with each type of determiner in the next few entries. Those aside, it is worth learning about determiners if you have young children because determiners feature in the primary-school grammar curriculum. Your child is likely to get a question like this:

● Underline all the determiners in the following sentence. 'She took two bottles back to his shop for the deposit.'

KEY POINT

Determiners are relatively new to the grammar scene. Some grammarians classify them as adjectives, and some don't. This issue will untangle with time. We're currently in an era when 'possessive adjectives', 'demonstrative adjectives' and the like are not classified as adjectives. That's pretty unhelpful, but hey ho. My advice? If you're a 'possessive adjective' type of person, start embracing the 'determiner' terminology. It's time. Let go.

Determiner (Article)

Articles are the words *'a'*, *'an'* and *'the'*. They define whether something is specific or unspecific.

The is called the definite article. It defines its noun as something specific (e.g. something previously mentioned or known, something unique or something being identified by the speaker).

- This is **the** lake.
  (This is a previously specified lake, i.e. one already known to the readers.)

A and *an* are called indefinite articles. They define their noun as something unspecific (e.g. something generic or something mentioned for the first time).

- This is **a** lake.

EASY EXAMPLES
- I'm not **a** troublemaker. I'm **the** troublemaker!
  (This means 'I'm not any old troublemaker. I'm the one you've all heard of.')
- **The** poets are only **the** interpreters of **the** gods. (Greek philosopher Socrates)
  (*The poets* and *the interpreters* are being identified. *The gods* are something known.)

WHY SHOULD I CARE ABOUT ARTICLES?
We're great at choosing between *a/an* and *the*, but we're not so great at choosing between *a* and *an*, and using the wrong one is by far the most common mistake involving articles.

Issue 1. Using the wrong indefinite article. Writers who dogmatically follow the rule that *an* precedes a vowel and *a* precedes a consonant often use the wrong indefinite article. *An* is used before a vowel sound, and *a* is used before a consonant sound. The word 'sound' is important because consonants – typically in abbreviations – can create vowel sounds (e.g. MOT, NTU), and vowels can create consonant sounds (e.g. *unicorn*, *united*, *Ouija*, *one-off*).

- Buy **a** house in **an** hour.
(*House* and *hour* start with the same three letters, but *house* starts with a consonant sound, while *hour* starts with a vowel sound.)
- I had **a** unique opportunity to strike **an** unexpected blow.

Be mindful of the distinction between initialisms (abbreviations spoken as individual letters) and acronyms (spoken as words).

- **An** MoD official and **a** MAFF official visited **an** NBC facility of **a** NATO country. ✔
  (The M and the N of the initialisms MoD (Ministry of Defence) and NBC (Nuclear Biological and Chemical) are pronounced *en* and *em*. The N and M of the acronyms NATO (North Atlantic Treaty Organization) and MAFF (Ministry of

Agriculture, Forestry and Fisheries) are pronounced *nn* and *mm*.)

The words *historic, historical, historian, horrific* and *hotel* start with a consonant sound, as soft as it might be. If you're drawn to *an historic* or *an horrific*, give your aitches more *huh* until you're comfortable with using *a*.

● The attraction of power can be **a** disease, **a** horrific disease. ✔

(Actor Liam Cunningham)

Issue 2. Writing a job title or an office name with a capital letter. A job title (e.g. president, judge, director) or the name of office (parliament, court, accounts section) is given a capital letter when it refers to a specific person or office, i.e. when it's a proper noun (see page 168). So, when the definite article (*the*) appears before such a title or name, there's a pretty good chance you'll need a capital letter. If the job title or office name is being used for its dictionary definition, i.e. as a common noun (see page 168), then don't use a capital letter.

● **The** King was **a** king among kings. ✔

(*The King* specifies an individual, but *a king* and *kings* do not. The first one is a proper noun. The other two are common nouns.)

● **The** Prime Minister said: 'Being **a** prime minister is a lonely job … you cannot lead from the crowd.' ✔ (Prime Minister Margaret Thatcher).

(*The Prime Minister* specifies an individual, but *a prime minister* does not.)

Issue 3. Capitalising 'The' when it starts a name (e.g. The Beatles). Some names (particularly band names) start with *The* (e.g. The Beatles, The Rolling Stones, The Sex Pistols). When such names appear in running text, you have a choice whether to write *The* or *the*. There's no consensus among the leading style guides on this point, so go with your preference.

● Did you download the The Clash album? ✗

(Logically, this is correct, but it's far too unwieldy. Most people would write 'Did you download the Clash album?'.)

Bear in mind that you might stumble across this issue with foreign names.

● Gina Vitale: The restaurant is called The La Trattoria.

Michael Felgate: The La Trattoria means The The Trattoria.

Gina Vitale: I know.

(This is from the 1999 Hugh Grant film *Mickey Blue Eyes*. With more clarity of thought, the owner might have called the restaurant La Trattoria.)

● Does it disturb anyone else that The Los Angeles Angels baseball team translates directly as The The Angels Angels? (Anon)

(There's no fix for this one. Just go with it.)

KEY POINTS
Use *an* before a vowel sound and *a* before a consonant sound.
When a job title (e.g. ambassador) or an office name (e.g. finance office) is preceded by *an* or *a* (as opposed to *the*), write it with a lowercase letter.

Determiner (Demonstrative)

A demonstrative determiner defines where its noun or pronoun is in relation to the speaker.

The demonstrative determiners (known as demonstrative adjectives in traditional grammar) are *this, that, these* and *those. This* and *these* define close things (geographically, psychologically or chronologically). *That* and *those* define distant things.

EASY EXAMPLES

In each example, the noun or pronoun being modified is underlined and the determiner is bold.

- **This** <u>shark</u> is pregnant.
- **That** <u>one</u> looks worried.
- In **these** <u>matters</u>, the only certainty is nothing is certain. (Writer Pliny the Elder)
- I regret **those** <u>times</u> when I've chosen the dark side. I've wasted time being unhappy. (Actress Jessica Lange)

WHY SHOULD I CARE ABOUT DEMONSTRATIVES?

There are three noteworthy issues related to demonstrative determiners.

Issue 1. Make sure it's clear what your demonstrative determiner refers to.

When you use a demonstrative determiner, do a quick check to ensure it's clear what your determiner refers to.

- **This** <u>issue</u> will be raised at the AGM.

  (What issue? If you can answer this question quickly because the answer is evident in the previous nearby text, then your determiner is safe.)

Knowing exactly what their determiners refer to, writers sometimes assume their readers do too. All too often though, readers don't. If your determiner could feasibly refer back to more than one thing, you've created ambiguity.

- The talk will cover America's nationally determined contribution (NDC) and the impact of a US–China trade war. **This** <u>issue</u> will also be addressed in sidebar meetings. ✗

  (Most readers would assume that *this* refers to *US–China trade war* because it's physically closer to the *this* than *NDC*, but it's not entirely clear. It could refer to either or both.)

If you spot possible ambiguity, a good option is to avoid the demonstrative determiner and just spell it out. ('The trade war will also be addressed in sidebar meetings' is one option.)

Issue 2. Consider using a demonstrative determiner and a noun to replace an ambiguous demonstrative pronoun. Demonstrative pronouns (see page 224) are just like demonstrative determiners except they stand alone and don't modify nouns. Demonstrative pronouns are even more prone to being ambiguous than demonstrative determiners.

● According to his Twitter feed, Professor Smith has been selected to lead a charity climb up Mount Everest. He will cease work on Monday to prepare. **That** surprised everybody. ✗

(It's unclear what *That* refers to. The ambiguity could be removed by using a demonstrative determiner and a noun, e.g. *That selection, That goal, That timing, That announcement.* Other options to kill the ambiguous *That* include *His selection* and *The announcement.*)

Issue 3. Make sure your demonstrative determiner and its noun match in number. *This* and *that* modify singular nouns. *These* and *those* modify plural nouns. This doesn't usually cause an issue for native English speakers except with the words *kind* and *type*.

● **These** <u>kind</u> of things. ✗
(It should be *kinds*.)
● **Those** <u>type</u> of issues. ✗
(It should be *types*.)

KEY POINT
If it's unclear what your demonstrative determiner refers to, spell it out.

Determiner (Possessive)

A possessive determiner sits before a noun (or a pronoun) to show who or what owns it.

The possessive determiners (known as possessive adjectives in traditional grammar) are *my, your, his, her, its, our, their* and *whose*.

EASY EXAMPLES

In the examples below, the possessive determiners are bold, and the nouns being modified are underlined. The table also shows how each possessive determiner corresponds to a personal pronoun.

Personal pronoun	Possessive determiner	Example
I	my	I do not choose that **my** <u>grave</u> should be dug while I am still alive. (Queen Elizabeth I)
you	your	If you want peace, you don't talk to **your** <u>friends</u>. You talk to **your** <u>enemies</u>. (Cleric Desmond Tutu)
he	his	If a man could have half of **his** <u>wishes</u>, he would double **his** <u>troubles</u>. (American founding father Benjamin Franklin)
she	her	She got **her** <u>looks</u> from **her** <u>father</u>. He's a plastic surgeon. (Comedian Groucho Marx)
it	its	Worry never robs tomorrow of **its** <u>sorrow</u>. It only saps today of **its** <u>joy</u>. (Author Leo Buscaglia)
we	our	How we spend **our** <u>days</u> is how we spend **our** <u>lives</u>. (Author Annie Dillard)
they	their	Men are like steel. When they lose **their** <u>temper</u>, they lose **their** <u>worth</u>. (Martial artist Chuck Norris)
who	whose	The key is to keep company only with people **whose** <u>presence</u> calls forth your best. (Greek philosopher Epictetus)

WHY SHOULD I CARE ABOUT POSSESSIVE DETERMINERS?

There are two noteworthy issues related to possessive determiners.

Issue 1. Use *their* instead of *his/her*. In English, we don't have a singular non-gender-specific possessive determiner that can be used for people. (We have *its*, but you

139

can't use *its* for people.) So, when your singular person could be male or female, you have two options.

Option A. Use *their*.
● Each owner is responsible for **their** dog. ✔
   (Using *their* to refer to a singular noun (here, *owner*) is acceptable. This is the best option.)
Option B. Use *his/her*.
● Each owner is responsible for **his/her** dog. ✔
   (This is acceptable, but it's clumsy.)

There used to be a third option:
Option C. Use *his* with a caveat. A common caveat at the beginning of formal documents used to be 'Throughout this document his means his/her.'
● Each owner is responsible for **his** dog.
   (Avoid this option. It's outdated.)

Issue 2. Don't confuse a possessive determiner with an identical-sounding contraction. Grammar mistakes with possessive determiners are rare, but spelling mistakes are common. Misspelling any of these (particularly if you make a habit of it) will smash your credibility. The four common spelling mistakes with possessive determiners are easy to fix because they're all made the same way – by confusing the possessive determiner with an identical-sounding contraction.

The contraction *it's* is not a possessive. *It's* is a contraction of *it is* or *it has*. If you can't expand your *it's* to *it is* or *it has*, then it's wrong.
● A country can be judged by the quality of **it's** proverbs. ✗
To some extent, this mistake is understandable because apostrophes are used for possession (e.g. *the dog's nose*). But *it's* has nothing to do with possession. Really, it doesn't.

The same is true for *you're* (a contraction of *you are*), *they're* (a contraction of *they are*) and *who's* (a contraction of *who is* or *who has*). Do not confuse these with *your*, *their/there* or *whose*.
● Even if you fall on <u>you're</u> face, <u>you're</u> still moving forward. ✗
   (The first *you're* is wrong. The second is correct.)
● Forgive your enemies, but never forget <u>there</u> names. ✗
● Never go to a doctor <u>who's</u> office plants have died. ✗

KEY POINTS
Use *their* to replace *his/her*.
If you can't expand your *it's*, *you're*, *they're* or *who's* to
the two-word version, then it's wrong.

Determiner (Quantifier)

Any determiner that refers, even loosely, to an amount or a quantity can be classified as a quantifier.

So, numbers (*one* dog, *two* dogs) are quantifiers. Not all quantifiers are so specific though. Many refer to an undefined amount or quantity. The most common ones are *any*, *all*, *many*, *much*, *several* and *some*. (These are called indefinite adjectives in traditional grammar.)

EASY EXAMPLES

In these examples, the quantifiers are in bold and the nouns being modified are underlined.

- **Many** <u>people</u> would sooner die than think. In fact, they do so. (Philosopher Bertrand Russell)
- I bought **some** <u>batteries</u>, but they weren't included. (Comedian Steven Wright)
- **Any** <u>kid</u> will run **any** <u>errand</u> for you, if you ask at bedtime. (Comedian Red Skelton)

WHY SHOULD I CARE ABOUT QUANTIFIERS?

Below are four commonly discussed issues related to quantifiers that precede nouns. (There are more issues related to quantifiers that stand alone (called indefinite pronouns in traditional grammar). These issues are covered in Indefinite Pronoun on page 227.)

Point 1. Use *fewer* with plural nouns and *less* with singular nouns. While there are some quirks with these (covered in Countable and Non-countable Nouns on page 180), that is the general rule.

- A low voter turnout is an indication of **fewer** <u>people</u> going to the polls. (Politician Dan Quayle)
- I prefer drawing to talking. Drawing is faster, and leaves **less** <u>room</u> for lies. (Swiss architect Le Corbusier)

A key point is that *less* is not always a determiner, even if it precedes a noun.

- The less men think, the more they talk. (Philosopher Montesquieu)

(As it is here, *less* is commonly an adverb. When it's an adverb, *fewer* isn't an option.)

Point 2. Save a word. Write 'all the' not 'all of the'. If you're unsure whether to use 'all the' or 'all of the' before a noun, use 'all the' because it saves a word. If you can't bear how it sounds without 'of', get over it.

- You can fool **all** <u>the people</u> some of the time, and some of the people **all** <u>the time</u>, but you cannot fool **all** <u>the people</u> **all** <u>the time</u>. ✔ (President Abraham Lincoln) (There must have been a strong urge to use 'all of the' because it would have chimed nicely with *some of the*. Here, succinctness trumped rhythm. Good skills, Abe.)

It's not the same deal with 'all my' (or any possessive determiner) or '*all of my*'. Grammatically, both are sound, but often omitting 'of' sounds awkward. Follow your instincts.

● **All** <u>my friends</u> left me when I was 12. ✔ (Singer Taylor Swift)
● All of my songs are autobiographical. ✔ (Taylor Swift)
  (Both are fine. Taylor followed her instincts.)

Point 3. Spell out the numbers one to nine but use numerals for the numbers 10 and above...or don't. It's your choice. Writers frequently ask whether they should write numbers as numerals (e.g. *11 cats*) or spell them out (e.g. *eleven cats*). It's a matter of style. Those who write business or technical documents tend to use numerals far more liberally than those writing stories or verse. If you want a more definitive answer though, the most common convention is to spell out the numbers one to nine but to use numerals for 10 and above. (This is by no means a rule.)

● Success is falling 9 times and getting up ten. (Singer Jon Bon Jovi)
  (Whoever transcribed this quotation stuck rigidly to the common convention. Such conventions are useful handrails to improve consistency when writing.)

Point 4. When writing numbers in full, hyphenate all numbers between 21 and 99 (less those divisible by 10). Regardless of where they appear within the whole number, all numbers between 21 and 99 (except, of course, the single-word numbers 30, 40, 50, 60, 70, 80 and 90) should be hyphenated.

● 51 = fifty-one
● 234 = two hundred and thirty-four
● 3,567 = three thousand five hundred and sixty-seven
  (There's no comma in the spelled-out version.)
● 25,223 = twenty five thousand two hundred and twenty three ✗
  (*Twenty five* and *twenty three* should be hyphenated.)

Of interest, Americans are likely to omit the word *and* when writing numbers in full.

KEY POINTS
To drink fewer coffees, buy less coffee.
Write '*all the*' not '*all of the*'.

Exclamatory Sentence

An exclamatory sentence conveys a strong emotion and ends with an exclamation mark (!).

EASY EXAMPLES
- You're late! (conveys anger or concern)
- We won! (conveys happiness or amazement)
- It's a boy! (conveys joy or surprise)
- No way! (conveys incredulity)
- I miss you! (conveys sadness)
- You're doing my swede in! (conveys frustration)

REAL-LIFE EXAMPLES
- You make the beds, you do the dishes and six months later you have to start all over again. I hate housework! (Comedian Joan Rivers)
- It's alive! It's alive! (Dr Frankenstein)

An exclamatory sentence is often preceded by an interjection.
- **Jeepers**, you're actually up before lunch!
  (Interjections can be followed by a comma for a mild effect.)
- **Oh!** Most miserable wretch that I am! Why have I not learnt how to swim? (Alexander the Great)
  (Interjections can be followed by an exclamation mark for a strong effect.)

Also of note is the use of *how, so, such* and *what* in exclamatory sentences.
- **How** adventurous you are!
- You're **such** an animal!
- I'm **so** full!
- **What** a great ending!

WHY SHOULD I CARE ABOUT EXCLAMATORY SENTENCES?
Don't overuse exclamatory sentences. An exclamatory sentence delivers a jolt of emotion. If you add emotion to everything, you add emotion to nothing.

Don't put an exclamation mark at the end of a declarative sentence (a matter-of-fact statement) just to highlight its importance. Your readers will quickly start to question your writing skills and even your sincerity if you make a habit of using exclamation marks and not word choice to portray the importance of a statement. Definitely don't use more than one exclamation mark.

KEY POINT
Use exclamatory sentences sparingly, and never use more than one exclamation mark

Figurative Language

Figurative language is the use of words in an unusual or imaginative manner.

EXAMPLES OF FIGURATIVE LANGUAGE

When most people think of figurative language, metaphors and similes spring to mind. However, the term covers a wide range of literary techniques.

A metaphor asserts that one thing is something that it literally is not.
- Google is a house of cards. (Businessman Steve Ballmer)

A simile likens one thing to another (usually achieved by the use of the word *like* or *as*).
- Doing something you like after doing something you love is like chewing on sawdust. (Entrepreneur Kimbal Musk)

Alliteration is the repetition of the same initial letter in successive words for effect.
- Smile. Speak. Serve.

Anastrophe (see page 86) is the deliberate changing of normal word order for emphasis.
- Deep into that darkness peering, long I stood there wondering, fearing.
  (Edgar Allan Poe's 'The Raven')

Assonance is the repetition of the same vowel sound in neighbouring words.
- I must confess that in my quest I felt depressed and restless. (from 'With Love' by Thin Lizzy)

Consonance is the repetition of the same consonant sound in neighbouring words.
- Increasing store with loss and loss with store. (Playwright William Shakespeare)

A euphemism is the use of agreeable or inoffensive words to replace rude or offensive ones.
- I am one, sir, that comes to tell you your daughter and the Moor are now <u>making the beast with two backs</u>. (William Shakespeare's Othello)

Hyperbole is an exaggeration or extravagant statement used for effect.
- I write for the same reason I breathe: if I didn't, I would die. (Writer Isaac Asimov)

An idiom is commonly used expression the meaning of which does not relate to the literal meaning of its words.
- A politician is an animal that can <u>sit on a fence</u> and yet <u>keep both ears to the ground</u>. (Journalist Henry Mencken)

A logosglyph* is a word that looks like what it means.
- Elizabeth has <u>eyes</u> like <u>pools</u>.
  (The word *eyes* looks like a pair of eyes. The 'oo' in *pool* depicts large, round eyes.)

*Logosglyph is a brand-new term, which I first encountered on an educational poster in 2015. It appeals to the eyes, in contrast to onomatopoeia, which appeals to the ears.

Onomatopoeia is the use of a word that sounds like what it represents.
- From the jingling and the tinkling of the bells. (Edgar Allan Poe's 'The Bells')

Personification is when non-human objects are given human traits.
- My computer throws a tantrum at least once a day.

A pun is a witticism that plays on the different meanings of a word or two words that sound alike but have different meanings.
- We must all hang together or assuredly we shall all hang separately.
  (American founding father Benjamin Franklin)

WHY SHOULD I CARE ABOUT FIGURATIVE LANGUAGE?

Figurative language will often feature a figure of speech, which is an expression that includes words not used in their literal sense. A figure of speech (typically a metaphor, simile, idiom, personification, hyperbole or euphemism) can be used to frame a point as something else in order to explain it.
- A man who waits for roast duck to fly into his mouth must wait a very, very long time. (French author Jules Renard)
  (This metaphor explains that things must be earned.)
- Love is like an hourglass, with the heart filling up as the brain empties. (Jules Renard)
  (This simile explains that love clouds the mind.)

Figurative language also includes techniques that might use words in their literal meanings (e.g. anastrophe, alliteration, assonance and consonance).
- Patient I am not.
  (The anastrophe provides emphasis. The words are used in their literal sense.)
- The best sushi chefs spot the finest fresh fish instantly. (Chef Nobu Matsuhisa)
  (The consonance and alliteration sharpen the focus on the words.)
- He bought her a ring with a choke-a-donkey diamond.
  (The assonance and alliteration sharpen the focus on the words.)

Regardless of whether the words are used in their figurative or literal sense, figurative language can help to keep your writing engaging.

KEY POINT
Use figurative language to:
- explain your idea with a comparison
- emphasise your idea
- make your writing more engaging.

Gender

Gender is a category of noun. A noun can have a masculine gender, a feminine gender or a neuter gender.

EASY EXAMPLES
- pig (neuter gender)
- sow (feminine gender)

    boar (masculine gender)

    pigpen (neuter gender)

MORE EXAMPLES
In English, the gender of a noun affects the pronouns we use in its place (e.g. *he, she, it*) and the possessive determiners (e.g. *his, her, its*).
- The **man** ripped his new coat, which **he** only bought yesterday.
- The **woman** lost her blue shoes, which **she** had never worn.
- The **dog** chewed its leather collar, which **it** hated.

While there are lots of gender-specific nouns in English (e.g. *actor, actress, prince, princess*), most nouns (e.g. *parent, cousin, teenager, teacher*) don't reflect gender until they're substituted for a pronoun or a possessive determiner.

In many languages, the spelling of a noun (as opposed to its meaning) often determines its gender. For example, if a noun ends *–a* in Russian or *–heit* in German, then it will be feminine. That's not how it works in English, where gender is directly linked to whether something is male, female or neuter. In English, nouns are often described as 'gender neutral' because the gender of a noun can change. Let's look at the noun *dog*:

Gender	Example
Neuter (We don't know the dog.)	**It** has lost **its** bone.
Masculine (We know it's a boy.)	**He** is admiring **his** large bone.
Feminine (We know it's a girl.)	**She** wants **her** Sunday bone.

Occasionally, a noun you'd expect to be neuter (e.g. *country, car, ship*) is treated as feminine to portray affection.
- France will defend herself.
- My Camaro has her creaks and groans, but she will get us there.
- She was loved by her crew before they smashed her on the beach.

WHY SHOULD I CARE ABOUT GENDER?
There are two issues linked to gender.

Issue 1. Finding an alternative to 'his/her'. Look at these sentences:
- Each person must understand where **he** fits in the team.
- Anyone who forgets **his** passport will be sent home.

What if they're not all male? Using *he* or *his* for unknown people was the accepted practice, but no longer. It is, of course, sexist and inaccurate. To resolve this, you could write:
- Each person must understand where **he/she** fits in the team.
- Anyone who forgets **his** or **her** passport will be sent home.

But, as those are clumsy solutions, lots of people naturally opt for this:
- Each person must understand where **they** fit in the team.
- Anyone who forgets **their** passport will be sent home.
  (This practice has been going on for centuries, so it sounds fine.)

Hang on a sec though. We now have *person* and *anyone* (both of which are singular) paired up with *they* and *their* (both of which are plural). Surely, they're grammar mistakes. Well, nowadays, they're not. Using a 'singular they' (as it's called) is formally accepted. In the past, tweed-clad teachers might have spluttered on their pipes if the antecedent of *they* or *their* was a singular noun or pronoun, but this wouldn't interfere with the vaping of today's trendy teachers – and with good reason. It's far tidier than the old alternatives. (As a matter of interest 'singular they' was nominated as the American Dialect Society's word of the year in 2015.)

It's not just *they* and *their* that can be singular. *Them* and *theirs* can be singular too. This issue commonly crops up with sentences including the pronouns *anyone*, *everyone* and *someone*. Here's the bottom line: you are safe to treat *they*, *their*, *them*, etc. as singular. If you really can't bear pairing them with a singular noun, reword your sentence to go 'all plural'.
- Players must understand where they fit in the team. ✔
- Students who forget their passports will be sent home. ✔

Issue 2. Choosing the right version of *blonde/blond*. The word *blond/blonde* changes depending on its gender.

Blonde is a noun meaning a fair-haired female. It is also an adjective used to describe a female with fair hair.
- The blonde has nice shoes.
(Here, *blonde* is a noun. We know it's a girl from the spelling.)

- I'm a white, blonde girl in the entertainment industry - it's so easy to fall into a world of pleasing everyone. (Actress Brie Larson)
  (*Blonde* is an adjective.)

Blond is a noun meaning a fair-haired male.
- The blond has nice shoes.　　　　(We know it's a boy.)

Blond is also an adjective used to describe anybody (regardless of their gender) with fair hair.

● The blond girl and the blond boy make a nice blond couple.

(As an adjective, *blonde* or *blond* can be used to describe females, but *blonde* is favoured in British English.)

Issue 3. Using gender-neutral pronouns for people who do not identify themselves as either male or female. Some people identify themselves as both male and female, others as neither male nor female. These people might ask you to use *they* (and of course *their, them, theirs, themself*) or just their name (e.g. *Sarah, Sarah's, Sarah's self*) instead of a pronoun when talking about them.

You might also have noticed other gender-neutral pronouns appearing. *Ey, per, sie, ve* and *zie* are all recently proposed alternatives to *he* or *she*, but at present none is showing any signs of entering into common usage. However, the use of *they* for a gender-neutral singular pronoun (or 'non-binary pronoun' as it's often called in this context) is deemed by a growing number of linguistics specialists to have a chance, particularly as it's used in a similar way already (*see Issue 1 on page 146*).

KEY POINT
Don't use *he/she* or *his/her* when someone's gender is unknown.
Use *they* or *their*.

Imperative Sentence

An imperative sentence gives a direct command. It can end in a full stop or an exclamation mark, depending on the forcefulness of the command.

EASY EXAMPLES
- Please tidy your room.
- Tidy your room!
- Please keep the noise down.
- Shut up!

REAL-LIFE EXAMPLES
Forceful commands end with an exclamation mark.
- Get out!
- Watch your mouth, young man!

Polite or gentle commands with a full stop.
- Pass the pepper.
- Don't forget to feed the pony.

Commands in the form of advice also end with a full stop.
- Don't count the days. Make the days count. (Boxer Muhammad Ali)
- If you don't want to feel alone, watch a horror before going to bed.

Be aware that not every sentence that ends with an exclamation mark is an imperative sentence. Exclamatory sentences, which are used to deliver a jolt of emotion, end in exclamation marks too.
- All the numbers on a roulette wheel add up to 666! (conveys astonishment)

WHY SHOULD I CARE ABOUT IMPERATIVE SENTENCES?
There are two points to consider when using imperative sentences.

Point 1. Use exclamation marks sparingly. When writing an imperative sentence, be mindful of how much force an exclamation mark adds.
- Be there at seven.
- Be there at seven!

There are two points to consider. First, your exclamation might be taken as more forceful than you meant. Second, if you use exclamation marks regularly, you diminish their power. (Remember that if you highlight everything, you highlight nothing.) Also, never use more than one exclamation mark! (That point is nearly worth two exclamation marks, but, actually, nothing is.) (*See also* Exclamation Mark on page 40.)

Point 2. Don't use *myself* with an order. The subject of an imperative sentence is an implied *you* (either singular or plural). This means an imperative verb can only be paired with *yourself* or *yourselves*.

● Please help <u>yourself</u>, mate.
    (The implied *you* is singular. Please (you) help yourself.)

● Ladies and gentlemen, please chat among <u>yourselves</u>.
    (The implied *you* is plural. Please (you) chat among yourselves.)

You cannot pair your imperative verb with other words of that type, e.g. *myself, himself, herself, ourselves*. (See also Emphatic Pronoun and Reflexive Pronoun on pages 225 and 226.)

● Please contact your manager or <u>myself</u> with any suggestions. ✗
    (Should be *me*.)
● Allow myself to introduce ... myself. ✗ (from *Austin Powers: International Man of Mystery*).
    (The first *myself* should be *me*.)

KEY POINT
You can't use *myself* with an imperative verb.

Indirect Question

An indirect question is a question embedded inside another sentence, either a statement, a question or an order.

EASY EXAMPLES

An indirect question (underlined) can be embedded in a statement, another question or an order.

- I wonder <u>whether Anne is happy</u>.

  (This is an indirect question within a statement, i.e. a declarative sentence. The direct question would be 'Is Anne happy?')
- Do you know <u>if anyone was listening</u>?

  (This is an indirect question within a question, i.e. an interrogative sentence. The direct question would be 'Was anyone listening?')
- Please find out <u>when the train is due</u>.

  (This is an indirect question within an order, i.e. an imperative sentence. The direct question would be 'When is the train due?')

REAL-LIFE EXAMPLES

- I wonder <u>whether other dogs think poodles are members of a weird religious cult</u>. (Comedian Rita Rudner)
- I want to know <u>why the universe exists, why there is something greater than nothing</u>. (Theoretical physicist Stephen Hawking)

MORE ABOUT INDIRECT QUESTIONS

When the direct question is a yes–no question, the indirect question starts with *if* or *whether*.

- I'm asking **if** <u>you are cold</u>. I'm asking **whether** <u>you are cold</u>.

  (The direct question is 'Are you cold?'. This is a yes–no question.)

When the direct question starts with a question word such as *how, what, when, where, which, who, whose* or *why*, the indirect question starts with the question word, but the word order is like a statement not like a question.

- I'm asking **what** <u>the time is</u>.

  (The direct question is 'What is the time?' Notice that the indirect question has the word order of a statement (*the time is*) rather than a question (*is the time*).)
- I don't know **who** <u>my grandfather was</u>; I am much more concerned to know **what** <u>his grandson will be</u>. (President Abraham Lincoln)

  (The direct questions are 'Who was my grandfather?' and 'What will his grandson be?'.)

WHY SHOULD I CARE ABOUT INDIRECT QUESTIONS?

There are two common issues related to indirect questions.

Issue 1. Don't use a question mark with a non-question. By far the most common mistake with indirect questions is using a question mark at the end of a sentence that isn't a question.

- She needs to know <u>where you're going</u>? ✗
- Tell the staff <u>if you feel cold</u>? ✗

Before using a question mark, make sure the whole sentence is a question.

- Does she need to know <u>where you're going</u>? ✔
- Will you tell the staff <u>if you feel cold</u>? ✔

Issue 2. Use *whether* unless you're presenting a condition. These two sentences are both grammatically sound, but they mean different things.

- Tell the staff **if** <u>you need a seat</u>.

    (This means tell the staff only if you need a seat. In other words, needing a seat is a condition that needs to be true before the staff are told. This is called a conditional sentence.)

- Tell the staff **whether** <u>you need a seat</u>.

    (This means tell the staff your seating needs. You either need a seat or you don't. Tell the staff either way. This is not a conditional sentence. See Conditional Sentence on page 111.)

Often *if* and *whether* are interchangeable when heading an indirect question, but if you're presenting a condition, you should use *if*.

KEY POINTS

An indirect question does not warrant a question mark – only a question does.

If and *whether* are not always interchangeable.

If heads a condition. *Whether* doesn't.

Infinitive Verb

An infinitive verb is a verb in its basic form. It is usually preceded by to *(e.g.* to run, *to* think).

EASY EXAMPLES

The infinitive form with the word *to* is called the *full infinitive* or the *to-infinitive*.

- Lee likes **to bake.**
- Give him a pamphlet **to read.**
- He went away **to rest.**

After certain verbs, the *to* is dropped. This happens most commonly after verbs like *can, could, may, might, must, shall, should, will* or *would* (see Auxiliary Verb on page 94). When the *to* is dropped, the infinitive form is called the *bare infinitive*.

- I can **resist** everything except temptation. (Playwright Oscar Wilde)
- You should **read** Leo Tolstoy by Warren Peace.

Bare infinitives follow other verbs. The main ones are *to feel, to hear, to help, to let, to make, to see* and *to watch*.

- They'll forget what you said but not how you made them **feel.** (Writer Carl Buechner)

An infinitive verb will not be the main verb in a sentence, which is known as a *finite verb*. (Now you can see where the word *infinitive* comes from.) In fact, infinitive verbs don't always function as verbs but like nouns, adjectives or adverbs.

- Lee likes **to bake.**
  (*To bake* is functioning as a noun. It could be replaced with the noun *baking*.)
- Give him a pamphlet **to read.**
  (*To read* is functioning as an adjective. It could be replaced with the adjective clause *that he can read*. It is describing *pamphlet*.)
- He went away **to rest.**
  (*To rest* is functioning as an adverb. It could be replaced with the adverbial clause *so he can rest*. It is an adverb of reason modifying the verb *went*.)

REAL-LIFE EXAMPLES

An infinitive phrase (underlined below) is the infinitive form of a verb (bold) plus all the bits that go with it (i.e. complements and modifiers).

- Wine is constant proof that God loves us and loves **to see** us happy. (American founding father Benjamin Franklin)
  (The infinitive phrase functions as a noun.)
- If one is wise, it is a profitable thing **to seem** foolish. (Greek tragedian Aeschylus)
  (The infinitive phrase functions as an adjective.)
- **To succeed** in life, you must be creative and persistent. (Businessman John Johnson)
  (The infinitive phrase functions as an adverb.)

If the term *infinitive phrase* comes up in a crossword, expect a clue like 'Group of words comprising an infinitive plus any complements and modifiers (10,6)'.

WHY SHOULD I CARE ABOUT INFINITIVE VERBS?

By far the most common question asked about infinitive verbs is 'Is a split infinitive a mistake?'. (A split infinitive occurs when an adverb is placed between the *to* and the verb (e.g. *to secretly plot*, *to knowingly act*). Here's the quick answer: no. For a longer answer, see Split Infinitive on page 241. That aside, here are two good reasons to think a little more about infinitives.

Point 1. An infinitive can usually replace *in order to*. To reduce your word count, you can usually replace *in order to* with *to* without any loss of meaning. In such cases, the infinitive phrase (underlined) is an adverb modifying a verb (bold).

● The doctors **joined** the A&E team ~~in order~~ to gain experience.

● In 2008, scientists discovered bacteria that **had adapted** ~~in order~~ to live in hairspray.

Even though it might add to your word count, *in order to* does have an advantage. Not only does it put a little more emphasis on the reason for the action, it also makes it clear that the text that follows is the reason for performing the action.

● Jack **built** a metal detector to find gold nuggets.
  (The underlined text could be an adjective modifying *detector*, meaning Jack's device is a gold-nugget-only detector.)

● Jack **built** a metal detector in order to find gold nuggets.
  (With *in order to*, it's clear that *to find gold nuggets* is an adverb modifying built. It tells readers why he built the metal detector, which readers will now take to be a standard metal detector.)

Mostly, *in order to* is used because writers think it sounds more highbrow. It's not, and it's often inefficient. That said though, *in order not to* (the negative version) flows far better than *not to*.

● In order not to offend anybody, in order not to seem to be partisan, the term 'terrorist' is virtually outlawed in US-run news agencies. (Journalist Kevin Meyers)
  (This reads far better than 'Not to offend anybody, not to seem to be partisan …'.)

Reason 2. Use the full infinitive to name the verb. When discussing grammar, the full infinitive (e.g. *to play*) is used to name the verb.

● The verb **to play** has the participles playing and played.

● In the present tense, **to be** has the forms am, is and are.

KEY POINTS

There's no need to actively avoid a split infinitive.
Use *in order to* in order to emphasise the reason. Otherwise, use just *to* to save two words.

Intensifier

An intensifier is a word that strengthens or weakens another word (typically the word immediately to its right). An intensifier can usually be removed from the sentence.

EASY EXAMPLES
- It's **very** cheap. Buy it **very** quickly.
- The test is **really** easy.
- She feels **quite** lonely.
- He hatched an **insanely** cunning plan.

REAL-LIFE EXAMPLES
- You can only enjoy life when you're **extremely** busy. (Actress Joséphine de La Baume)
- Nothing to me feels as good as laughing **incredibly** hard. (Actor Steve Carell)
- I don't see myself as a philosopher. That's **awfully** boring. (Author and philosopher Ray Bradbury)

  (Of note, negative-sounding words such as *awfully*, *dreadfully* and *terribly* can also provide strength.)

Intensifiers (also known as *boosters* or *amplifiers*) tend to modify adjectives, but they can modify adverbs too.
- In *Jaws*, they used their state-of-the-art animatronic shark **very** sparingly because it kept breaking down. (Actor Tom Ellis)

Despite the name, intensifiers can also weaken words.
- I don't need much money. I lead a **fairly** simple life. (TV presenter Karl Pilkington)
- I make things up. It would be **pretty** boring to write about real people. (Author Kristin Gore)

WHY SHOULD I CARE ABOUT INTENSIFIERS?
There are three reasons to care about intensifiers.

Reason 1. Intensifiers make you look lazy. Intensifiers are widely considered a sign of lazy writing. It is better to achieve intensity through word choice not intensifiers.
- **extremely** angry ✗   outraged ✔
- **very** tasty ✗   delicious ✔

With a strong adjective, there's no need for an intensifier, which is why 'very delicious' and 'extremely delicious' sound unnatural.

Intensifiers also fade with time. *Awfully* and *terribly* are good examples as they no longer exude the strength of the power words *awe* and *terror*. They have lost their shock value.

To overcome the diminishing effect of intensifiers, some writers (especially in informal writing) double up their intensifiers.

- She tried **very very** hard. ✗ (yuk)
- Tomorrow's meeting is **so terribly** important. ✗ (yuk)

Using two intensifiers highlights that you don't have the skills to find the right words. This practice might be efficient in, say, a text, but don't 'double up' in anything else.

- 'What's that word that means you know lots of words?'
  'Articulate.'
  'Yeah, that's it. I'm **very very** articulate.'

Reason 2. Using too many intensifiers is ineffective and a bit melodramatic.
Intensifiers can be effective if you limit their use. If you were to use the word *very* just once in a document, your readers would understand that *very* really did mean *very*. But be aware that using intensifiers (especially overusing them) can portray you as melodramatic. Often, less is more.

- Emily is **very** badly behaved, **very** loud and **extremely** disruptive. ✗
  (This overuse of intensifiers suggests the teacher is unable to cope and raises a question about professionalism. Through formal training or experience, senior executives avoid words like *very* and *extremely*, which do little to portray a sense of calm and control.)

Reason 3. Some words shouldn't be intensified. Some words shouldn't be intensified. A non-gradable adjective (e.g. *impossible*, *unanimous*, *dead*) is one that expresses an idea to its maximum degree (see also page 128). If an adjective is truly non-gradable, then it stands to reason that it can't be strengthened or weakened. Something can't be very dead. Here are 10 common non-gradable adjectives: *absolute, dead, fatal, impossible, inevitable, principal, unanimous, unavoidable, unique, universal*.

Be aware though that many of these non-gradable adjectives have nuanced meanings that allow them to be graded. *Unique* causes most debate. *Unique* means 'the only one of its kind,' but, depending on which dictionary you use, it can also mean 'special' or 'unusual'. In the first meaning, you could make a case for *very unique* being wrong but not in the second. There may also be times when *unique* in the first meaning is gradable (e.g. 'This system is fairly unique.'). Remember that we're dealing with language here not logic. Of course, those who detest terms like *very unique* (and they are many) could challenge the increasingly common, watered-down meanings of *unique*, but they'd be arguing on a point of vocabulary not grammar. Just as *literally* no longer means *literally*, so *unique* no longer means *unique*. Let's move on.

KEY POINTS
In formal writing, don't use an intensifier until you really need one.
When you write *very*, stop. Is it lazy writing? Is it melodramatic?

Interjection

An interjection is a word added to a sentence (usually at the start) to convey an emotion such as surprise, disgust, joy, excitement or enthusiasm.

EASY EXAMPLES
- **Hey!** Get off that grass!   **Good,** now we can move on.

Some interjections are sounds.
- **Phew!** That was close!   **Mmm,** my compliments to the chef.

Some are more than one word.
- **Oh, really?** I doubt that.   **Holy moly!** She won!

They're not always at the start of a sentence.
- It is cold, **indeed.**

REAL-LIFE EXAMPLES
- **Well**, it's one a.m. Better go home and spend some quality time with the kids. (Homer Simpson)
- **Yes**, anything worth doing is worth doing poorly until you can do it well. (Author Zig Ziglar)
- **Ah!** Don't agree with me! When people agree with me, I feel I must be wrong. (Playwright Oscar Wilde)

WHY SHOULD I CARE ABOUT INTERJECTIONS?
Recognising an interjection will help you to choose the punctuation that follows it. If your interjection is not a question (and most aren't), you have a choice. You can use a comma, a full stop or an exclamation mark. Commas and full stops are used for mild interjections, while exclamation marks are used for stronger expressions of emotion.
- **Crikey!** Think before you speak!

The choice between a comma and a full stop depends on your desired flow of text. When an interjection is mid-sentence, offset it with commas.
- I think, **well**, if they attack one personally, it means they've not a single political argument left. (Prime Minister Margaret Thatcher)

Interjections can be impactful and insert some pep into a business document. Too much interjection-invoked pep, however, will make you look scatty.

KEY POINTS
Use a comma or a full stop after a mild interjection as you think fits best.
For a stronger blurt, use an exclamation mark.

Interrogative Sentence

An interrogative sentence is one that asks a direct question and ends in a question mark. (It is another term for question.)

EASY EXAMPLES
- Eva, have you seen my other ball?
- What is the name for a unit of power?
- Would you prefer noisy or nosey neighbours?

REAL-LIFE EXAMPLES
There are three main types of question: yes/no questions, question-word questions, and choice questions.
- Is it possible to succeed without any act of betrayal? (Film director Jean Renoir)
  (This is a yes/no question.)
- Why are diplomatic cables secret? (Lawyer Elliott Abrams)
  (This is a question-word question, the response to which is information.)
- Are protein bars classified as biscuits or cakes?
  (This is a choice question, the answer to which is in the question.)

WHY SHOULD I CARE ABOUT INTERROGATIVE SENTENCES?
There are two noteworthy points to consider.

Point 1. Don't use a question mark for non-question. The biggest issue related to interrogative sentences is writers thinking a non-question deserves a question mark. This error occurs when the statement contains an indirect question (see page 155).
- I want to know if it's finished? ✗
- I wonder if I'll ever find my torch? ✗
  (These are not questions but statements. They should end in full stops.)

Point 2. Use a rhetorical question to introduce a topic or to make a statement diplomatically. Rhetorical questions (see page 230) are questions that are not expected to elicit an answer. They can be used to introduce a subject or to make a point softly or diplomatically.
- Lecture title: 'Is the Loch Ness Monster Dead?'
  (Often used as titles, rhetorical questions help to pique the audience's interest.)
- £60 billion for the HS2 rail link. Is it worth it?
  (This rhetorical question is saying in a non-antagonistic way that HS2 is not value for money.)

KEY POINT
It's a common mistake to use a question mark after a statement containing an indirect question. (I wonder if that's true? ✗)

Limiting Modifier

Limiting modifiers restrict the words they modify. The most common limiting modifiers are *almost, hardly, nearly, just, only* and *merely.*

EASY EXAMPLES
- Martin knows **hardly** anybody.
- Martin **hardly** knows anybody.
- **Only** Martin eats pears.
- Martin eats **only** pears.

REAL-LIFE EXAMPLES
- Space is **only** an hour's drive away if your car could go straight upwards. (Astronomer Fred Hoyle)
- Human beings have an **almost** infinite capacity for taking things for granted. (Writer Aldous Huxley)

WHY SHOULD I CARE ABOUT LIMITING MODIFIERS?
Pay attention when placing your limiting modifier (especially *only*). A limiting modifier can make a sentence ambiguous.
- Jack **only** eats ice cream.

This could be telling us that Jack eats nothing but ice cream, but it could mean Jack does nothing to the ice cream other than eat it (he doesn't make it). To avoid ambiguity, place your limiting modifier immediately to the left of the word(s) it governs (underlined).
- Jack **only** <u>eats</u> ice cream.
  (Jack does not make the ice cream.)
- Jack eats **only** <u>ice cream</u>.
  (Jack does not eat sorbet.)
- **Only** <u>Jack</u> eats ice cream.
  (Jill does not.)

In speech, you can get away with an ambiguously placed limiting modifier, but be more precise when writing. In these quotations, the limiting modifiers are not immediately to the left of the words they govern, so, technically, they are ambiguous.
- Everyone is born with genius, but most people **only** <u>keep</u> it a few minutes. ✗
  (Composer Edgard Varese)
  (*Only a few minutes* is sharper.)
- I don't give a damn for a man that can **only** <u>spell</u> a word one way. ✗
  (Writer Mark Twain)
  (*Only one way* is sharper.)

KEY POINT
Place *only* immediately to the left of the word(s) it governs.

Linking Verb

A linking verb is used to re-identify or to describe its subject.

EASY EXAMPLES

In each example, the linking verb is bold and the subject is underlined.

- <u>Alan</u> **is** a vampire.
  (The subject is re-identified as a vampire.)
- <u>Alan</u> **is** thirsty.
  (The subject is described as thirsty.)

The word, phrase or clause that follows a linking verb to re-identify or describe the subject is called the *subject complement*. In the following examples, everything after the linking verb is the subject complement.

- <u>He</u> **seems** too drunk to deliver his speech.
- <u>The soup</u> **tastes** garlicky.
- <u>His voice</u> **sounds** as flat as a pancake.

REAL-LIFE EXAMPLES

The most common linking verb is the verb *to be* (in all of its forms, e.g. *am, is, are, was, were, will be, was being*).

- <u>Lawyers</u> **were** children once. (Poet Charles Lamb)
- <u>The only thing that interferes with my learning</u> **is** my education.
  (Physicist Albert Einstein)

Other common linking verbs include *to appear, to become* and *to seem* or relate to the five senses (*to look, to feel, to smell, to sound* and *to taste*).

- <u>A new book</u> **smells** great. <u>An old book</u> **smells** even better. <u>An old book</u> **smells** like ancient Egypt. (Author Ray Bradbury)
- <u>It</u> **sounds** really corny, but inner beautiful shows on the outside, for sure.
  (Model Kate Moss)
- Once made equal to man, **woman** <u>becomes</u> his superior. (Greek philosopher Socrates)
- <u>It</u> always **seems** impossible until it's done. (President Nelson Mandela)
- <u>Whatever makes an impression on the heart</u> **seems** lovely in the eye.
  (Persian poet Saadi)

Linking verbs do not express actions. The verbs *to be, to become* and *to seem* are always linking verbs, but others can be linking verbs or non-linking verbs depending on the context.

- <u>Tony</u> always **smells** like the soup.
  (Here, *smells* is a linking verb. It describes *Tony*, the subject.)

- Tony always smells the soup.
  (Here, *smells* is not a linking verb. A linking verb does not express an action.)
- He **felt** sick when he felt the heat.
  (The first *felt* is a linking verb, but the second *felt* isn't.)

WHY SHOULD I CARE ABOUT LINKING VERBS?

Linking verbs do not cause serious problems for native English speakers, but here are two issues that sometimes arise.

Issue 1. Don't use an adverb after a linking verb. Occasionally when speaking, you will hear someone (usually someone who is quite grammar savvy) use an adverb instead of an adjective after a linking verb. That's wrong.

- Your hair **smells** amazingly. ✗

(This error occurs because speakers know that adverbs (here, *amazingly*) modify verbs. Nevertheless, the subject complement (the thing that follows a linking verb to re-identify or describe the subject) will always be a noun or an adjective. Here, the adjective *amazing* would have been correct.)

Mistakenly using an adverb instead of adjective is quite rare. It's more common the other way around.

- The process is working fantastic. ✗
  (It should be *fantastically*.)

Issue 2. 'It was me' and 'It was I' are both acceptable. A common question related to linking verbs is whether to say 'It **was** me' or 'It **was** I'. You can say either. 'It was me' is what everyone says (and so is acceptable), and 'It was I' fits the ruling that subject complements are in the subjective case. (*See also* Subjective Case on page 97.)

KEY POINT

Use an adjective (not an adverb) after a linking verb to describe your subject.

Misplaced Modifier

A misplaced modifier is a word or group of words that does not clearly link to what it is intended to modify. A misplaced modifier makes the meaning of a sentence ambiguous or wrong.

EASY EXAMPLES

- We will not sell paraffin to anyone <u>in glass bottles</u>. ✗
  (The intended meaning is usually clear from context. This is obviously not about people in glass bottles.)
- Talking <u>quickly</u> annoys people. ✗
  (Does *quickly* apply to *talking* or *annoys*? See also Squinting Modifier on page 242.)
- <u>Having read your letter</u>, my parrot has since died. ✗
  (*Having read your letter* does not apply to anything in the sentence. See also Dangling Modifier on page 126.)

REAL-LIFE EXAMPLES

- 'He was a hero at his last police station. He once shot a robber <u>with a Kalashnikov.</u>'
  'Great, where did he get that?'
  'No, the robber had the Kalashnikov.' (from the film *Hot Fuzz*)

One well-known example of a misplaced modifier turns out not to be one:

- One morning I shot an elephant in my pyjamas. How he got into my pyjamas I'll never know. (Comedian Groucho Marx)

WHY SHOULD I CARE ABOUT MISPLACED MODIFIERS?

A misplaced modifier makes your sentence ambiguous or wrong. You can avoid this by placing your modifier next to whatever it's modifying (or putting some distance between the modifier and whatever it's not meant to be modifying).

Let's fix some the examples above. In these examples, the word being modified is bold.

- We will not sell **paraffin** <u>in glass bottles</u> to anyone. ✔
  (This has been fixed by moving the modifier next to the word being modified.)
- **Talking** <u>quickly</u> is a sure way to annoy people. ✔
  (This has been fixed by rewording the sentence and by putting the modifier next to the word being modified.)
- <u>Having read your letter</u>, **I** would like to inform you that my parrot has since died. ✔
  (This has been fixed by introducing the thing being modified into the sentence.)

Be careful with modifiers. These are both correct but have different meanings.

- He lost <u>nearly</u> **$5,000** in Las Vegas. (This means he lost just under $5,000.)
- He <u>nearly</u> **lost** $5,000 in Las Vegas. (This could mean he lost nothing.)

KEY POINT
Put your modifier next to whatever it's modifying.

Mood

Mood is the form a verb takes to show how it is to be regarded (e.g. as a fact, a command, a wish, an uncertainty). There are three moods in English: indicative, imperative and subjunctive.

EXAMPLES OF THE INDICATIVE MOOD

The indicative mood states a fact or asks a question.

- When you forgive, you change not the past but the future.
  (1960s radio host Bernard Meltzer)
- Why is the King of Hearts the only one without a moustache?

EXAMPLES OF THE IMPERATIVE MOOD

The imperative mood expresses a command or a request.

- Get out!
- Forgive your enemies, but never forget their names. (President John F Kennedy)

EXAMPLES OF THE SUBJUNCTIVE MOOD

The subjunctive mood is complicated. It is used to express a hypothetical situation. For example, it shows a wish, a suggestion, a demand or a condition contrary to fact.

- He wishes it were him.
  (This is a wish. Note the use of *were* instead of *was*.)
- I suggest he be told.
  (This is a suggestion. Note the use of *be* instead of *is*.)
- I demand he apologise.
  (This is a demand. Note the use of *apologise* instead of *apologises*.)
- If I were you, I'd leave.
  (This is a condition contrary to fact. Note the use of *were* instead of *was*.)

Here are some quotations that use the subjunctive mood (see also page 248).

Hypothetical Situation	Example
Expressing a wish	Don't wish it ~~was~~ were easier; wish you were better. (Entrepreneur Jim Rohn)
Making a suggestion	I suggest a chip ~~is~~ be put in future robots' brains to shut them off if they have murderous thoughts. (Physicist Michio Kaku)
Making a demand	The demand I make of my reader is that he ~~devotes~~ devote his whole life to reading my works (Novelist James Joyce)
Expressing a condition contrary to fact	When I hear a man preach, I like to see him act as if he ~~was~~ were fighting bees. (President Abraham Lincoln)

WHY SHOULD I CARE ABOUT MOOD?

Native English speakers create sentences in the indicative and imperative moods easily. The same is not always true of the subjunctive mood. There are two good reasons to care about mood.

Reason 1. The subjunctive mood is a thing, so use it. Outside set expressions (e.g. *If I were you, God bless you*), writers can get away with not using the subjunctive mood because, even though a verb in the subjunctive usually sounds pleasing to the native ear, the non-subjunctive version does too.

● I demand he <u>apologise</u>. ✔ (Subjunctive version)
  (This is correct, and it sounds natural.)
● I demand he apologises. ✔ (Non-subjunctive version)
  (Almost nobody would challenge this nowadays.)

It is likely that the subjunctive mood will continue to be trodden on by its non-subjunctive alternatives until, maybe sadly for some, its use outside set terms is considered archaic. But, we're not there yet, so you should use it. Why? Well, for one, you'll get to say 'subjunctive mood' when your colleague questions your quirky verb. Better though, your verb will be correct and sound natural.

Reason 2. Verb mood plays a big part in some foreign languages. Mood is a term you will hear when learning foreign languages (many of which, like Russian and Spanish, have more changes than our 'optional' ones), so it's worth having a basic understanding of mood to assist with cracking their verb changes.

KEY POINT
The subjunctive mood – use it or lose it.

Non-finite Verb

A non-finite verb is a verb form that does not show tense or have a subject.

A non-finite verb is never the main verb in a sentence. (That's a finite verb.) Non-finite verbs can function as nouns, adjectives and adverbs or combine with a finite verb for verb tense (see page 213) or voice (see page 259).

EASY EXAMPLES

There are three types of non-finite verbs: gerunds, infinitives and participles. (On this page, the non-finite verb is bold and the finite verb (the main verb) is underlined.)

Type	Telltale sign	Example (function)
Gerund	The -ing ending	Lee likes **playing** rugby. (noun)
Infinitive	Usually preceded by to	He wants **to play** rugby. (noun) He wants a game **to play**. (adjective) He begged **to play**. (adverb)
Participle	Present participle: -ing ending	Lee was the **playing** reserve. (adjective) We watched Lee **playing** rugby. (adjective) He is **playing** badly. (verb tense)
	Past participle: usually ends -ed, -d, -t, -en, or -n	The set-piece **played** failed. (adjective) He has **played** two games. (verb tense) The set-piece was **played** by Lee. (voice)

MORE EXAMPLES OF GERUNDS, INFINITIVES AND PARTICIPLES

A gerund (see also page 185) is a noun formed from a verb. All gerunds end –ing.

- Discovery consists of **seeing** what everybody has seen and **thinking** what nobody has thought. (Biochemist Albert Szent-Gyorgyi)
- The root of **suffering** is attachment. (Buddha).

Gerunds maintain some verb-like properties (e.g. they can take objects and be modified by adverbs). Therefore, a gerund will often appear in a gerund phrase, which consists of the gerund and any objects and modifiers. (The gerund phrases are in italics.)

- I started by **photographing** *birds in my garden*. (Film producer Seymour Belvoir)
- Art is **making** *something out of nothing* and **selling** *it*. (Musician Frank Zappa)

An infinitive (see also page 153) is the base form of a verb. Usually preceded by *to*, an infinitive can function as a noun, an adjective or an adverb.

- **To win** was everything.
  (Functioning as a noun. Compare this with 'The victory was everything.')
- It is the competition **to win**.
  (Functioning as an adjective. Compare this with 'It is the top competition.')
- The man paid **to win**.
  (Functioning as an adverb. Compare this with 'The man paid so he could win.' *So he could win* is an adverbial clause.)

An infinitive often appears in an infinitive phrase (in italics), which consists of the infinitive and any objects and modifiers.

- She needed **to find** *a lot of money quickly*. (noun)
- I showed her the best way **to make** *a Yorkshire pudding*. (adjective)
- He set the camera **to film** *whatever was eating his chickens*. (adverb)

Not all infinitives are preceded by *to*. Infinitives also feature in verb chains after verbs like *could, may, should* and *would* (i.e. auxiliary verbs) and verbs like *to make* and *to let*.

- If the highest aim of a captain were to preserve his ship, he <u>would</u> **keep** it in port forever. (Saint Thomas Aquinas)
- <u>Let</u> **them** eat cake. (Queen of France Marie Antoinette)

A participle (see page 213) is a verb form that can function as an adjective. Present participles end *-ing* and past participles usually end *-ed, -d, -t, -en*, or *-n*.

- A **stirring** dwarf we do allowance give before a **sleeping** giant.
  (Playwright William Shakespeare)
  (There are two present participles functioning as adjectives.)
- Food is an important part of a **balanced** diet. (Author Fran Lebowitz)
  (The past participle is functioning as an adjective.)

Often, a participle heads up a participle phrase (italic), which functions as an adjective.

- **Drawing** *on my fine command of the English language*, I said nothing.
  (Writer Robert Benchley)
- **Connected** *entirely by canals and footbridges*, the Dutch village of Giethoorn has no roads.

Participles are also used to form verb tenses.

- I <u>was</u> **eating** beans by candlelight for a decade. (Actor Eric Andre)
  (A present participle helps to form the past progressive tense.)
- I <u>have</u> **taken** more out of alcohol than alcohol <u>has</u> **taken** out of me.
  (Prime Minister Winston Churchill)
  (A past participle helps to form two examples of the present perfect tense.)

WHY SHOULD I CARE ABOUT NON-FINITE VERBS?

Here are two good reasons to give more thought to non-finite verbs.

Reason 1. Gerunds can reduce your word count and improve reading flow.
The overuse of normal nouns (i.e. not gerunds) and the prepositions needed to make those nouns work can make a sentence jolty and unnecessarily long.

- The use of urine for the cleaning of teeth was a common practice in the time of the Romans.

This sentence has way too many nouns. It's long and stuffy, and it doesn't flow naturally. As a rule, a well-placed verb is the best way to fix a jolty, noun-filled sentence, but gerunds – being a bit verb-like themselves – are also useful.

- **Cleaning** teeth with urine was common in Roman times.

(This sharper nine-word version features a gerund phrase. It flows far better than the noun-y 19-word version.)

Of course, a few other things have happened here to reduce 19 words to nine (e.g. *in the time of the Romans* became *in Roman times*), but the very act of looking to replace a rabble of nouns and prepositions with some sleek gerunds or verbs will drive those other changes too. Overusing nouns is particularly common in a business setting, because writers feel that noun chains make their writing sound more corporate. *See also Gerund Noun on page 185.*

Reason 2. Participles allow a sentence structure that lets you say two or more things tidily. You will know that it's a good idea to mix up your sentence structures (e.g. short ones, long ones, active ones, passive ones) to keep your readers engaged. Participles can help with this. They can be used to create a great sentence structure that lets you say two or more things about the subject, not only in an efficient way but also in a way that adds variety to your sentence structures.

- *Always **willing** to entertain others' ideas,* Jack is adept at building trust through regular, open and honest communication.
- ***Demonstrating** level-headedness in all business dealings,* Jill listens actively and engages appropriately when in disagreement.

This participle-phrase-upfront structure is particularly useful when writing personal appraisals. Clearly, you shouldn't write every sentence in this style, but the odd one will give that sentence-structure variety and help you to shoehorn in more observations.

KEY POINTS

Using the verb-like properties of gerunds creates shorter, better-flowing sentences. As well as adding variety to your sentence structures, using participle phrases upfront lets you cram more info into your sentences.

Noun

A noun is the word used to represent a person, animal, place, thing or idea. Everything we talk about is represented by a word that names it. That 'naming' word is called a noun.

EASY EXAMPLES
- *People:* soldier, Alan, cousin, lawyer
- *Animals:* aardvark, rat, shark, Mickey
- *Places:* house, London, factory, shelter
- *Things:* table, Brooklyn Bridge, chisel, nitrogen, month, inch
- *Ideas:* confusion, kindness, faith, Theory of Relativity, joy

Every noun can be categorised as either a common noun or a proper noun. Most nouns are common nouns. Common nouns refer to generic things (e.g. cousin) whereas proper nouns are the names of specific things (e.g. Edward). Depending on its meaning or structure, a common noun can usually be further categorised as at least one of the following: abstract, concrete, collective, compound, countable, uncountable or gender-specific. We'll cover each of these separately over the next few pages, along with noun phrases, noun clauses, gerunds and verbal nouns.

Noun (Common and Proper)

A common noun is the word for something, e.g. boy, cat, lake, bridge. A proper noun is the given name for something, i.e. its own name (e.g. Michael, New York, Rover). Proper nouns are capitalised.

EASY EXAMPLES
The difference between common nouns and proper nouns is clear when they're side by side:

Common noun (generic)	Proper noun (specific)
boy	Callum
sailor	Adam
mother-in-law	Janice
town	Milton Keynes
bridge	Golden Gate Bridge
tower	Eiffel Tower
street	Crow Court
cat	Rocky

REAL-LIFE EXAMPLES

The common nouns are underlined and the proper nouns are in bold:

- **Walt Disney** got the <u>inspiration</u> for **Mickey Mouse** from a tame <u>mouse</u> at his <u>desk</u> at **Laugh-O-Gram Studio** in **Kansas City**.
- With <u>members</u> all around the <u>globe</u>, the **Flat Earth Society** believes the **Earth** is flat and horizontally infinite.
  (*Globe* is a common noun, but *Earth* is the name of our planet.)
- <u>Turkeys</u> aren't from **Turkey**, but there are lots of <u>turkeys</u> in **Turkey**.
  (A common noun is written with a lowercase letter unless it starts a sentence.)

WHY SHOULD I CARE ABOUT COMMON AND PROPER NOUNS?

You can't use proper nouns in Scrabble. That's the first good reason to care about proper nouns. Here are six issues related to common and proper nouns.

Issue 1. Don't capitalise a common noun because it's an important word. Do not give a word that isn't a proper noun (or derived from one) a capital letter just because it's an important word in your sentence.

- As a valued <u>Client</u>, you have been selected for a special <u>Gift</u>. ✗
- We live in an age when <u>Pizza</u> gets to your home before the emergency services. ✗
- Lisa, <u>Vampires</u> are make-believe, like elves, gremlins and **Eskimos**. ✗
  (Homer Simpson)
  (*Vampires* is wrong. *Eskimos* is correct. It's a proper noun.)

Issue 2. Use capital letters for just the principal words in a title. It's a common convention when writing a name or a title to use capital letters only for the principal words (see Title Case on page 251). All words are principal words except articles (*a, an, the*), conjunctions (e.g. *and, but, or*) and prepositions (e.g. *on, in, with*).

- Tower of London
- Snow White and the Seven Dwarfs
- The Last of the Mohicans
  (A non-principal word (here, *The*) gets a capital letter if it starts the title.)
- Leonardo da Vinci / Ludwig van Beethoven
  (Apply this to the prepositions in foreign names too, but beware exceptions, e.g. Dick Van Dyke.)

Issue 3. Do not write the seasons (e.g. summer) with uppercase letters. The names of the seasons are not proper nouns. They are written with lowercase letters. Using a capital letter for a season is an understandable mistake given that the days of the week and months are written with capitals. But it's still a mistake.

- In the <u>autumn</u>, on a **Monday** in **October**, I saw thousands of <u>geese</u> fly south for the <u>winter</u>.

Issue 4. Write the points of the compass with lowercase letters. Do not use a capital letter for a direction (e.g. *north, south)*, unless the word forms part of a name.
- Take ten paces **East** and then dig. ✗
- Paddle <u>west</u> as far as **West Bridgford**. ✓

Be aware though that geographical areas with names like *The North, The South East* and *The North West* are proper nouns and written with capital letters.(There's a lot of leniency on whether to capitalise *The. See* Article on page 135.)

This issue can get complicated. Should you write *North Wales* or *north Wales, Central Europe* or *central Europe*? Some argue that north Wales and central Europe aren't recognised areas, so shouldn't be all capitals. Others say they are recognised areas. If you can't find a good reference book to copy, consider the following points before making your decision. If you're still unsure, go for the non-capitalised version.
- How well is the area defined? Is it like South Africa (well defined) or southern Africa (vaguely defined)?
- How common is the term?
- What would your readers expect?
- How does the written version look aesthetically?

Issue 5. Write *the Sun* and *the Moon* with capital letters. Our moon is called the Moon, and our sun is called the Sun. Therefore, the words to denote our moon and our sun can be either proper nouns or common nouns depending on context.
- The <u>moon</u> orbiting **Earth** is called the **Moon**. ✓
  (The first *moon* is a common noun, but *the Moon* (its name) is a proper noun.)
- The largest <u>moon</u> orbiting **Jupiter** is **Ganymede**. ✓
  (If you lived on Jupiter, this issue would go away.)

Imagine you had a dog called Dog. It's the same issue. If you write *the* Moon/Sun but *a* moon/sun, you'll probably have used capital letters correctly.

Issue 6. Write terms like *Director* and *Claims Department* with capital letters if they refer to specific people or departments. With job titles and the names of departments, it's often unclear whether a term is a common noun or a proper noun. Pay attention to the context. Treat such terms as proper nouns when they refer to specific people or offices, otherwise use lowercase letters.
- According to the **President,** he has done more than any other <u>president</u>. ✓
- I run the **Finance Office**. I've worked in <u>finance offices</u> since I left school. ✓
  (More often than not, the capitalised version will be preceded by *the*.)
- I know my **Dad** is looking down on us. He's not dead – just very condescending. ✓
  (Comedian Jack Whitehall)
  (*Mum* and *dad* are given capital letters when they refer to a specific parent.)

KEY POINT
Don't capitalise a common noun just because it's an important word.

Noun Phrase

A noun phrase is a noun and all modifiers (even just *a* or *the*).

A noun doesn't usually stand by itself as a single word in a sentence.
- <u>Man</u> proposes, but <u>God</u> disposes. (German canon Thomas à Kempis)

(This example features two nouns without any modifiers. That's rare.)

It's far more common for a noun to be accompanied by modifiers. Here's the list of nouns on page 168 again. This time, each entry has at least one modifier, making it a noun phrase.
- *People*: the <u>soldier</u>, my <u>cousin</u>, dopey <u>Alan</u>, the lawyer with the big nose
- *Animals*: that <u>aardvark</u>, one <u>rat</u>, a <u>shark</u>, funny <u>Mickey</u>
- *Places*: the <u>house</u> on the corner, inner <u>London</u>, dirty <u>factory</u>, no <u>shelter</u>
- *Things*: this <u>table</u>, our <u>Brooklyn Bridge</u>, the sharp <u>chisel</u>, that <u>nitrogen</u>, last <u>month</u>, an <u>inch</u>
- *Ideas*: utter <u>confusion</u>, some <u>kindness</u>, your <u>faith</u>, the <u>Theory of Relativity</u>, a <u>joy</u>

EASY EXAMPLES

Like any noun, a noun phrase can function as a subject (see page 243), an object (see page 191) or a complement (see below) within a sentence. In each example below, the noun phrase is bold and the head noun is underlined.
- **<u>Singing</u> in the bath** relaxes me.

   (The noun phrase is the subject of the verb *relaxes*.)
- I know **the back <u>streets</u>**.

   (The noun phrase is the direct object of the verb *know*.)
- She was **the <u>devil</u> in disguise**.

   (The noun phrase is a subject complement.)

As most nouns feature in noun phrases, let's look quickly at the definition for 'phrase'.
- A phrase has at least two words and functions as one part of speech.

It follows therefore that a 'noun phrase' functions as a noun. We can test this because a noun can be replaced by a pronoun (e.g. *he, she, it, them*). For each example above, we can replace each noun phrase with a pronoun.
- **It** relaxes me.
- I know **them.**
- She was **him/he.**

   (Grammarians are still scrapping over whether this should be *him* or *he*. See page 198.)

REAL-LIFE EXAMPLES

- **This <u>man</u>** has **a nice <u>smile</u>**, but he's got **iron <u>teeth</u>**. (Soviet Foreign Minister Andrei Gromyko)

   (The pronoun test: *He* has *one*, but he's got *them*.)

- I never learned from **a <u>man</u> who agreed with me**. (Science-fiction writer Robert Heinlein)
  (The pronoun test: I never learned from *him*.)
- **Every <u>man</u> of courage** is **a <u>man</u> of his word**. (Dramatist Pierre Corneille)
  (The pronoun test: *He* is one.)

In the last example, *courage* and *word* are both nouns, but they're not the head nouns of the phrases. They're both part of prepositional phrases (see page 209) modifying the head nouns. The last thing to say about noun phrases is that they can be headed by pronouns as well as nouns, and they can be quite long.

- **<u>Anybody</u> who wants the presidency so much that he'll spend two years organising and campaigning for it** is not to be trusted with the office.
  (Journalist David Broder)
  (*Anybody* is a pronoun. The rest of the noun phrase is an adjective clause (see page 221) modifying the head 'noun'. Here's the pronoun test: *He* is not to be trusted with the office.)

Noun Clause

A noun clause has a subject and verb (like all clauses) and functions as a noun. Lots of noun clauses start with *that, how* or a *wh-* word (*what, who, which, when, where, why*).

EASY EXAMPLES
In each example, the noun clause is bold
- I saw **how the accident happened**.
- I know **who said that**.

The two noun clauses above are both direct objects. Like all nouns, a noun clause can function as a subject, an object or a complement.
- **Whoever smelt it,** dealt it.
  (The noun clause is the subject.)
- I will give **what you said** some thought.
  (Here, it's the indirect object – that's rare!)
- My command is **whatever you wish**.
  (Here, it's the subject complement.)

REAL-LIFE EXAMPLES
- **That he believes his own story** is remarkable. (Author Jerome Blattner)
  (Noun clause as subject. Starting a sentence with a noun clause beginning *That* is acceptable, but it grates on lots of people's ears. Many writers prefer 'The fact that ...'.)

- My relationships are between me and **whomever I am with,** not between me and the world. (Actress Lili Reinhart)
  (Noun clause as object.)
- Liberty means responsibility. That is **why most men dread it.**
  (Playwright George Bernard Shaw)
  (Noun clause as subject complement.)

So, we started with defining a noun as a 'naming' word, and now we're talking about nouns being clauses functioning as subjects, objects or complements. To respect the followers of contemporary grammar, who would see you hang for describing a noun as a naming word, here's another definition: a noun is any word or group of words that could be replaced by a pronoun. And, if that's not a great definition, it's certainly a great test.

It's even more complicated than that. Grammar ninjas can dissect noun clauses into phrases (they don't recognise the term 'noun clause' at all). If that's you, you're probably reading the wrong book.

- A cynic is <u>a man who looks around for a coffin when he smells flowers</u>.
  (Journalist H L Mencken)
  The underlined text above is functioning as a noun (a subject complement). As it includes subjects (*who* and *he*) and verbs (*looks* and *smells*), you might think it meets the criteria to qualify as a noun clause. It's not though. It's a noun phrase. Those subjects and the verbs feature in the adjective clause '*who looks around for a coffin when he smells flowers*', describing *a man*. ('*When he smells flowers*' is an adverbial clause embedded in that adjective clause.) Hey, if you can follow that, you're well down the path between sentence butcher and sentence surgeon.

WHY SHOULD I CARE ABOUT NOUN PHRASES AND CLAUSES?

Most native English speakers form noun phrases and noun clauses without giving the grammar a second thought. So, if the truth be told, understanding how they function isn't particularly useful unless you're required to teach them. That said, here are two common issues associated with multi-word nouns.

Issue 1. When a noun phrase is the subject of a verb, ensure that the verb agrees with the head noun. Do not be tricked into making the verb agree with the nearest noun (here, *bullets*). When a noun phrase is the subject of a verb, the head noun governs the verb.

- **The Spitfire's nine-yard <u>belt</u> of bullets** give us the term 'the full nine yards'. ✘
  (The head noun in this noun phrase is *belt*. All the other words in the noun phrase are modifiers. As *belt* is singular, the verb *give* is wrong. It should be *gives*.)

Issue 2. Choose the right version of *who* and *whom* at the start of a noun clause. *Who* is the subject of a verb. *Whom* isn't. It's the same deal with *whoever* and *whomever*.

● My relationships are between me and **whomever I am with**.

   (Here, *whomever* is the object of the preposition *with*.)

● My relationships are between me and **whoever is interested**.

   (Here, *whoever* is the subject of the verb *is*. Note that the clause *whoever is interested* is the object of the preposition *between*, but that doesn't mean that *whoever* becomes *whomever*. If your *whoever* is the subject of a verb, then *whoever*, not *whomever*, is correct.)

If this made no sense to you whatsoever, just go with *who* or *whoever* every time. First, they're more common, but second, most grammarians agree that *whom* and *whomever* are on their last legs in English. They're going the same way as *hither* and *thither*.

KEY POINT

When a noun phrase is the subject of a verb, don't let the modifiers divert your eye from the head noun, as it must govern the verb.

Noun (Abstract and Concrete)

Abstract nouns refer to intangible things, i.e. things you can't perceive with one of your five senses. Concrete nouns are the opposite.

Abstract nouns refer to invisible things such as an emotion (e.g. *anger, joy*), a feeling (e.g. *anxiety, pleasure*), a quality (e.g. *courage, patience*), a concept (e.g. *charity, deceit*), a state (e.g. *freedom, luxury*) or a moment (e.g. *birthday, childhood*). It's helpful to think of an abstract noun as something you can't perceive with one of your five senses, i.e. *seeing, hearing, touching, smelling* and *tasting*.

Concrete nouns are things you can perceive with one of your five senses. (Be aware that classifying a noun as concrete (underlined below) or abstract (bold below) may depend on context or even the classifier's definition of perceivable.)

- My next <u>work</u> of art will require some hard **work**.
(No one would argue that the underlined *work* in this sentence is a concrete noun. However, the bolded *work* is more subjective. When it means 'a task needing effort', *work* is generally classified as an abstract noun. But, some argue that you can feel *work* and would classify it as concrete too.)

Some nouns will be abstract in one meaning but concrete in another.
- You may be able to fool the voters but not the <u>atmosphere</u>.
(Environmental scientist Donella Meadows)
(When *atmosphere* means 'the envelope of gases around the Earth', it's concrete.)
- Moscow had an intense **atmosphere** of darkness and secrecy. (Author Alan Furst)
(When *atmosphere* means 'the pervading mood of a place', it's abstract.)

WHY SHOULD I CARE ABOUT ABSTRACT AND CONCRETE NOUNS?

Poets like abstract concepts but not abstract nouns. Many creative writers consider abstract nouns 'the enemy'. Even though abstract nouns cover many of the topics that poets like to address (e.g. love, sadness, loneliness), poets know that using these words or their derivatives (e.g. I was in love; he was sad; she was lonely) tells their readers little. For poets, the challenge is often to capture abstract feelings using concrete nouns (i.e. things that can be perceived with one of your five senses).
- …and my bicycle never leaned against the garage as it does today, all the dark blue speed drained out of it. (from '*On Turning Ten*' by Poet Laureate Billy Collins)
(The poet uses concrete nouns to express the abstract idea of ageing.)

KEY POINT
If writing a poem, consider expressing abstract ideas using concrete nouns.

Noun (Collective)

A collective noun is a word used to represent a group of people, animals or things (e.g. *team*, *crowd*, *committee*, *flock*, *choir*).

EASY EXAMPLES

Some collective nouns are quite versatile.

- a **pack** of thieves, a **pack** of wolves, a **pack** of cards, a **pack** of lies

Collective nouns that describe a specific group of animals are called terms of venery.

- **colony** of ants, **parliament** of owls, **cloud** of bats, **mob** of kangaroos, **murder** of crows

WHY SHOULD I CARE ABOUT COLLECTIVE NOUNS?

There are two good reasons to care about collective nouns.

Reason 1. Collective nouns can be singular or plural. Should you write 'the group is' or 'the group are'? Well, both can be right. You should treat a collective noun as singular or plural depending on the sense of your sentence.

- The **shoal** <u>was</u> moving north.
  (*Shoal* is singular, considered as one unit.)
- The **shoal** <u>were</u> darting in all directions.
  (*Shoal* is plural, considered as lots of individuals)
- In Rome, there is always an incredible **crowd** that <u>follows</u> me. (Boxer Muhammad Ali)
  (*Crowd* is singular, hence *follows* not *follow*.)
- Tennis can be tough when the **crowd** <u>are</u> spitting on you. (Tennis player Lleyton Hewitt)
  (Lleyton said 'the crowd <u>are</u>' because only a few in the crowd would have spat at him, compelling him to consider the crowd as individuals and not as a single unit.)

As a rule, treat a collective noun as singular unless you have a good reason not to. If your decision to go singular or plural feels uncomfortable, add a term like '*members of*' to force a plural.

- The **audience** <u>is</u> happy.
- The members of the **audience** <u>are</u> all wearing comedy wigs.

Once you've decided whether your collective noun is singular or plural, stay consistent throughout your sentence.

- The **group** <u>is</u> happy with <u>their</u> performance. ✗
  (*is* = singular / *their* = plural)
- The **group** <u>is</u> happy with <u>its</u> performance. ✔
  (*is* = singular / *its* = singular)

Reason 2. Using the 'wrong' collective noun can be a useful writing technique.
While some collective nouns (e.g. *pack*, *group*) can be used with different things, most
can't. For example, you probably shouldn't say:

- a **bouquet** of wolves, a **swarm** of students, a **litter** of ships ✗

But hang on. The term '*a swarm of students*' conjures an image of lots of students in
a frenzy, which would be an effective and interesting way to describe that situation.
Therefore, deliberately using the wrong collective noun can add a useful connotation.

- a **pack** of ships
  (ships hunting likes wolves or thieves – it brings pirates to mind)
- a **forest** of soldiers
  (thousands of stationary soldiers standing shoulder to shoulder)
- A **flock** of men is more easily driven than a single one. (Economist Richard Whately)
  (men behaving like sheep, with no individual will of their own)

KEY POINT
Treat a collective noun as singular unless the context highlights
the individuals in the group.

Noun (Compound)

A compound noun is a noun made from at least two words.

EXAMPLES

Compound nouns can be written with spaces, without spaces and with hyphens.

- *With spaces:* swimming pool, grey matter, fish tank, Iron Man
- *Without spaces:* shotgun, housework, eyelid, Batman
- *With hyphens:* laughing-gas, daughter-in-law, Spider-man

Most compound nouns are made up with the following components:

- *noun + noun:* bath tub, seaman
- *adjective + noun:* full moon, highway, whiteboard.

Other common combinations include:

- *verb + noun:* breakfast
- *noun + verb:* sunrise
- *preposition + noun:* influx
- *preposition + verb:* overthrow
- *verb + preposition:* checkout.

WHY SHOULD I CARE ABOUT COMPOUND NOUNS?

There are three good reasons to care about compound nouns.

Reason 1. Choosing the right version (i.e. the version with spaces, nothing or hyphens). Choosing the right or best form of a compound noun can be a nightmare. Some compound nouns were always the one-word version (e.g. *keyboard*). Some two-word ones have transitioned to a one-word version (e.g. *snow man* to *snowman*). Some are transitioning (e.g. *eye opener* to *eyeopener* and *ice cream* to *ice-cream*), and some are not (e.g. *peace pipe*). Some compound nouns were always the hyphenated version (e.g. *self-control*), whereas some two-word ones have transitioned to a hyphenated version (e.g. *play off* to *play-off* and soon *playoff*). Some exist in two versions (e.g. *ice-axe* or *ice axe* but not *iceaxe*). Some exist in all three versions (e.g. *chatroom, chat-room, chat room*).

For the best chance of hitting the right or best version, do the following checks:
Check 1. Check if your spellchecker accepts the one-word version. If it does, then happy days – you're done.

Check 2. Check if the hyphenated version exists using a dictionary. (NB: You can't use your spellchecker. It will only check the spelling of the sub-words either side of the hyphen. Yeah, thanks for that, Microsoft.) If it does exist, you're done.

Here's some guidance on the types of compound nouns that should always be hyphenated:

- nouns in the form role-role (e.g. *student-athlete*, *soldier-poet*, *boy-child*)
- nouns with a preposition in the middle (e.g. *man-of-war*, *brothers-in-arms*)
- titles of relatives with *great* (e.g. *great-grandmother*, *great-great-grandson*)
- fractions written in full (e.g. *two-thirds*, *one-quarter*)
- titles with *vice* and *elect* (e.g. *president-elect*, *vice-chair*)
- words with *self* (e.g. *self-awareness*, *self-restraint*).

Check 3. You're now left with the two-word version, which you should use unless it makes your sentence ambiguous.
- I like braising steak. ✘
  (This is a type of steak, not an activity. *Braising-steak* eliminates the ambiguity.)
- I need a wire fastener. ✘
  (This a fastener for wires, not one made of wire. *Wire-fastener* eliminates the ambiguity.)

Check 4. If there's no ambiguity, use the two-word version. However, you might want to consider a hyphen to prevent reading stutter.
- Domain names and websites are the new real-estate. (Entrepreneur Marc Ostrofsky)
Hyphenated compound nouns stand out as single grammatical entities, making them easier to read. Be careful not to hyphenate a well-established two-worder though (e.g. fish tank, Iron Man).

Reason 2. Forming the plural of a compound noun. Compound nouns with hyphens (e.g. brother-in-law) and compound nouns with spaces (e.g. Knight Templar) usually form their plurals by pluralising the principal word.
- I used to have two brothers-in-law. One was a karate expert, who joined the army. The first time he saluted, he killed himself. ✔ (Comedian Henny Youngman)
- The Knights Templar were a sort of medieval SAS. ✔ (Historian Dan Jones)
When there's no obvious principal word, add -s (or -es) to the end of the compound (e.g. forget-me-nots).

Reason 3. Creating the possessive form of a compound noun like
mother-in-law. With a compound noun like *mother-in-law*, the possessive form is created by adding *'s* to the end, regardless of whether it is singular or plural.

Singular	Plural
brother-in-law's manners	brothers-in-law's habits
colonel-in-chief's arrival	colonels-in-chief's meeting

KEY POINT
When writing a compound noun, use the one-word version if it exists.
If it doesn't, use the hyphenated version if it exists. If it doesn't, use the two-word version, but consider hyphenating it if the hyphen eliminates ambiguity or makes reading easier.

Noun (Countable and Uncountable)

A countable noun is a noun with both a singular and a plural form
(e.g. dog/dogs, pie/pies). A non-countable noun is a noun without
a plural form (e.g. oxygen, patience).

Non-countable nouns usually fall into one of the following categories:

Category	Example
Concept	bravery, honesty, intelligence
Activity	homework, playing, reading
Food	bread, butter, milk
Gas	air, helium, smoke
Liquid	petrol, water, wine
Material	chalk, cloth, concrete
Item Category	clothing, furniture, luggage
Natural Phenomenon	gravity, humidity, sunshine
Particles	dust, flour, salt

MORE ABOUT COUNTABLE AND
NON-COUNTABLE NOUNS

Only a countable noun (underlined below) can be preceded by a number or a/an
(bold below).

● There are **three** faithful <u>friends</u>: **an** old <u>wife</u>, **an** old <u>dog</u>, and ready money.
(American founding father Benjamin Franklin)
(*Friends*, *wife* and *dog* are countable. You can't say 'two monies' or 'a money', so
money must be a non-countable noun. Clearly, money can be counted, but
remember we're talking about the grammatical qualities of the noun money, not
physical notes and coins.)

Only a countable noun can be preceded by *many*, *several* or *fewer* (these are determiners
used with plurals). Similarly, only a non-countable noun can be preceded by *much* and
less (these are the determiners used with singular concepts).

● You can learn **many** <u>things</u> from children – how **much** patience you have, for instance.
(Writer Franklin Jones)
(*Things* is countable. *Patience* is non-countable.)

Some nouns can be non-countable in one context but countable in another. This
happens most commonly with nouns that refer to food and liquid.
● Do we have **much** coffee left? I need **a** <u>coffee</u> in the morning.
(The first *coffee* is a non-countable noun (note *much*). The second is countable
(note *a*).)

● The Middle East produces much fine cheese. For example, Israel is famous for baby <u>cheeses</u>.

The easiest way to determine whether a noun is countable or non-countable is to have a go at pluralising it or putting *a* or *an* in front. If you can't, you're looking at a non-countable noun.

WHY SHOULD I CARE ABOUT COUNTABLE AND NON-COUNTABLE NOUNS?

There are three noteworthy issues related to countable and non-countable nouns.

Issue 1. Use *fewer* with plurals and *less* with non-countable nouns. Use fewer when referring to people or things in the plural (e.g. *lawyers, dogs, pies*).

● One merit of poetry few will deny: it says more and in **fewer** <u>words</u> than prose. ✔
  (French writer Voltaire)
● Our perfect companions never have **fewer than four** <u>feet</u>. ✔
  (Novelist Sidonie Colette)

There's a quirk. Use *less than* (as opposed to *fewer than*) with numbers used with times and measurements. (If *feet* in the last example had referred to the distance, *less than* would have been correct.)

● Unemployed? Get a great job in **less than three** <u>months</u>. How? Learn to program. ✔
● Butterflies cannot fly if their body temperature is **less than 86** <u>degrees</u>. ✔

Use *less* with non-countable nouns (e.g. *money, smoke, time, snow*).
● Talk of recession offends me. I'm delighted bankers have **less** money. ✔
  (Actor Chris O'Dowd)
● It takes **less** time to do it right than to explain why you didn't. ✔
  (Poet Henry Longfellow)

Issue 2. Be careful with *number of*, *amount of* and *quantity of*. Writers are sometimes unsure whether to use 'number of', 'amount of' or 'quantity of'. Let's start with the easy one.

Number of is used with plural nouns (underlined). Mistakes with *number of* are rare.
● The grand aim of all science is to cover the greatest **number of** empirical <u>facts</u> by logical deduction from the smallest **number of** <u>hypotheses</u> or <u>axioms</u>. ✔
  (Scientist Albert Einstein)

Amount of is used with non-countable nouns. It is particularly well suited to concepts that are not easily measured.

- He harbours a certain **amount of** disdain towards her. ✔
- I regret the enormous **amount of** travel my work required. ✔
  (Astronaut Neil Armstrong)
- The **amount of** <u>women</u> in London who flirt with their own husbands is perfectly scandalous. It is simply washing one's clean linen in public. ✘ (Oscar Wilde)
  (*Women* is plural. It's a countable noun. This should be '*The number of women*'.)

Quantity of is used with countable and non-countable nouns. It fits particularly well with concepts that can be measured (especially inanimate ones).

- Greatness is an unusual **quantity of** a usual <u>quality</u> grafted upon a common man. ✔
  (US politician William Allen White)
  (*Quality* is a countable noun. A quality is measurable, and it's inanimate.)

Unlike 'amount of' and 'number of', the expression 'quantity of' carries a connotation of accuracy.

- When women and men can shed an equal **quantity of** <u>tears</u> in public, that's when we'll have equal power. ✔ (US ambassador Madeleine Kunin)
  (*Tears* is a countable noun. Even though tears are difficult to count or measure, 'quantity of' works well here because of the connotation of accuracy.)
- The strength and power of a country depends absolutely on the **quantity of** good <u>men</u> and <u>women</u> in it. ✔ (Art critic John Ruskin)
  ('Quantity of' works well because of the connotation of accuracy.)

Let's keep examining the idea that 'quantity of' is used with something measurable. The term 'amount of sleep' is far more common than 'quantity of sleep' because we tend to talk about the quality of sleep, which is a difficult thing to measure.

- Those who succeed seem to need a stupefying **amount of** sleep. ✔
  (Actor Quentin Crisp)

However, some do quantify sleep by measuring it in hours.

- Lifestyle factors such as work schedules and stress affect the **quantity of** your sleep. ✔
  (This is from the National Sleep Foundation, which talks a lot about hours of sleep.)

Too complicated? If you're still unsure whether to use 'amount of' or 'quantity of' because you can't decide whether your singular, inanimate concept is measurable or not, then you might be able to avoid the issue by wedging in a plural word and rewording.

amount/quantity of bread?	>	a number of <u>loaves</u> of bread ✔
amount/quantity of sugar?	>	a few <u>cubes</u> of sugar ✔

Issue 3. If you precede your noun with a term like 'a lot of' or 'a pound of', check you've aligned your verb. Expressing quantity with a non-countable noun is typically done by preceding it with an inexact expression (e.g. *some, a lot of, much, a bit of*) or an exact measurement (e.g. *a spoonful of, two kilograms of, an hour of, three pinches of*). When using an expression with *of* in, the word before *of* is the head word and governs the verb.

● Two bags of cheese **has** been left outside. ✗
   (*Bags* is the head word. It should be *have* not *has*.)
● A box of the cheeses **have** been left outside. ✗
   (*Box* is the head word. It should be *has* not *have*.)

So, when using an expression with the format 'A of B', remember that A is the head word. This means the expression is singular if A is singular but plural if A is plural. It doesn't matter one jot to the verb whether B is singular or plural…ordinarily.

I say 'ordinarily' because there are some quirks. When using expressions like *a lot of B, half of B, the majority of B* or *a percentage of B*, the expression is singular if B is singular but plural if B is plural.

● A lot of cheese **has** been left outside. ✔
● A lot of cheeses **have** been left outside. ✔
(*See also* Subject on page 243.)

KEY POINTS
Use *fewer* with plural nouns. Use *less* with singular nouns. Use *less* with numbers when they quantify dates or measurements.
With an expression in the format 'A of B', A governs the verb.

Noun (Gender-specific)

A gender-specific noun refers to something specifically male or female.

EASY EXAMPLES
- king, uncle, drake (male duck), wether (a castrated male sheep or goat)
- queen, niece, vixen (female fox), sow (female pig)

The following are not gender-specific nouns. Without further context, these are gender-neutral nouns.
- soldier, shark, lawyer, person

WHY SHOULD I CARE ABOUT GENDER-SPECIFIC NOUNS?
The following three issues are worthy of note.

Issue 1. Using the word *actress*. Some feel that using the word *actress*, which emerged long after *actor*, engenders gender inequality. As a result, the gender-neutral usage of *actor* is now common. There are no female versions of nouns like *doctor*, *politician*, *pilot* and *beggar*, so it's a fair point.

Issue 2. Using the word *chairman*. Not everyone treats the noun *chairman* as a gender-specific noun, and it is regularly used for men and women. However, many consider it a masculine noun, and when the appointed person is female, they opt for *chairwoman* (a term that has been in use since at least the seventeenth century). So, some will think *chairman* is just for men, and some won't. This issue is often avoided by using the gender-neutral terms *chairperson* or *chair*.

The fire and rescue services avoided the same issue with *fireman* by introducing *firefighter*. Royal Mail has kept the distinction, using *postman* and *postwoman*, but, informally, will use the gender-neutral *postie*. It's become bit of minefield. Some might view your use of the *-man* version as sexist while others view your avoidance of it as sexist. My advice? Go *chair*.

Issue 3. Choosing the right version of *blonde/blond*. The word *blonde* denotes a fair-haired female. As an adjective, it describes a female. The word *blond* denotes a fair-haired male. As an adjective, it can be used to describe men (common) or women (rare in the UK). (*See also* Gender on page 146.)

KEY POINTS
Actor can refer to males and females who act.
Chairperson is a bit contrived. Use *chair*.

Noun (Gerund)

A gerund is a noun formed from a verb (e.g. *drinking* from the verb to *drink*, *driving* from the verb to *drive*, *visiting* from the verb to *visit*). All gerunds end *-ing*.

EASY EXAMPLES

Unlike a normal noun, a gerund maintains some verb-like properties. Like a verb, a gerund can take a direct object and be modified with an adverb.

- **drinking** a flagon
  (The gerund *drinking* has a direct object, *a flagon*.)
- **driving** erratically
  (The gerund *driving* is modified with an adverb, *erratically*.)
- regularly **visiting** the hospital
  (The gerund *visiting* is modified with an adverb, *regularly*, and has a direct object, *the hospital*.)

REAL-LIFE EXAMPLES

- You can tell a lot about a fellow's character by his way of **eating** jellybeans.
  (President Ronald Reagan)
- Generosity is **giving** more than you can, and pride is **taking** less than you need.
  (Writer Kahlil Gibran)

A gerund will often be at the head of a gerund phrase. A gerund phrase (underlined) consists of a gerund, its objects and all modifiers.

- <u>**Eating** blackberries quickly</u> will make you ill.
- I like to play blackjack. I'm not addicted to **gambling**. I'm addicted to <u>**sitting** in a semicircle</u>. (Comedian Mitch Hedberg)
  (*In a semicircle* is an adverbial phrase that modifies the gerund *sitting*.)
- Discovery is <u>**seeing** what everybody has seen</u> and <u>**thinking** what nobody has thought</u>. (Biochemist Albert Szent-Gyorgyi)
  (The direct objects of the gerunds are *what everybody has seen* and *what nobody has thought*. They are both noun clauses. Don't forget that nouns (just like adverbs and adjectives) are often phrases or clauses (not just single words). This is a key point for unpicking sentences.)
- <u>**Eating** blackberries without washing them</u> will make you ill.
  (*Without washing them* is an adverbial phrase modifying the gerund *eating*. Note that it has its own internal gerund phrase, *washing them*.)

Even though all gerunds end *-ing*, not every word ending *-ing* is a gerund. Present participles also end *-ing*. Like gerunds, present participles are formed from verbs (making them verbals), but they are not used as nouns. Present participles are used as adjectives or to form verbs in a progressive tense.

- **Running** the tap will clear the air pocket. (gerund)
- Can you fix the <u>running</u> tap? (present participle as an adjective)
- The tap was <u>running</u> for an hour. (present participle forming a tense)

WHY SHOULD I CARE ABOUT GERUNDS?

Using gerunds and gerund phrases comes easily to native English speakers, and, as a rule, gerunds do not cause many writing issues. In fact, gerunds come so easily, they're great for creating natural, flowing sentences.

Use gerunds to write shorter, better-flowing sentences. One of the biggest failings with business writing is using too many nouns (normal nouns, I mean, not gerunds), making sentences sound stilted.

- We will discuss the reprimand of John for being in violation of the regulations. ✗

Writers often favour nouns (and the prepositions needed to make those nouns work) to make their writing sound more corporate. Usually, that's bad judgement because overusing nouns tends to make text harder to read as well as jolty and stale. Cleaner, smoother sentences are best achieved with verbs (see page 255), but gerunds (given they're pretty verb-like themselves) are good too.

- We will discuss **reprimanding** John for **violating** the regulations. ✔

(This nine-word version featuring two gerunds is far smoother than the 14-word version above. It saves time, brain cells and ink.)

KEY POINT

~~The replacement of~~ Replacing a normal noun with a gerund can help with ~~the creation of~~ creating a shorter, smoother sentence.

Number

Number is a grammatical category. In English, the two number categories are *singular* and *plural*. These two categories relate to nouns, pronouns, determiners and verbs. In other words, a noun, a pronoun, a determiner or a verb can be described as *singular* or *plural*.

EASY EXAMPLES

The word *singular* refers to a quantity of one. The word *plural* refers to more than one. Here are some easy examples of nouns, pronouns, determiners and verbs in the two number categories:

Word Type	Singular	Plural
Noun	cat, mouse	cats, mice
Pronoun	I, he	we, they
Determiner	this, his	these, their
Verb	is, was	are, were

Here's an example sentence with all singular words and one with all plural words:
- That man stalks her. (singular determiner, noun, verb and pronoun)
- They smoke those leaves. (plural pronoun, verb, determiner and noun)

REAL-LIFE EXAMPLES

These examples use just singular words.
- A balanced diet means a cupcake in each hand.
- It's simple. If it jiggles, it's fat. (Actor Arnold Schwarzenegger)

These examples use just plural words.
- When officers on bikes arrest people, do they put them in their baskets?
- They succeed because they think they can. (Roman poet Virgil)

MORE ABOUT NUMBER

Some words change when their grammatical number changes. For example, nouns tend to add an *s* (e.g. *cat* becomes *cats*), verbs might drop an *s* (e.g. *he plays* becomes *they play*) and one or two determiners change their forms (e.g. *that* becomes *those*).

Compared to many other languages, we have it relatively easy because lots of words (especially adjectives) don't change at all when their grammatical number changes. For example, we say *smelly dog* and *smelly dogs*. The word *smelly* doesn't change. That's not the case in many other languages:
- French: *chien malodorant* becomes *chiens malodorants*
- German: *stinkender Hund* becomes *stinkende Hunde*
- Spanish: *perro maloliente* becomes *perros malolientes*

We're good at ensuring our nouns, pronouns, determiners and verbs agree in number. More specifically, we're good at ensuring the following:

Determiners agree in number with nouns
- **This love** is silent. (Playwright TS Eliot)
  (Singular determiner with a singular noun.)
- **These accolades** get in the way. (Singer Bob Dylan)
  (Plural determiner with a plural noun.)

Determiners agree in number with pronouns
- I write my own quotations…except **this one**. I stole **this one** from somebody really clever. (Author Brian Celio)
  (Singular determiner with a singular pronoun.)
- I want to be one of **those ones**: a legend. (Rapper Ty Dolla Sign)
  (Plural determiner with a plural pronoun.)

Nouns agree in number with verbs
- A **fly flies**. (Singular noun with a singular verb.)
- **Flies fly**. (Plural noun with a plural verb.)

Pronouns agree in number with verbs
- **Everything is** self-evident. (Philosopher René Descartes)
  (Singular pronoun with a singular verb)
- **Some are** wise and **some are** otherwise. (Poet Tobias Smollett)
  (Plural pronoun with a plural verb)

WHY SHOULD I CARE ABOUT NUMBER?
We usually get grammatical number right, but we're not infallible. Here are 11 number-related issues.

Issue 1. Don't make the wrong noun agree with the verb. In a construction like 'a box of videos' or 'an assortment of chocolates', the verb must agree with the head noun (here, *box* or *assortment* not *videos* or *chocolates*). *See also* Subject on page 243.
- An assortment of chocolates **are** available from the shop. ✘
  (It should be *is*. The verb must agree with *assortment*, which is singular.)

Issue 2. Treat 'either' and 'neither' as singular. Even though they seem to refer to two things, 'either' and 'neither' are singular.
- Quorn nuggets or quorn chilli? Er, neither **is** my preference. ✔
- Either of the twins **is** available. ✔

Issue 3. Treat 'each of' as singular. 'Each' is singular. Don't treat it as plural when it appears in an expression like 'each of us' or 'each of the children'.
- Each of my garments **is** something special in itself. ✔ (Fashion designer Givenchy)
- Each of us **bears** his own hell. ✔ (Roman poet Virgil)

Issue 4. Make sure *these* and *those* agree with their noun. *These* and *those* modify plural nouns. Be careful when using the words *kind* and *type*.
- These kind of things. ✘   (It should be *kinds*.)
- Those type of issues. ✘   (It should be *types*.)

Issue 5. Be aware that terms unlike 'and', terms like 'along with', 'together with' and 'as well as' do not increase the number of the subject.
- Bill and Ben **are** the Flowerpot Men. ✔ (*And* increases the number.)
- Bill as well as Ben **is** a Flowerpot Man. ✔ (*As well as* does not increase the number.)

Issue 6. Be aware that 'or' and 'nor' do not increase the number. Unlike 'and', 'or' and 'nor' do not increase the number.
- Bill or Ben **is** guilty of breaking the sunflower. ✔
- Neither Bill nor Ben **has** a clue about gardening. ✔

Issue 7. Be aware that collective nouns can be singular or plural. A collective noun is a word that represents a group (e.g. *choir*, *shoal*, *team*). A collective noun can be singular or plural depending on the context. See *also* page 176.
- The flock **is** moving away. ✔
  (When considered as one unit, a collective noun is singular.)
- The flock **are** scattering in different directions. ✔
  (When the focus is on the individuals in the group, a collective noun is plural.)

Issue 8. Be aware that 'none' can be singular or plural. Even though some of your readers might expect you to treat it as singular, 'none' can be singular or plural.
- None of us **is** happy. ✔   None of us **are** happy. ✔

If your 'none' translates best as 'not one of', treat it as singular. If it translates best as 'not any of', treat it as plural. (See *also* Subject on page 243.)

Issue 9. Be aware that terms like 'half of', 'the majority of', and 'a percentage of' can be singular or plural. These expressions are singular when they refer to something singular but plural when they refer to something plural.
- Half of my life **has** put the other half in the grave. ✔ (French dramatist Pierre Corneille)
  (*Half* is singular because it refers to *life*, which is singular.)

● Half of the American people **have** never read a newspaper, and half have never voted. One hopes it is the same half. ✔ (Writer Gore Vidal)

(*Half* is plural because it refers to *people*, which is plural.)

Issue 10. Be aware that terms like 'all of' and 'some of' can be singular or plural. Terms such as 'all of', 'any of', 'more of', 'most of' and 'some of', i.e. ones that feature indefinite pronouns (see page 227), are singular when they precede something singular but plural when they precede something plural.

● Most of the story **does not** make sense. ✔

(*Most* is singular because it precedes *story*, which is singular.)

● Most of the people **do not** realise it, but we're part of something much bigger than ourselves, and we're all connected in some way…not just through Facebook. ✔

(*Most* is plural because it precedes *people*, which is plural.)

Issue 11. Treat 'a number of' as plural, but 'the number of' as singular.

● A number of people **are** still sleeping rough in the town. ✔
● The number of people sleeping rough **is** growing. ✔

KEY POINTS
Don't be distracted by plural modifiers. (His collection of coins **are** valuable. ✗)
Remember that 'either', 'neither' and 'each' are singular.

Object

An object is a noun or pronoun governed by a verb or a preposition. There are three kinds of objects: direct object, indirect object and object of a preposition.

EXAMPLES OF DIRECT OBJECTS

The direct object of a verb is the thing being acted upon. You can find the direct object by finding the verb and asking 'what?' or 'whom?'. In each example below, the verb is in bold and the direct object is underlined.

- Please **pass** the butter.
  (Step 1: Find the verb. Verb = *pass*)
  (Step 2: Ask 'what?'. Q: Pass what? A: *the butter*)

- The people who **cast** the votes **do not decide** an election. The vote counters do. (Soviet leader Joseph Stalin)
  (Step 1: Find the verbs. Verbs = *cast* and *do not decide*)
  (Step 2: Ask 'what?' for each verb. Q: Cast what? Do not decide what? A: *the votes* and *an election*.)

Direct objects can be pronouns too.
- **Don't eat** me. **I have** a wife and kids! **Eat** them! (Homer Simpson)
  (Step 1: Find the verbs. Verbs = *don't eat*, *have* and *eat*)
  (Step 2: Ask 'what?' for each verb. Q: Don't eat whom? Have what? Eat whom? A: *me*, *a wife and kids* and *them*)

The verb could be a phrasal verb (e.g. *to put down*, *to give up*, *to recover from*).
- My cat **is recovering from** a massive stroke. (Comedian Darren Walsh)
  (Step 1: Find the verb. Verb = *is recovering from*)
  (Step 2: Ask 'what?' Q: Is recovering from what? A: *a massive stroke*)

It can get complicated.
- The cat **wants** to eat our goldfish.
  (Step 1. Find the verb. Verb = *wants*)
  (Step 2. Ask 'what?'. Q: Wants what? A: *to eat our goldfish*)
  (That seems easy enough, but note that the direct object has its own verb and direct object. (Q: Eat what? A: *our goldfish*.))

Don't forget that the term *noun* does not necessarily mean a single word. An object can be a single-word noun (e.g. *dog*, *goldfish*, *man*), a pronoun (e.g. *her*, *it*, *him*), a noun phrase (e.g. *the doggy in the window*, *to eat our goldfish*, *a man about town*) or a noun clause (e.g. *what the dog saw*, *how the goldfish survived*, *why man triumphed*).

EXAMPLES OF INDIRECT OBJECTS

The indirect object is the recipient or beneficiary of the action (more often than not, it's a person). You can find the indirect object by finding the verb and direct object (see above) and then asking 'for or to whom?'. In each example below, the direct object is in bold and the indirect object is underlined.

● Give a girl **the right shoes**, and she can conquer the world. (Actress Marilyn Monroe)
   (Q: Give 'the right shoes' to whom? A: *a girl*)

● Show me **a hero**, and I'll write you **a tragedy**. (Author F. Scott Fitzgerald)
   (Q: Show 'a hero' to whom? A: *me*)
   (Q: Write 'a tragedy' for whom? A: *you*)

● Never tell people **how to do things**. Tell them **what to do**, and they will surprise you with their ingenuity. (General George Patton)
   (Q: Never tell 'how to do things' to whom? A: *people*)
   (Q: Tell 'what to do' to whom? A: *them*)

Often, the word *to* or *for* will be present, making identification of the indirect object easier.
● When giving jewellery as a present, I'm giving **protection** to someone I care about.
   (Actress Sofia Boutella)

Indirect objects aren't always people. Every now and again, you might have to ask 'for or to what?' as opposed to 'whom?'.
● Be ashamed to die until you have won **some victory** for humanity.
   (Educational reformer Horace Mann)

EXAMPLES OF OBJECTS OF PREPOSITIONS

The object of a preposition is the noun or pronoun governed by it. In each example below, the object of the preposition is underlined and the preposition is in bold.
● **in** silence   **without** prejudice   **to** me, **to** you   **by** whom

The object of a preposition is usually the noun or pronoun immediately to the right of the preposition.
● Failure cannot cope **with** persistence. (Author Napoleon Hill)
● Turn your wounds **into** wisdom. (Talk-show host Oprah Winfrey)

The object of preposition will often be accompanied by modifiers, which can precede or follow an object of a preposition. The whole caboodle – the preposition (bold), the object of the preposition (underlined) and all of its modifiers – is called a prepositional phrase (italic).
● When I was younger, I felt like a man trapped *inside a woman's body*. Then I was born. (Comedian Yianni Agisilaou)

● You cannot work **with** <u>men</u> who won't work with you.
(Businessman John Harvey Kellogg)
(It can get complicated. Here, the prepositional phrase (italic) has another prepositional phrase '**with** <u>you</u>' nested within it.)

Also of note, the whole caboodle less the preposition (bold) will be something functioning as a noun. In other words, it will be a single-word noun, a noun phrase (see page 171) or a noun clause (see page 172). When the object of the preposition is a noun clause, the head 'noun' will be a word like *that*, *how* or a 'wh'-word (*what*, *who*, *which*, *when*, *where*, *why*).

● I saw a documentary **on** <u>how</u> ships are kept together. Riveting!
(Comedian Stewart Francis)

MORE ABOUT OBJECTS

Only transitive verbs can have a direct or indirect object. When a verb can take a direct object, it's called a transitive verb. Some verbs cannot take direct objects. They're known as intransitive verbs.

● Malcolm fell badly.
(Step 1: Find the verb. Verb = *fell*)
(Step 2: Ask 'what?'. Q: Fell what? A: *Nothing*. You can't fall something. Therefore, there's no direct object. The verb *to fall* is intransitive. (*See also* Transitive and Intransitive Verbs on page 256.)

Linking verbs don't have a direct object. Don't confuse subject complements with direct objects. If you ask 'what?' with a linking verb, you'll find a subject complement not the direct object.

● Peter is happy.
(Step 1: Find the verb. Verb = *is*)
(Step 2. Ask 'What?'. Q: Is what? A: *happy*.)

On this occasion, *happy* is not the direct object. The 'What?' test doesn't work with linking verbs. Look at this example:

● You **are** a funny guy. I **will kill** <u>you</u> last.
(*Funny guy* is not a direct object. It's a subject complement following a linking verb. The verb *to kill* is transitive (so not a linking verb) and *you* is its direct object. See *also* Linking Verb on page 160.)

Objects are in the objective case. In English, this only affects pronouns (but not all pronouns).

● She saw <u>him</u>.
(The pronoun *him* (the direct object of *saw*) is the objective-case version of *he*.)
● Give <u>them</u> the money.
(The pronoun *them* (the indirect object of *give*) is the objective-case version of *they*.)

● Dance with _her_. She wants to dance with <u>you</u>.

(The pronoun _her_ (the object of the preposition _with_) is the objective-case version of _she_. The pronoun _you_ is one of the ones that doesn't change. Unless you're planning on learning a foreign language, don't worry about this too much. We all do this stuff naturally.)

Verbals can have direct objects too. A verbal is a word derived from a verb. Verbals function as nouns or adjectives. They can be infinitives (e.g. _I like_ **to read**,), gerunds (e.g. _I like_ **reading**), and participles (_e.g. my_ **reading** _glasses_). Here are some examples of verbals (in bold) with direct objects (underlined):

● As a kid, I was made **to walk** <u>the plank</u>. We couldn't afford a dog. (Comedian Gary Delaney)

(_To walk_ is an infinitive (see page 153). Q: To walk what? A: _the plank_)

● **Driving** <u>a time machine</u> is annoying because your kids are always asking, 'Are we then yet?'. (Comedian Paul Taylor)

(_Driving_ is a gerund (see page 185). Q: Driving what? A: _a time machine_)

● **Watching** <u>the London Marathon</u>, I noticed one runner dressed as a chicken and another as an egg. I thought: 'This could be interesting.' (Comedian Paddy Lennox)

(_Watching_ is a participle (see page 213). Q: Watching what? A: _the London Marathon_)

WHY SHOULD I CARE ABOUT OBJECTS?

Yup, that's a lot of terminology for stuff you do naturally, but there are three good reasons to think more carefully about objects.

Reason 1. Making sure your subject and verb agree. The object of a preposition cannot be the subject of a verb.

● A box **of** <u>magazines</u> are under the stairs. ✗
● A box **of** <u>magazines</u> is under the stairs. ✔

Don't be fooled by the proximity of the object of the preposition to the verb. You have to ensure the subject (_box_) and the verb agree in number. This error is particularly common with the word _each_ (which is singular).

● Each **of** the guide <u>dogs</u> are assigned a trainer. ✗
● Each **of** the guide <u>dogs</u> is assigned a trainer. ✔

(Don't be fooled by _dogs_ being plural. Remember that the object of a preposition (here, _dogs_) cannot be the subject of a verb.)

Be aware though that with some expressions (e.g. _half of_, _proportion of_, _percentage of_, _majority of_), the object of the preposition does influence the verb.

● A worrying percentage **of** <u>skin</u> **is** missing. ✔ (_skin_ means that _percentage_ is singular)
● A high percentage **of** <u>the students</u> have failed. ✗ (_students_ means that _percentage_ is plural)

See also subject-verb agreement in Subject on page 243.

Reason 2. Use *if* and *whether* correctly. Writers are sometimes unsure whether to use *if* or *whether* after a preposition. Use *whether*.

● It's a moral question **about** <u>whether we have the right to exterminate species.</u> ✔
  (Naturalist Sir David Attenborough)
  (Put another way: Use *whether*, not *if*, to head up the object of a preposition.)

Reason 3. Don't confuse *who* and *whom*. *Who* is never an object, but *whom* always is. Use *who* for a subject but *whom* for an object.

● The paper slates <u>whom</u>? ✔ (direct object)
● Show <u>whom</u> the money? ✔ (indirect object)
● I met two men, one of <u>whom</u> was a bit too good at dancing. ✔
  (object of a preposition)

It's the same deal with *whoever* and *whomever*. This means *who* and *whoever* almost never follow a preposition. It can happen though.

● Islam was interpreted to give the ruler absolute power, which was a convenient interpretation **for** <u>whoever was the ruler.</u> ✔
  (Egyptian Vice President Mohamed ElBaradei)
  (Even though it follows a preposition (*for*), *whoever* is correct. It's the subject of *was*.)

Of interest, writers never confuse pairings like *he/him* and *they/them*. Well, they're no different from the *who/whom* pairing. If you're not following this, just use *who* for everything. It's way more common, and many consider *whom* obsolete. It's certainly on its last legs. (Warning: Using *who* wrongly isn't a disaster. Using *whom* wrongly is.)

KEY POINTS
Don't let the object of a preposition drag your eye away
from the subject of your verb.
(Each of the seven billion people <u>have</u> a reason. ✗)
(A long list of issues <u>were</u> considered. ✗)

Paragraph

A paragraph is a distinct section of writing covering one topic. It will usually contain more than one sentence. A paragraph starts on a new line. Sometimes, the first line of a paragraph is indented or numbered.

EXAMPLES

The perfect paragraph will start with a topic-introducing sentence (underlined in the example below) or a sentence that provides a logical link to the previous paragraph. It will have more detailed sentences in the middle (normal text in the example), and it will end with a concluding sentence (underlined). It will cover only one topic from start to finish.

● <u>Sharks are a group of fish characterised by a cartilaginous skeleton, five to seven gills and pectoral fins that are not fused to the head.</u> Today's sharks are classified within the *Selachimorpha* clade, a sister group to the rays. However, the term 'shark' has also been used for extinct members of the subclass *Elasmobranchii* outside the *Selachimorpha*, such as *Cladoselache*. <u>Under this broader definition, the earliest known sharks date from more than 420 million years ago.</u>

A paragraph could be part of a text that informs people, describes something, critiques something, compares things, persuades people, lists a process, makes an argument, offers a solution or narrates a story. The level of detail will vary from text to text. All this diversity means that it's not always easy to determine what 'one topic' means when dividing your text into paragraphs. For example, you could have a one-topic paragraph describing Venus with the next paragraph describing Mars, or a one-topic paragraph describing the colours of a sunset with the next paragraph describing its reflection in the sea.

If you're getting the sense that the word 'topic' is a bit too grand for a measly paragraph, then think of a paragraph as a distinct section of writing that covers one aspect of your topic. That's the point. Sometimes, a paragraph will be an aspect of a topic, sometimes it will be a topic within an issue, sometimes it will an issue within an argument ... a narrative, a process, a comparison, whatever. Whatever the scope of your paragraph, it should be neatly bounded as one ... well, topic. If you prefer *aspect* instead of *topic*, go with that.

WHY SHOULD I CARE ABOUT PARAGRAPHS?

There are three noteworthy points related to paragraphs. One is a good tip, one is a style convention, and one is an observation.

Point 1. In business writing, use paragraph titles. A good tip for business writing is to give each paragraph a title that summarises it. This serves two purposes. It ensures your paragraph topic is neatly bounded, and the title will assist busy executives to skim.

● **The new building will cost £400K.** The new building will be more expensive than the initial estimate. The new regulations have delayed the start of the building, and they stipulate deeper foundations. As a result, the cost will rise by 25% to £400K.

You could use a single-word title for your paragraph (e.g. **Cost**), but it wouldn't be as useful. Alternatively, you can concoct a paragraph title in your head (without physically writing it). This is a useful tip to ensure your paragraph covers one topic neatly.

Point 2. Use several 'opening' quotation marks if your quotation covers more than one paragraph. When a quotation contains multiple paragraphs (or is a text with lots of new lines), a common convention is to use an opening quotation mark at the start of each paragraph (to remind your readers that they're still reading a quotation) but only one closing quotation mark at the end of the last paragraph. Look at this example:

> In 1912, the publisher Arthur C. Fifield sent Gertrude Stein the following rejection letter shortly after receiving her manuscript:
>
> 'Dear Madam,
>
> 'I am only one, only one, only one. Only one being, one at the same time. Not two, not three, only one. Only one life to live, only sixty minutes in one hour. Only one pair of eyes. Only one brain. Only one being. Being only one, having only one pair of eyes, having only one time, having only one life, I cannot read your M.S. three or four times. Not even one time. Only one look, only one look is enough. Hardly one copy would sell here. Hardly one. Hardly one.
> 'Many thanks. I am returning the M.S. by registered post. Only one M.S. by one post.
>
> 'Sincerely yours,
> 'A. C. Fifield'

Only the last 'paragraph' (here, the name) gets a closing quotation mark.

Point 3. Your online readers won't read lengthy texts, so use your discretion to keep your paragraphs short. In print, an unbroken lengthy text looks daunting – on a screen, doubly so. Therefore, dividing a long text into bite-sized chunks is essential for keeping your readers engaged. If we're being strict, each of your paragraphs should neatly encapsulate one topic, but, as we've mentioned, the definition of 'topic' is pretty slack, and this often gives you some wriggle room to play with your paragraph lengths.

KEY POINT
Keep your paragraphs neatly bounded under one topic by using paragraph titles.

Person

Person is a category used to distinguish between (1) those speaking, (2) those being addressed and (3) those who are neither speaking nor being addressed (i.e. everybody else). These three categories are called the first person, the second person and the third person.

In grammar, the personal pronouns (*I, you, he, she, it, we, you, they*) are grouped into one of the three categories.

● **The First Person.** This category is used for the point of view of the speaker or a group that includes the speaker. A basic sentence in the first person would typically start 'I [did something]' or 'We [did something]'. (In grammar, the first-person personal pronouns are *I, me, we* and *us*.)

● **The Second Person.** This category is used for those being spoken to. A basic sentence in the second person would start 'You [did something]'. (In grammar, the second-person pronoun is *you*.)

● **The Third Person.** This category is used for everyone else. A basic sentence in the third person would start 'He [did something]', 'She [did something]' or 'They [did something]'. (In grammar, the third-person pronouns are *he, him, she, her, it, they* and *them*. The third person also includes all other nouns, e.g. *Fritz, Germans*.)

The personal pronouns are further categorised into singular and plural, giving six categories overall. The table below shows the pronouns in the six person categories and in the various cases.

	Person	Subjunctive Case	Objective Case	Possessive Determiner	Possessive Pronoun
Singular	First person singular	I	me	you	mine
	Second person singular	you	you	your	yours
	Third person singular	he/she/it	him/her/it	his/her/it	his/hers/its
Plural	First person plural	we	us	our	ours
	Second person plural	you	you	your	yours
	Third person plural	they	them	their	theirs

See also Case, Possessive Determiner and Possessive Pronoun on pages 97, 139 and 220.

EASY EXAMPLES

The idea of grammatical person is used in some everyday terms:

● *First-person gaming.* In video games, first-person games show the viewpoint of the player's character. In other words, when I play the game, the graphics are rendered from my perspective (i.e. what I can see).

● *First-person narrative.* In storytelling, a first-person narrative relays events using 'I' or 'we'.

● *Third-party insurance.* Third-party insurance protects against the claims of others. Here's more: I (the first party) am insured by you, the insurer (the second party), to protect me against them (the third party).

WHY SHOULD I CARE ABOUT PERSON?

The overwhelming majority of native speakers – even those who've never heard the term *grammatical person* before – use all the pronouns and adjectives in the table on page 198 flawlessly. Nevertheless, there are two good reasons to be familiar with the person categories.

Reason 1. Understanding the person categories is useful for learning a foreign a language. Understanding terms like 'first person singular' and 'third person plural' is useful when learning a foreign language because the vast majority of teachers and reference books use these terms to explain how grammar works (especially verbs). Also, being familiar with the person categories allows you to anticipate what's to come. Put another way, you can now enter your first foreign-language lesson with an empty version of the table in your head and think, 'Bring it on. Just fill in the gaps.'

Reason 2. Choosing the right person can help portray the right image. Yup, I'm still talking about grammatical person. If you want to portray a personal touch or show responsibility for your actions, write in the first person; i.e. use 'I' or 'we'.

● I will handle your claim within 24 hours.

If you want to portray formality or distance yourself from your actions, write in the third person; i.e. use 'he', 'she', 'it', 'they' or nouns.

● Lees Ltd will handle your claim within 24 hours.

If you really wanted to distance yourself from your actions, you could also write in the passive voice (see page 63).

● Your claim will be handled within 24 hours.

KEY POINTS

I advise you to write in the first person for that personal touch.
The author advises you to write in the third person to portray more formality.
You are advised to write in the passive voice if you really want to hide under the quilt.

Phrasal Verb

A phrasal verb is a multiword verb. A phrasal verb consists of a main verb and at least one other word (often a preposition, e.g. up, in, back).

EASY EXAMPLES
- to catch up
- to give in
- to go back

REAL-LIFE EXAMPLES
More often than not, a phrasal verb has a different meaning to the verb on its own (underlined). For example, *to catch up* does not mean the same as *to catch*.
- Aching to know why she **broke up** with him, he <u>broke</u> the window and **broke in**. (The phrasal verbs do not mean the same as *to break*.)
- If you **drop out** or <u>drop</u> the baton, we will **drop back** to last place.

MORE ABOUT PHRASAL VERBS
Some phrasal verbs are transitive (see page 256), which means the action of the verb is done to something. The thing being acted upon is called the direct object (underlined).
- **Fill in** <u>the form</u> as quickly as possible.
- Did you **go over** <u>those reports</u> last night?

Some phrasal verbs are intransitive (i.e. they do not take a direct object).
- If you're unhappy, **stand up**.
- Do not **give in**.

Some phrasal verbs can be transitive or intransitive depending on their meaning.
- She will **show up** <u>the opposition</u>. (Transitive. It means 'She will embarrass the opposition.')
- She will **show up** soon. (Intransitive. It means 'She will appear soon.')

Some transitive phrasal verbs are separable. This means the direct object appears between the verb and the preposition.
- I will **make** <u>you</u> **up** to look like a princess.
- She **talked** <u>her father</u> **into** letting her attend the party.

Some transitive phrasal verbs are inseparable. This means the direct object cannot appear between the verb and the preposition.
- She **looks up to** <u>her sister</u>.
- You must **stick to** <u>the plan</u> at all costs.

And, there are lots of transitive phrasal verbs that can be used in a separable way or an inseparable way.

- He **looked** <u>my address</u> **up** on the National Voter Register.   (separable way)
- He **looked up** <u>my address</u> on the National Voter Register.   (inseparable way)
- He **looked up** <u>it</u> on the National Voter Register. ✗   (inseparable way)
  (It's a quirk. You can't use the inseparable way with a pronoun (here, *it*). Good luck explaining that if you're an English teacher!)

WHY SHOULD I CARE ABOUT PHRASAL VERBS?

There are three good reasons to avoid phrasal verbs and two good reasons to embrace them.

Reason to Avoid 1. Phrasal verbs sound informal. Phrasal verbs tend to derive from our Germanic heritage. As the Germanic elements in our language stem from the language of the common people, phrasal verbs are usually easy on the ear and easily understandable. That's all good. The downsides, however, are that phrasal verbs can seem informal. Therefore, in business and academic writing, there's a leaning towards the one-word Latinate verbs, i.e. those which derive from Latin via our French heritage. Latinate verbs sound more formal because they stem from the language of our aristocracy.

- We'll all **get together** in the foyer. (okay, if a little informal)
- We will <u>congregate</u> in the foyer. (possibly preferable if some formality is required)

- We've **put** the meeting **off** until Tuesday. (okay, if a little informal)
- The meeting is <u>postponed</u> until Tuesday. (possibly preferable if some formality is required)

Reason to Avoid 2. Some phrasal verbs eat up your word count unnecessarily.
Some phrasal verbs include prepositions that don't add anything. Delete them.
- I cannot **face up** to this problem. (okay)
- I cannot face this problem. (better, more succinct)

- She will not **stand for** shoddy work. (okay)
- She will not stand shoddy work. (better, more succinct)

If the phrasal verb sounds better, go with it.
- Even I don't **wake up** looking like Cindy Crawford. (Model Cindy Crawford)
  (It's possible to use *wake* without *up*, but it doesn't sound as natural.)

Reason to Avoid 3. A phrasal verb often sticks a preposition at the end of your sentence. It doesn't matter how many times we're told it's okay to end a sentence in a preposition. There are still wads of people who think it isn't okay. So, for now, if you can easily avoid ending a sentence in a preposition, you might as well. Think of it as a game, not a rule.

- It is a situation I will not **put up with**. (okay)
- It is a situation I will not tolerate. (safer and more succinct)

- Can you **sort** it **out**? (okay)
- Can you resolve it? (safer and more succinct)

Reason to Embrace 1. A phrasal verb might better fit your image. When choosing words for business correspondence, you must consider the character of your business. For example, auditors like KPMG might write 'Terms and Conditions of the Contract', while Virgin Media might write 'The stuff you need to know'. You must know your 'writing voice'. If you're a formal bunch, you should probably steer clear of phrasal verbs, but if you're a down-with-the-kids outfit, phrasal verbs and other simple vocabulary might be a good fit.

- We would not expect you to tolerate a second-rate service. (corporate)
- Don't **put up with** bad service. (engaging)

Reason to Embrace 2. Phrasal verbs are easily understood. Phrasal verbs are often more familiar than Latinate verbs.

- The framework is required to concatenate the disparate elements.
  (This might sound business-like, but there's a risk it won't be understood.)
- The framework is required to **join up** each element.
  (This is clearer and safer.)

Often, the clarity and naturalness afforded by a phrasal verb is worth the informality.

KEY POINT
Phrasal verbs will eat up your word count.
Many phrasal verbs sound natural but also informal. Use them or avoid them to tune to your 'writing voice'.

Predicate

The predicate is the part of a sentence (or clause) that tells us about the subject. To put it another way, the predicate is everything that is not the subject.

EASY EXAMPLES

In the examples below, the predicate is underlined. (The subjects of the sentences aren't.)

- Elvis lives.
- Adam lives in Bangor.
- The girls in our office are experienced instructors.

REAL-LIFE EXAMPLES

At the heart of every predicate is a verb (bold in the examples).

- True friends **appear** less moved than counterfeit. (Greek poet Homer)
- Words empty as the wind **are** best left unsaid. (Greek poet Homer)
- With $10,000, we **would be** millionaires! We **could buy** all kinds of useful things like … love. (The other Homer)

MORE ABOUT PREDICATES

A clause contains a subject and predicate too. The examples below are all clauses, not sentences.

- who **lives** with our mother (The subject is *who*.)
- which **was** somewhat unexpected (The subject is *which*.)
- that **points** to the North Pole (The subject is *that*.)

Spotting predicates can get quite complicated because it's not uncommon for a clause with its own predicate to feature within a sentence-level predicate.

- Sarah **is** my youngest sister, who lives with our mother;

(Look at the clause 'who lives with our mother'. It has its own subject ('who') and its own predicate ('lives with our mother'). The clause is part of the longer, underlined, sentence-level predicate.)

If you find yourself discussing predicates, it won't be too long before you come across the terms *compound predicate*, *predicate adjective* and *predicate nominative*.

Compound Predicate. A compound predicate tells us two (or more) things about the same subject (without repeating the subject). This is a simple predicate:

- Rachel **lives** in Dublin.
   (This tell us just one thing about the subject (*Rachel*). It is a simple predicate.)

These are examples of compound predicates:

- Rachel **lives** in Dublin and **speaks** Irish. (This tell us two things about the subject.)
- The telegram **was** late but **contained** exciting news.

Remember that a compound predicate tells us at least two things about one subject. So, the following sentence is **not** an example of a compound predicate:

● Rachel **lives** in Dublin, and she **speaks** Irish.
(This is a compound sentence (see page 238). It does not have a compound predicate. It has two subjects (*Rachel* and *she*), each with one simple predicate.)

This one does have a compound predicate:

● Rachel and her brother **live** in Dublin and **speak** Irish.
(The predicate tells us two things about the subject (*Rachel and her brother*). Even though the subject has two elements, it's still just one subject. This is called a compound subject.)

Predicate Adjective. A predicate adjective is an adjective that describes the subject of a linking verb (see page 160). Linking verbs are divided into the 'status' verbs (e.g. *to be, to appear, to become, to continue, to seem, to turn*) and the 'sense' verbs (e.g. *to feel, to look, to smell, to taste, to sound*). In these examples, the linking verbs are in bold and the predicate adjectives are underlined.

● No one **is** happy all his life long. (Greek tragedian Euripides)
● I **feel** beautiful when my makeup **looks** great. (Model Khoudia Diop)

Predicate Nominative. A predicate nominative (also called a *predicate noun*) is a word or group of words that completes a linking verb and renames the subject. (A predicate nominative is always a noun or a pronoun.) In these examples, the linking verbs are in bold and the predicate nominatives are underlined.

● Your proposal **was** a risk.
● Diamonds **are** a girl's best friend, and dogs **are** a man's best friend. Now you know which sex has more sense. (Actress Zsa Zsa Gabor)
(Note that a predicate nominative is often a noun phrase, i.e. a noun made up of more than one word.)

A predicate nominative can be made up of more than one noun. In other words, it can be a compound predicate nominative.

● Your proposal **was** an opportunity and a risk.
● I **will be** your employer, your advisor and your friend.
(The underlined texts are both compound predicate nominatives.)

Predicate nominatives and predicate adjectives are known as *subject complements*.

WHY SHOULD I CARE ABOUT PREDICATES?

Jeepers, that's a lot of terminology to describe how we construct sentences, especially as we all do it on autopilot. Right now, you're probably thinking that you don't need to know about predicates. But, actually, there are two good reasons to learn about them.

Reason 1. Be clear on when to use a comma before 'and'. Writers often ask whether they need a comma before 'and' (The answer applies equally to other conjunctions like 'but' and 'or'.) Here's the rule: When 'and' joins two independent clauses (i.e. clauses that could stand alone as sentences), use a comma. Look at these two correctly punctuated sentences:

- John is smart and articulate. ✔
- John is smart, and he is articulate. ✔

Let's examine the first example. Even though it has a compound predicate adjective that tells us two things about the subject (*John*), it is a simple sentence (i.e. it's just one independent clause). That's why there's no comma before 'and'.

The second example is a compound sentence. It has two independent clauses, either of which could stand alone as a sentence. That's why there is a comma before 'and'. So, when 'and' is used to merge two 'sentences' into one, use a comma. When 'and' is used to make two points about the same subject (i.e. when it's just a compound predicate), don't.

Reason 2. Don't use an adverb when you need a predicate adjective. With some linking verbs (bold), writers feel the need to use an adverb because they know that adverbs, not adjectives, modify verbs.

- The soup **tastes** brilliantly. ✘
- The soup works brilliantly. ✔

After any linking verb, the subject complement modifies the subject (here, *the soup*) not the verb (here, *tastes*). That's why the adjective *brilliant* is right and the adverb *brilliantly* is wrong. Incorrectly using an adverb occurs most commonly with the 'sense' linking verbs, especially *to feel* and *to smell*.

- Don't **feel** badly. ✘ (This should be *bad*.)
- His **breath** smells terribly. ✘ (This should be *terrible*.)

KEY POINTS

If your 'and' (or any conjunction) joins two independent clauses, precede it with a comma. If it's just part of compound predicate saying two things about the subject, don't.
Remember that your soup tastes *brilliant* not *brilliantly*.

Preposition

A preposition is a word (often a short word) that precedes a noun or a pronoun to show the noun's relationship to another word in the sentence.

Here is list of common prepositions: *above, about, across, against, along, among, around, at, before, behind, below, beside, between, by, down, during, except, for, from, in, inside, into, like, near, of, off, on, since, to, toward, through, under, until, up, with, within.*

EASY EXAMPLES

In the examples below, each preposition (bold) shows us the relationship between the word *book* and the word *wizard*.

- The book **about** the wizard
- The book **near** the wizard
- The book **behind** the wizard

When you're first learning about prepositions, it might be useful to think of them as 'anywhere a mouse could go'.

- The mouse is **behind** the clock / **near** the clock / **under** the clock / **inside** the clock. (The prepositions show us the relationship between *the clock* and *the mouse*. This tip works because lots of prepositions show the relationship between two words by expressing their locations relative to each other.)

REAL-LIFE EXAMPLES

- The difference **between** stupidity and genius is that genius has its limits. (Physicist Albert Einstein)
  (*Between* shows the relationship between *stupidity* and *genius*.)
- I cook **with** wine. Sometimes, I even add it **to** food. (Actor W C Fields)
  (*With* shows the relationship between *wine* and *cook*. *To* shows the relationship between *food* and *add*.)
- If you've nothing nice to say **about** anybody, sit **next to** me. (Writer Alice Longworth)
  (*About* shows the relationship between *anybody* and *to say*; *next to* shows the relationship between *me* and *sit*. Note that a preposition can be more than one word e.g. *close to, ahead of, in front of, according to*.)

WHY SHOULD I CARE ABOUT PREPOSITIONS?

There are four common issues involving prepositions.

Issue 1. Using the wrong case after a preposition. The word or words that follow a preposition are called the object of a preposition (see page 192). The object of a preposition is always in the objective case. This just means that words like *I, she, we* and *they* change to *me, her, us* and *them* when they follow a preposition (e.g. *about me, with her, for us, against them*).

- It is a present **from** my wife and I. ✘
- **Between** you and I ✘
  (These are both wrong because *I* cannot be the object of the preposition)
- It is a present **from** me and my wife. ✔
- **Between** you and me ✔

Ironically, many people use terms like 'from my wife and I' and 'between you and I' with a highbrow tone, believing them to be grammatically pure. They're wrong.

Another one that catches people out is using *who* after a preposition. *Who* becomes *whom* in the objective case (i.e. *who* is to *whom* as *he* is to *him* or *they* is to *them*).

- You went with who? ✘
- You went with whom? ✔

The word *whom* is on its last legs – some sources already list it as obsolete. So, if you're unsure whether to use *who* or *whom*, use *who*. Even if it's wrong, it'll be acceptable. If you use *whom* wrongly, it'll look as if you're trying to be clever … and failing.

Issue 2. Confusing prepositions with other words. Writers sometimes confuse prepositions with other words. Here are the top five mistakes. *See also* Easily Confused Words chapter on page 266.

- Writing the adverb *too* (which means 'overly' or 'as well') instead of the preposition *to* (which has several meanings including 'towards' and 'for').
- Writing the preposition *of* instead of *have* when writing *could've*, *should've* or *would've* in full.
- Writing the noun *dependant* (a person, usually a child or spouse) instead of *dependent* in the preposition *dependent on* ('reliant on').
- Writing the preposition *past* ('beyond') instead of *passed* (past tense of 'to pass').
- Writing the preposition *between* (usually used with two distinct points) instead of the preposition *among* (in the middle of a group).

Issue 3. Some phrasal verbs (i.e. multi-word verbs) have prepositions that do not add anything. When you encounter one of these, delete the prepositions to improve succinctness.

- Thinking about being an adult, facing ~~up to~~ your problems, facing ~~up to~~ your insecurities, is difficult for everybody. (Actress Mary Elizabeth Winstead)
  (The original had the prepositions. It's a bit sharper without them.)

Issue 4. Keeping writing succinct. Lots of people think it's an error to end a sentence in a preposition because, as we've just covered, a preposition is supposed to sit before a noun. (That is, after all, how preposition gets its name.) Therefore, if the preposition is the last word in a sentence, it can't sit before anything. So, there's some logic to this ruling. However, this issue is more complicated, and the best way to summarise it is by saying that, in the overwhelming majority of cases, it's perfectly acceptable – from a grammatical perspective – to end a sentence in a 'preposition'. (I'll explain the quotation marks later.)

Here's the rub. Even though you'd probably be correct in ending your sentence with a 'preposition', you should be mindful that a fair few of your readers will think it's a grammar mistake or sloppy writing. As we haven't trained ourselves to strike through this so-called ruling, we can't ignore it. I like to think of 'avoiding a preposition at the end of a sentence' as a game rather than a rule.

Here's an example.
● It is a scenario I have not thought **of**.
(This is natural sounding, but it ends in a preposition.)
Let's restructure our sentence.
● It is a scenario <u>of</u> **which** I have not thought.
(This sounds unnatural and contrived. On the plus side, our preposition now sits before the pronoun *which*, and that fits the rule for siting a preposition.)

But, it sounds terrible, so let's keep playing the game. Let's reword our sentence again.
● It is a scenario I have not considered.
(Yes! This sounds natural, and it does not end in a preposition. This keeps everyone happy … except those people who think we shouldn't pander to those who still think you can't end a sentence in a preposition.)
So, for now, I'm advising you become a panderer to this non-ruling. But if restructuring your sentence makes it sound contrived, and you can't reword it, then just let the preposition at the end ride. If you're questioned on it, fight like a dog, because you'll be in the right.

Now, why was 'preposition' in quotation marks earlier in this section? Well, quite often, your sentence will end in something that looks like a preposition but isn't. It could be part of a phrasal verb (see page 200), which is a verb made up of a verb and another word (either a preposition or a particle), e.g. *fill in, stick to, catch up, catch out*. Quite often, these words must be next to each other, and that's often a factor in your sentence structure.

KEY POINT
Don't say 'between you and I' or 'from my wife and I'. They're both wrong.

Prepositional Phrase

A prepositional phrase is a phrase that starts with a preposition and ends with noun or a pronoun.

EASY EXAMPLES
In these examples, the prepositional phrase is underlined and the preposition is bold.

- A singer **with** passion
- Keep **in** time

- A town **near** London
- He acts **without** thinking.

It gets a bit more complicated than shown above, because the noun can be anything that plays the role of a noun (see page 168).

- It's a present **from** her.
  (The 'noun' is a pronoun.)
- She stole it **from** the man across the street.
  (This is a noun phrase.)
- It's obvious **from** what he said.
  (And this is a noun clause.)

The noun that follows the preposition is called the object of a preposition (see page 192). There will often be modifiers in the object of the preposition making it a noun phrase.

- I sat **with** Simba.
  (There are no modifiers in this example.)
- I sat **with** the wonderful Simba.
  (With the modifiers *the* and *wonderful*, the object of the preposition is now a noun phrase.)

Prepositional phrases function as either adjectives or adverbs (i.e. they are adjectival phrases or adverbial phrases). Here are some prepositional phrases functioning as adjectives.

- Please buy the scarf **with** dots.
  (The prepositional phrase describes the noun *scarf*. We could have written 'dotted scarf', which proves that *with dots* is functioning as an adjective.)
- The man **on** the radio has a boring voice.
  (The prepositional phrase describes *The man*.)

Here are some prepositional phrases functioning as adverbs.

- Lee raised his small mackerel **with** utmost pride.
  (The prepositional phrase modifies the verb *raised*. It is an adverb of manner; i.e. it tells us how he raised it. We could have written 'proudly raised', which proves that *with utmost pride* is functioning as an adverb.)
- **Before** the war, Chris played football for Barnstoneworth United.
  (The prepositional phrase modifies the verb *played*. It is an adverb of time.)

209

● Lee lives **in** that fridge.
(The prepositional phrase modifies the verb *lives*. It is an adverb of place.)

REAL-LIFE EXAMPLES

In these examples, the prepositional phrases are functioning as adjectives.

● The best defence **against** the atom bomb is not to be there when it goes off.
(1949 *British Army Journal*)

● In 1938, *Time* magazine chose Adolf Hitler for Man **of** the Year.

● Red sky **at** night, shepherds' delight. Blue sky **at** night, day.

These prepositional phrases are functioning as adverbs.

● I used to work **in** a fire-hydrant factory. You couldn't park **near** the place.
(Comedian Steven Wright)

In the example below, the first prepositional phrase functions as an adjective while the second functions as an adverb.

● A mathematical formula **for** happiness: reality divided **by** expectations. There are two ways to be happy: improve your reality or lower your expectations. (Author Jodi Picoult)

It can get quite complicated.

● A raisin dropped **in** a glass **of** fresh champagne will bounce up and down continuously **from** the bottom **of** the glass **to** the top.
(Here, *in a glass of fresh champagne* is a prepositional phrase functioning as an adverb. It includes its own prepositional phrase (*of fresh champagne*) functioning as an adjective. Similarly, *from the bottom of the glass to the top* is functioning as an adverb. It includes a prepositional phrase (*of the glass*) functioning as an adjective.)

WHY SHOULD I CARE ABOUT PREPOSITIONAL PHRASES?

There are three good reasons to care about prepositional phrases.

Reason 1. Avoid ambiguity when placing your prepositional phrase. Ambiguity with prepositional phrases can be a real issue.

● Joe fed the shark **in** the cage.
(Does the prepositional phrase tell us where Joe was when he fed the shark, or does it tell us which shark Joe fed? In other words, is *in the cage* functioning as an adverb modifying *fed* or an adjective modifying *shark*? If you read it as an adverb (i.e. telling us where Joe was), you might assume there was just one shark. If you read it as an adjective (i.e. the shark that was in the cage), you would assume there were other sharks.)

You can usually eliminate ambiguity by rewording your sentence. (Don't be surprised if your rewording hacks your original sentence to shreds.)

● Joe was **in** the cage when he fed the shark.

Often, context means there's no genuine ambiguity.

- Never ruin an apology **with** an excuse. (American founding father Benjamin Franklin)
  (This is clearly telling you how not to ruin an apology as opposed to telling what type of apology not to ruin; i.e. the prepositional phrase is functioning as an adverb not an adjective.)
- Joe hit the burglar **with** a hammer.
  (So, who had the hammer? Often, a standalone sentence will be ambiguous (as this example is), but if the surrounding context eliminates the ambiguity, you will get away with not rewording your sentence.)

The ambiguous examples so far have involved uncertainty over whether the prepositional phrase is functioning as an adverb or an adjective. Sometimes, that's clear, but ambiguity (often humorous ambiguity) can also occur when it's unclear what a prepositional phrase is modifying.

- Simon and his mother were reunited **after** 52 years **in** McDonald's. ✘ (ambigious)
  (What? They spent 52 years in McDonald's?)

When you use a prepositional phrase, do a quick check to see whether it could potentially be modifying something else in your sentence. Try to bear in mind that even though it's clear to you what it's modifying, it might not be clear to your readers. If your prepositional phrase is ambiguous, move it next to (usually immediately to the right of) whatever it's meant to be modifying. If that makes your sentence too unwieldy, reword the whole thing.

- Simon and his mother were reunited **in** McDonald's **after** 52 years. ✔
- Joe hit **with** a hammer the burglar. ✘
  (This is too unwieldly. Let's reword it.)
- Joe used a hammer to hit the burglar. ✔

Reason 2. Don't treat a prepositional phrase as the subject of your verb.
Don't confuse the noun in a prepositional phrase as the subject of the verb.

- A box **of** knives were found at the scene. ✘
  (Here, the subject is not *knives*. It is *box*. Therefore, the verb should be singular and not plural: 'A box of knives was found at the scene.')
- A combination **of** factors were the cause of the crash. ✘
  (*Combination* is singular. The subject is not *factors*.)

- Bernard Shaw hasn't an enemy in the world, and none **of** his friends like him.
  (Playwright Oscar Wilde) ✘
  (Marking this wrong is a little harsh, but try to treat *none* as singular (if for no other reason than many of your grammar-savvy readers will want it to be singular). Therefore, 'none of his friends likes him' is a bit safer.)

Reason 3. The noun in a prepositional phrase influences the verb with an expression like *most of, some of, half of, majority of* and *99 percent of*. The noun in a prepositional phrase influences the verb when the subject is an indefinite pronoun (a word like *all*, *any*, *more*, *most* and *some*), which can be singular or plural depending on context.

- Most **of the cake** has been eaten. ✔
  (The noun in the prepositional phrase (*cake*) is singular. Therefore, *most* is treated as singular.)
- Most **of the cakes** have been eaten. ✔
  (The noun in the prepositional phrase (*cakes*) is plural. Therefore, *most* is treated as plural.)
- Some **of the worst mistakes of my life** have been haircuts. ✔ (Singer Jim Morrison)
  (The head noun in the prepositional phrase modifying *some* is *mistakes*. Therefore, *some* is treated as plural. The prepositional phrase *of my life* functions as an adjective modifying *mistakes*. Yeah, it can get complicated.)

So, when modified by a prepositional phrase, an indefinite pronoun (e.g. *most*, *some*, *all*) adopts the number of the noun in the prepositional phrase. Got that? Now, here's your two-for-one bonus. This ruling also applies to common terms like *half of*, *majority of* and *percentage of*, which can also be singular or plural. Such expressions are singular when they refer to something singular but plural when they refer to something plural.

- Democracy is the recurrent suspicion that more than half **of the people** are right more than half the time. ✔ (Writer Elwyn Brooks White)
  (*People* is plural, so *half* becomes plural. Therefore, *are* is correct.)
- Half **of the world** knows not how the other half lives. ✔ (Poet George Herbert)
  (*World* is singular, so *half* becomes singular. Therefore, *knows* is correct.)

KEY POINT
A prepositional phrase can function as an adjective or an adverb. Make sure it's clear what role yours is playing and what word it's modifying.

Present Participle and Past Participle

Formed from a verb (e.g. *to stew*), a participle is a word that can be used as an adjective (e.g. *the stewing steak*), to form a verb tense (e.g. *I have been stewing the steak for hours*) or to form the passive voice (e.g. *the steak was stewed for hours*).

There are two types of participle:
- The present participle (ending *-ing*).
- The past participle (usually ending *-ed*, *-d*, *-t*, *-en*, or *-n*).

EASY EXAMPLES

Participles as Adjectives. Here are some participles being used as adjectives:

The Verb	The Present Participle	The Past Participle
rise	the rising sun	the risen sun
boil	the boiling water	the boiled water
break	the breaking news	the broken news

Participles for Verb Tense. Here are some participles being used to form verb tenses:

The 4 Past Tenses	Participle Type	Example
simple past tense		I wrote
past progressive tense	present	I was <u>writing</u>
past perfect tense	past	I had <u>written</u>
past perfect progressive tense	both	I had <u>been</u> <u>writing</u>
The 4 Perfect Tenses		**Example**
simple present tenses		I go
present progressive tense	present	I am <u>writing</u>
present perfect tense	past	I have <u>written</u>
present perfect progressive tense	both	I have <u>been</u> <u>writing</u>
The 4 Future Tenses		**Example**
simple future tense		I will go
future progressive tense	present	I will be <u>writing</u>
future perfect tense	past	I will have <u>written</u>
future perfect progressive tense	both	I will have <u>been</u> <u>writing</u>

Past Participles for Passive Voice. Here are some past participles forming the passive voice. (NB: A sentence is in the passive voice when its subject (*The song* in these examples) does not perform the action of the verb but has the action performed to it. See also Voice on page 259.)

- The song was <u>written</u> by monks.
- The song is being <u>refined</u> by scholars.
- The song will be <u>translated</u> into Irish by the Rialtas na hÉireann.

REAL-LIFE EXAMPLES

Let's take a look at some real-life examples.

Present Participles as Adjectives

- If you pick up a <u>starving</u> dog and make him prosperous, he will not bite you. This is the principal difference between a dog and a man. (Writer Mark Twain)
- A <u>laughing</u> man is stronger than a <u>suffering</u> man. (French novelist Gustave Flaubert)

Past Participles as Adjectives

- Painting is the <u>frozen</u> evidence of a performance. (US artist Chuck Close)
- Language exerts <u>hidden</u> power, like the Moon on the tides. (Author Rita Mae Brown)

Present Participles Forming Verb Tense

- When, in school, they **were <u>teaching</u>** algebra, I **was <u>studying</u>** differential equations at home. (Theoretical physicist George Gamow)
- Be kind, for everyone you meet **is <u>fighting</u>** a hard battle. (Philosopher Philo)

Past Participles Forming Verb Tense

- Education is what remains after one **has <u>forgotten</u>** what one **has <u>learned</u>** in school. (Theoretical physicist Albert Einstein)
- Wars **have** never **<u>hurt</u>** anybody except the people who die. (Artist Salvador Dali)

Past Participles Forming The Passive Voice

- If you sit on the lid of progress, you **will be <u>blown</u>** to pieces. (Industrialist Henry Kaiser)
- Ornamental deer heads are bad, but it's worse when they've streamers in their antlers because then you know they were enjoying themselves when they **were <u>shot</u>.** (Comedian Ellen DeGeneres)

MORE ABOUT PRESENT PARTICIPLES AND PAST PARTICIPLES

Let's take a closer look at participle phrases and perfect participles.

Participle Phrases. Participles often feature in participle phrases. A participle phrase (italicised in examples opposite) consists of the participle and any words (i.e. objects, modifiers or complements) needed to complete the thought. A participle phrase functions as an adjective. (In these examples, the nouns modified by the participle phrases are in bold.)

- **That puppy** _wearing_ the bandana is a little rascal.
- Lee, do you dream of **scones** _crammed_ with cream?
- _Whistling_ the same tune as always, **Ted** touched the front of his cap with his forefinger as she dismounted.
- _Stunned_ by the blow, **Mike** gathered his senses and searched for the pepper spray.
- The inventor of the bagpipes was inspired when he saw a **man** _carrying_ an indignant, asthmatic pig under his arm. Unfortunately, the instrument's sound never equalled the purity of the **sound** _achieved_ by the pig. (Film director Alfred Hitchcock)

Perfect Participles. These are formed by putting the present participle _having_ in front of a past participle, e.g. _having paid, having arrived._ A type of participle phrase, a perfect participle functions as an adjective that indicates a completed action.

- **Three German planes**, _having lost_ their way during a mission to destroy a target in France, dropped 69 bombs on Freiburg by mistake.
- Clever stuff stimulates me. _Having said that_, I love to see a drunk granny doing the can-can at a wedding on You've Been Framed. (Actor Simon Pegg)

WHY SHOULD I CARE ABOUT PRESENT PARTICIPLES AND PAST PARTICIPLES?

There aren't too many serious writing issues linked to participles, but here are four good reasons to think about them a little more clearly.

Reason 1. Use a participle phrase to say two or more things about your subject tidily. A fronted participle phrase can be used to create a sentence structure that lets you say two or more things about a subject efficiently.

- _Communicating_ well upwards, downwards and laterally, **John** has managed expectations across the program and ensured that all projects remain oriented towards the program objective.
  (The participle-phrase-upfront structure has allowed three observations about John to be shoehorned into one sentence.)
- _Having displayed_ a cooperative spirit from the outset, **John** has become a role model for those seeking to share research ideas and techniques.
  (Here, it has allowed two observations about John to be recorded in a chronologically tidy way.)

Don't write every sentence in this style, but the odd one will give your text variety and help you to cram more information into fewer sentences. This structure is particularly useful when writing personal appraisals. (See also Non-finite Verb on page 165.)

Reason 2. Punctuate your participle phrases correctly. Here are some general guidelines to help with placing and punctuating a participle phrase.

When a participle phrase is at the front of a sentence, offset it with a comma and put the noun being modified immediately after the comma.
- _Removing_ his glasses, **the professor** shook his head with disappointment. ✔

When a participle phrase follows the noun it's modifying, don't use a comma.
- Scandal is **gossip** _made_ tedious by morality. ✔ (Playwright Oscar Wilde)

However, if the participle phrase is nonessential (i.e. you could delete it or put it in brackets), then offset with a comma (or two commas if it's mid-sentence). (You could also use dashes or brackets.)
- The yellow **Ferrari**, _unregistered_ in the UK and probably _stolen_ in France, was used as the get-away car. ✔

When a participle phrase is at the end of your sentence and not immediately after its noun, offset it with a comma to help show that it's not modifying whatever is to its left.
- **The boys** loved their boxing gloves, _wearing_ them even to bed. ✔

Reason 3. Avoid dangling modifiers, especially when using fronted participle phrases. A dangling modifier (see page 126) is an error caused by failing to use the word that the modifier is meant to be modifying.

- _Having taken_ the anti-malarial tablets religiously, the malaria diagnosis came as a shock. ✘
  (The italicised text is a participle phrase headed by a perfect participle. It's meant to be an adjective to a noun (or a pronoun), but that noun doesn't feature in the sentence.)

- _Overcome_ by emotion, the whole speech was delivered in two- and three-word bursts. ✘
  (The italicised participle phrase is meant to be an adjective to a noun, but the noun is missing.)

To avoid a dangling modifier, assume that any participle phrase you put at the start of a sentence is 'dangling' (i.e. isn't modifying anything) until you've written the noun (or pronoun) it is modifying. Let's correct these examples.

- _Having taken_ the antimalarial tablets religiously, **Sarah** was shocked by the malaria diagnosis. ✔
- _Overcome_ by emotion, **he** delivered the whole speech in two- and three-word bursts. ✔

Reason 4. Avoid misplaced modifiers when using participle phrases. With a dangling modifier, the noun being modified is missing. With a misplaced modifier (see page 162), the noun being modified is too far away. To avoid a misplaced modifier, make sure it's obvious which noun (or pronoun) your participle phrase is modifying. Often, context will tell your readers which noun the modifier belongs to, but a misplaced modifier will – at the very least – cause a reading stutter and portray you as a clumsy writer. Sometimes, a misplaced modifier causes a sentence to be genuinely ambiguous.

● The **meerkats** are acutely aware of the eagles, _scurrying from burrow to burrow._ ✗
(This is clumsy and potentially ambiguous – if you knew nothing about meerkats or eagles. Note also that if the comma were missing, this sentence would be wrong (as opposed to clumsy) because it would mean _the eagles that are scurrying from burrow to burrow._)

● _Tattered_ but not _ripped_, Lee handed **the ticket** to the doorman. ✗
(This is potentially ambiguous, especially if you knew Lee.)

● **Tim** saw David Attenborough, _filming the leatherback turtles for Blue Planet._ ✗
(This is clumsy. There are better ways to avoid ambiguity than relying on that comma.)

The best way to avoid a misplaced modifier with a participle phrase is to put it next to the noun it's modifying. Let's fix the examples above.

● _Scurrying from burrow to burrow,_ **the meerkats** are acutely aware of the eagles. ✔
● Lee handed **the ticket**, _tattered but not ripped,_ to the doorman. ✔
● When he was filming the leatherback turtles for Blue Planet, Tim saw David Attenborough. ✔
(Rewording your sentence is often a good idea.)

KEY POINTS

Use a participle phrase to say something about your subject before you've even mentioned your subject. That's cool.

Put your participle phrase next to its noun. If there isn't a noun, you're dangling (and that's never good).

Pronoun

A pronoun is a word used in place of a noun (or a noun phrase).

For most of us, the pronouns that leap to mind are the personal pronouns (e.g. *I, you, he, she, they*), but these are just one type of pronoun. There are nine types:

- personal pronouns (e.g. *he, they*)
- possessive pronouns (e.g. *his, its*)
- relative pronouns (e.g. *which, who*)
- demonstrative pronouns (e.g. *this, these*)
- emphatic pronouns (e.g. *itself, himself*)
- reflexive pronouns (e.g. *itself, himself*)
- indefinite pronouns (e.g. *none, several*)
- interrogative pronouns (e.g. *which, what*)
- reciprocal pronouns (e.g. *each other, one another*)

Pronoun (Personal)

A personal pronoun takes the place of people or things. The personal pronouns are *I, you, he, she, it, we* and *they*.

- Man is what **he** believes. (Playwright Anton Chekhov)
  (*He* takes the place of the noun *man*.)
- Give a girl the right shoes, and **she** can conquer the world. (Actress Marilyn Monroe)
  (The pronoun *she* is used in place of a girl, which is a noun phrase. Pronouns are used primarily to avoid repetition.)

We can't talk about pronouns without mentioning antecedents (*see also* page 87), which are underlined throughout this entry. The antecedent of a pronoun is the thing represented by the pronoun. So, in the first example above, *man* is the antecedent of *he*.

- My wife bought some batteries, but **they** weren't included.
  (Comedian Steven Wright)
  (*Some batteries* is the antecedent of the pronoun *they*.)

The personal pronouns above are all subjective personal pronouns, because they're the subjects of verbs. There's also the objective form of personal pronouns (e.g. *me, him, her*), which is used when the pronoun is not the subject of a verb, i.e. when it's an object (see page 191).

- Get the facts first, then distort **them**. (Author Mark Twain)
- Conscience is the only incorruptible thing about **us**. (Author Henry Fielding)
  (Often, the antecedent is not mentioned but understood from context. Here, the antecedent of *us* is *mankind*.)

WHY SHOULD I CARE ABOUT PERSONAL PRONOUNS?

Native English speakers nearly always use the correct personal pronouns, and there are few serious mistakes associated with them, but here are two noteworthy points.

Point 1. The subjective pronoun *I* can't be the object of a verb or a preposition.

● They found my wife and **I** under a snowdrift. ✗
  (The subjective pronoun *I* must be the subject of a verb. Here, it's the direct object of the verb *found*. It should read 'They found me and my wife…'.)

● Keep this between **you** and **I**. ✗
  (The term 'between you and I' is always wrong. 'It should be between you and me')

Point 2. This is good stuff for learning a foreign language. Knowing personal-pronoun terminology will help with learning a foreign language. If you're a native English speaker, whether you know it or not, you currently select a personal pronoun having first determined its number, person, case and gender.

● *Number:* Is the personal pronoun representing something singular or plural?

● *Person*: Is the personal pronoun representing something in the first person, i.e. the speaker himself or a group that includes the speaker (*I*, *we*), the second person, i.e. the speaker's audience (*you*), or the third person, i.e. *everybody else* (*he*, *she*, *it*, *they*)?

● *Gender*. Is the personal pronoun representing something male, female or neuter?

● *Case*: Is the personal pronoun functioning as a subject or an object?

So, when you say something as simple as '**We** like **him**', your brain has whipped through that list twice, making eight decisions on personal pronouns. It's flash processing. However, when you start learning a foreign language (particularly in the classroom), this grammar processing is done far more consciously. If you understand our grammar terms, you'll absorb their language *mucho más rápido*.

KEY POINTS

Don't use a term like 'my wife and I' unless it's the subject of a verb.
Never say 'between you and I'.

Pronoun (Possessive)

A possessive pronoun shows possession.

The possessive pronouns are *mine*, *yours*, *his*, *hers*, *ours* and *theirs*.

● I always check if the art across the street is better than **mine**. (Artist Andy Warhol)
● Humans are the only animals that have children on purpose with the exception of guppies, who like to eat **theirs**. (Satirist P J O'Rourke)

Be aware that *my*, *your*, *his*, *her*, *its*, *our* and *their* (called possessive adjectives in traditional grammar but possessive determiners in contemporary grammar) can also be classified as pronouns because they too replace nouns.

● Is that the Queen's hat? No, it's **her** crown.
(*Her* replaces *the Queen*. That's why it's classified as a pronoun. See possessive determiners on page 139.)

WHY SHOULD I CARE ABOUT POSSESSIVE PRONOUNS?

By far the most common mistake related to possessive pronouns is including an apostrophe with *yours*, *hers*, *ours* or *theirs*. There are no apostrophes in any possessive pronouns.

● There are gods above gods. We have **ours**, and they have **theirs**. That's what's known as infinity. (Poet Jean Cocteau)

KEY POINT
Don't put an apostrophe in *yours*, *hers*, *ours* or *theirs*.

Pronoun (Relative)

A relative pronoun introduces a clause that describes a noun. (The clause is called an adjective clause.)

The relative pronouns are *that, which, who, whom* and *whose.* The following relative pronouns introduce adjective clauses (underlined) that provide information necessary to identify their nouns. (Note that there are no commas.)

- Education is the most powerful weapon **which** <u>you can use to change the world</u>. (President Nelson Mandela)
- An atheist is a man **who** <u>has no invisible means of support</u>. (Canadian politician John Buchan)

The following relative pronouns introduce adjective clauses that give unnecessary but interesting information about their nouns. (Note that there are commas.)

- The United Nations, **whose** <u>membership comprises almost all the states in the world</u>, is founded on the principle of the equal worth of every human being. (UN Secretary-General Kofi Annan)
- The man Dickens, **whom** <u>the world at large thought it knew</u>, stood for all the Victorian virtues even as his novels exposed the greed and cruelty of the Victorian age. (Author Robert Gottlieb)

WHY SHOULD I CARE ABOUT RELATIVE PRONOUNS?

Here are the top five questions related to relative pronouns:

Question 1. Do you put a comma before *which* or *who*? The answer is sometimes yes and sometimes no. This applies to all relative pronouns, not just *which* and *who*. (Actually, it doesn't apply to *that*, but we'll cover that later.) Look at these two examples using *who*:

- The man **who** <u>won last week's lottery</u> gave all his money to a donkey sanctuary.
- My neighbour, **who** <u>won last week's lottery</u>, gave all his money to a donkey sanctuary.

These two sentences are nearly identical, but one has commas and one doesn't. It all depends whether the adjective clause (the underlined text) specifies its noun. If it does (as in the first example, where it specifies *the man*), then don't use commas. If it doesn't (as in the second example, where it's just additional information about *my neighbour*), then use commas.

This example is also correct.

- My neighbour **who** <u>won last week's lottery</u> gave all his money to a donkey sanctuary.

This time, the adjective clause is specifying *my neighbour*. We're now talking about *my lottery-winning neighbour* as opposed to any neighbours who didn't win the lottery. So, you have to think carefully about whether an adjective clause specifies or doesn't.

Good tip: Treat the commas like brackets. If you'd happily put brackets around the adjective clause, then use commas because the clause will just be additional information. Similarly, if you'd happily delete the clause, then it must be just additional information.

***That* is different.** Lots of Americans, and increasingly Brits, insist on using *that* instead of *which* without a comma (i.e. when *which* heads an adjective clause that specifies its noun).

- The dog **which** bit the postman has returned ✔ (but Americans would whinge).
- The dog **that** bit the postman has returned ✔ (for everybody).

Both are correct, but some find the top one a little awkward. When a clause specifies its noun, it's called a restrictive clause. When it's just additional information, it's called a non-restrictive clause (see page 232). So, *which* can head a restrictive adjective clause (without commas) or a non-restrictive one (with commas), but, if you're writing for Americans, use *that* for the former.

- My dog gives a trust **which** / **that** is total.
  (Both options work for a restrictive clause.)
- My dog gives total trust, **which** / **that** is very endearing.
  (Only *which* works with a non-restrictive adjective clause.)

Had the question been 'Do you put a comma before that?', the answer would've been quick. No.

- How can you govern a country **which** has 246 varieties of cheese?
  (French President Charles de Gaulle)
  (This translation of de Gaulle's quotation is fine, but for many, *that* would've read better.)
- War should only be declared by the authority of the people, **whose** toils and treasures are to support its burdens, instead of the government **which** is to reap its fruits. (US President James Madison)
  (The first adjective clause is non-restrictive (just additional information about *the people*). The second is restrictive (specifies *the government*). Get it?)

Using a comma before a word like *which* is not an aesthetics thing. It's not a fly-by-the-seat-of-your pants thing. It's a depends-on-the-intended-meaning thing.

Question 2. Can you use *whose* for inanimate things? Yes. *Who* is used for people. *Which* is used for things. *Whose* is used for people and things.

- Even in moments of tranquillity, Murray Walker sounds like a man **whose** trousers are on fire. (TV presenter Clive James)
- An invasion of armies can be resisted, but not an idea **whose** time has come. (French poet Victor Hugo)
  (*Whose* has been used with something inanimate (*idea*). That's acceptable.)

Question 3. When do you use *whom*? Here's the rule: Use *who* when it's the subject of verb (shown in bold), otherwise use *whom*.

- Never lend your car to anyone **who** *calls* you mum.
  (*Who* is the subject of the verb *calls*.)
- Never lend your car to anyone **whom** you *have given* birth to.
  (Author Erma Bombeck)
  (*Whom* is not the subject of *have given*. *You* is.)

Many consider *whom* to be obsolete. So, if you're unsure whether to use *who* or *whom*, use *who*. (*See also* Prepositions on page 206.)

Question 4. Can you use *that* for people? Yes. *That*, like *whose*, can be used for people or things. But try to use *who* instead of *that* with people (especially in formal writing). Some of your readers might find *that* with people a little uncouth.

- The dog **that** bit the postman. ✔
- The postman **that** bit the dog.
  (NB: This isn't popular.)

Question 5. What's the difference between *whose* and *who's*? *Who's* is a contraction. It is short for *who is* or *who has*. If you can't expand your *who's* to one of those, then use *whose*.

- A weed is a plant **who's** virtues have never been discovered. ✗
  (It should be *whose*.)

KEY POINT

If you'd happily put your adjective clause in brackets, then it doesn't specify its noun. Offset it with commas.

Pronoun (Demonstrative)

A demonstrative pronoun specifies something previously mentioned or something in the speaker's surroundings

The demonstrative pronouns are *this*, *that*, *these* and *those*.

- Some people get so rich they lose all respect for humanity. **That** is how rich I want to be. (Comedian Rita Rudner)
- **Those** are my principles. If you don't like them ... well, I have others. (Groucho Marx)

WHY SHOULD I CARE ABOUT DEMONSTRATIVE PRONOUNS?

When using a demonstrative pronoun, make sure the link to its antecedent (see page 87) is obvious. Typically, the antecedent of a demonstrative pronoun is close by in the previous text. In these two examples, the links to the antecedents (underlined) are not ambiguous.

- My court case isn't a trial. **This** is a lynching. (Pathologist Jack Kevorkian)
- Curious people are interesting people; I wonder why **that** is.
  (Comedian Bill Maher)

You must ensure your demonstrative pronoun's antecedent is clear.

- The next intake of recruits will receive four presentations on the new procedures. **These** are scheduled to start in mid-August. ✗
  (The antecedent of *these* is ambiguous. It could be *the recruits*, *the presentations* or *the procedures*.)
- Everything I buy is vintage, so my house smells funny. **That** is why I'm single. ✗
  (Actress Lucy Liu)
  (Is the antecedent of *that* the whole idea, her buying habits or the house smell? It's ambiguous.)

Such ambiguity occurs because a writer knows what the antecedent is and assumes others will spot it with the same clarity. Unfortunately though, that clarity doesn't always shine through the words. Ambiguity most often occurs when a writer has expressed a multi-component idea and then starts a sentence with a term like 'This means', 'This explains' or 'This is why'.

If you find yourself starting a sentence this way, ask yourself, 'What means? 'What explains?' or 'What is why?' If the answer doesn't leap out at you, consider a rewrite or a demonstrative determiner and a noun to spell it out more clearly.

- The next intake of recruits will receive four presentations on the new procedures. These presentations are scheduled to start in mid-August. ✔

KEY POINT
If your sentence starts with something like 'This is',
make sure it's clear what 'This' is.

Pronoun (Emphatic)

An emphatic pronoun is paired with another noun or pronoun (underlined) to emphasise it.

The emphatic pronouns are *myself, yourself, herself, himself, itself, ourselves, yourselves* and *themselves*.

- <u>The Queen</u> **herself** attended the party.
  (*The Queen* is the noun being emphasised. *The Queen* is the antecedent of *herself*.)
- Nothing is impossible for <u>the man who</u> doesn't have to do it **himself**.
  ('Weiler's Law')
- Learn from others' mistakes. <u>You</u> won't live long enough to make them all **yourself.** (Anon)

WHY SHOULD I CARE ABOUT EMPHATIC PRONOUNS?

Using an emphatic pronoun is far slicker than **bolding** a word, WRITING IT IN UPPERCASE LETTERS or <u>underlining</u> it. When speaking, you can emphasise a word with your voice, so there's an alternative to using an emphatic pronoun. In writing, however, the alternatives are often unwieldy or ambiguous.

An emphatic pronoun just provides emphasis, but that's a pretty important job. It's often the reason the sentence exists.

- <u>She</u> will attend the reception drinks **herself**.

An emphatic pronoun can be removed from a sentence without affecting the sentence's core meaning.

KEY POINT

Emphatic pronouns emphasise. That itself is a good reason to learn about them.

Pronoun (Reflexive)

A reflexive pronoun is paired with another noun or pronoun to show it is acting on itself.

Reflexive pronouns have a different function to emphatic pronouns, but they're the same words (*myself, yourself, herself, himself, itself, ourselves, yourselves* and *themselves*). In these examples, the subject (underlined) is the antecedent of the reflexive pronoun.

- <u>Alison</u> does not trust **herself**.
- <u>I</u> often quote **myself**. It adds spice to my conversation. (Playwright George Bernard Shaw)
- If <u>the world</u> blew **itself** up, the last voice would an expert's saying it's impossible. (Actor Peter Ustinov)

WHY SHOULD I CARE ABOUT REFLEXIVE PRONOUNS?

'You' can't do something to 'myself'; only 'I' can. The most common mistake involving reflexive pronouns is using one when the subject of the verb (underlined) is not doing something to itself.

- <u>He</u> did it to **myself**. ✗
- <u>I</u> did it to **myself**. ✔
- <u>He</u> did it to **himself**. ✔

Most often, writers make this mistake because they think *myself* sounds more formal than *me*.

- <u>He</u> insulted the doctor and **myself**. ✗
- Please pass any comments to the director or **myself**. ✗
  (This example has the implied subject *you*, i.e. 'Please [will you] pass any comments …'. See Imperative Sentence on page 149.)

Here are better versions.

- He insulted me and the doctor. ✔
- Please pass any comments to me or the director. ✔
  (Note how *me* now comes first. If it didn't, these sentences would sound awkward, and that also contributes to writers going for *myself*.)

The antecedent of *myself* is always *I*. If *I* isn't doing something to *myself*, then *myself* is wrong. Ironically, lots of people who mistakenly use *myself, yourself*, etc. do so believing a reflexive pronoun sounds more highbrow than the correct personal pronoun (*me, you*, etc.).

Oh, and don't write *hisself* … ever. It's *himself*.

KEY POINT
Myself and *yourself* are not posh versions of *me* and *you*.
(Only *I* can touch *myself*.)

Pronoun (Indefinite)

**An indefinite pronoun refers to a person or a thing
without being specific.**

The most common indefinite pronouns are *any, anyone, anything, each, everybody, everyone, everything, few, many, no one, nobody, none, several, some, somebody* and *someone*.

- I don't know **anything** about music. In my line, you don't have to. (Singer Elvis Presley)
- A classic is **something** that **everybody** wants to have read and **nobody** wants to read. (Writer Mark Twain)

Do not confuse indefinite pronouns with indefinite determiners (also called quantifiers or, in traditional grammar, indefinite adjectives). An indefinite pronoun (bold) stands alone. An indefinite determiner (underlined) modifies a noun or a pronoun.

- <u>Some</u> people have so <u>much</u> respect for their superiors they have **none** left for themselves. (Playwright George Bernard Shaw)
- <u>Each</u> **one** of us alone is worth **nothing**. (Revolutionary Che Guevara)
  (Indefinite determiners can even modify indefinite pronouns.)

MORE ABOUT INDEFINITE PRONOUNS

Indefinite pronouns can be singular or plural.

- Always singular: *another, anybody, anyone, anything, each, either, enough, everybody, everyone, everything, less, little, much, neither, nobody, no one, nothing, one, other, somebody, someone* and *something*.
- Always plural: *both, few, fewer, many, others* and *several*.
- Singular or plural: *all, any, more, most, none, some* and *such*.

WHY SHOULD I CARE ABOUT INDEFINITE PRONOUNS?

There are four noteworthy issues related to indefinite pronouns.

Issue 1. *None* can be singular or plural. Your retiring English teacher might tell you that none is always singular, but that's outdated.

- **None** of the students is expected to get an A.
- **None** of the students are expected to get As or Bs.

If your *none* best translates as *not one of*, go singular. If it best translates as *not any of*, go plural. That's the usual advice given, but it's not great because *not any of* sounds awkward, which steers writers away from going plural with *none*. Follow your instincts, but if you're still unsure, go singular. If you find yourself treating *none* as singular with a singular *they* or *their* (see Issue 4), go plural throughout.

- **None** of the students <u>has</u> done <u>their</u> homework. ✗
  (*None* is singular (hence *has*). Using *their* is acceptable, but it's untidy.)
- **None** of the students <u>have</u> done <u>their</u> homework. ✔
  (*None* is plural (hence *have*). Using *their* is natural.)

227

Issue 2. *Either* and *neither* are singular, even though they naturally refer to two things.

- **Either** of the brothers <u>are</u> welcome to attend. ✘
  (It should be 'is welcome to attend'.)
- Men's anger about religion is like two men quarrelling over a lady **neither** of them <u>care</u> for. ✘ (1st Earl of Halifax Edward Wood)
  (It should be 'neither of them cares for'.)

Issue 3. Some indefinite pronouns (e.g. *all*, *some*) can be singular or plural. The indefinite pronouns *all*, *any*, *more*, *most* and *some* are singular when they refer to something singular but plural when they refer to something plural.

- **More** of <u>them</u> were needed.
  (*Them* is plural; therefore, *were* is correct.)
- **More** of it <u>was</u> needed.
  (*It* is singular; therefore, *was* is correct.)

This point gets a little more complicated when the indefinite pronoun is used with a collective noun (e.g. *crowd*, *team*).

- **Most** of the crowd <u>is</u> leaving. ✔
- **Most** of the crowd <u>are</u> waving their national flags. ✔

When used with a collective noun (see page 176), an indefinite pronoun is singular if you envisage it representing a single body but plural if you envisage it representing individuals.

Issue 4. Words like *someone* and *anyone* are gender neutral, but it's not always easy to keep that neutrality. The singular indefinite pronouns that represent people (e.g. *anyone*, *each*, *everyone*, *no one*, *nobody*, *someone*) are gender neutral, and this can cause problems.

- **No one** knows what <u>he</u> can do till <u>he</u> tries. (Latin writer Publilius Syrus)
  (Why *he*? This also applies to women.)
- From **each** according to <u>his</u> abilities, to **each** according to <u>his</u> needs.
  (Revolutionary Karl Marx)(Why *his*?)

This problem is easy to fix. You can reword or go or plural:

- People don't know what <u>they</u> can do till <u>they</u> try. ✔
- From **each** according to <u>their</u> abilities, to **each** according to <u>their</u> needs. ✔

(Acceptable. See also Possessive Determiner on page 139.)

KEY POINTS
None can be singular or plural. Follow your instincts.
Either and *neither* are singular. Don't follow your instincts.

Pronoun (Interrogative)

An interrogative pronoun is used to ask a question.

EASY EXAMPLES

The interrogative pronouns are *what, which, who, whom* and *whose.*

- **Which** is worse, failing or never trying?
- **What** is originality? Undetected plagiarism. (Dean of St Paul's Cathedral William Inge)

The other, less common interrogative pronouns are the same as the ones above but with the suffix *-ever* or *-soever* (e.g. *whatever, whichever, whatsoever, whichsoever*). They're used for emphasis or to show surprise. The antecedent (see page 87) of an interrogative pronoun is the answer to the question.

- **Whatever** did you say?
- **Whomsoever** did you find?

MORE ABOUT INTERROGATIVE PRONOUNS

Interrogative pronouns can also be used to create indirect questions (underlined). *See also* Indirect Question on page 151.

- Do you know **what** this is?
  (The interrogative pronoun *what* heads an indirect question in a question.)
- I want to know **what** this is.
  (Here, *what* heads an indirect question in a statement.)

Do not confuse interrogative pronouns with interrogative determiners (called interrogative adjectives in traditional grammar), which look the same as interrogative pronouns.

- Which feat is the greater?
  (This is not an interrogative pronoun. The word *which* modifies *feat.* Therefore, it's a determiner.)

Also, do not confuse interrogative pronouns with interrogative adverbs (*how, when, why, where*), which are also used to ask questions. Interrogative adverbs ask about the time, place, reason or manner an action occurs.

- **When** will the game start?
- **Why** is common sense seldom common practice?
  (Management guru Eliyahu Goldratt)

How is also used to ask about amounts, quantities and degrees.

- **How** much cake have you got?
- **How** many skittles have you eaten?

Let's unpick this example:

● **Who** are you and **how** did you get in here?

I'm a locksmith. And ... I'm a locksmith. (from the TV series *Police Squad!*)

(The answer to the interrogative pronoun *who* is the noun phrase *a locksmith*. The answer to the interrogative adverb *how* is the, albeit unstated, adverbial phrase 'by virtue of being a locksmith'. The answer to a question starting with an interrogative pronoun will be a noun, typically a person, place or thing. The answer to an interrogative adverb will be an adverb, typically words that specify a time, place, reason or manner.)

Interrogative determiners and adverbs have been included in this entry on pronouns because they too have antecedents (the answers to the questions they ask). Like some other determiners (see page 131), that makes them pretty 'pronouny' (or *pronominal*, as they say).

WHY SHOULD I CARE ABOUT INTERROGATIVE PRONOUNS?

There are two good reasons to care about interrogative pronouns.

Reason 1. Punctuating sentences correctly. Only questions get question marks. It sounds obvious, but it's not uncommon for writers to use a question mark at the end of a non-question featuring an indirect question (underlined).

● I want to know **who** told you? ✗

(This is not a question. It's a statement. It should end in a full stop.)

● Can you tell me **who** told you? ✔

Reason 2. Creating rhetorical questions. Interrogatives can be used to ask a rhetorical question (a question for which no answer is expected). Posing a rhetorical question (see also page 158) is an efficient and engaging way of making a point or introducing a new idea.

● **What** is a weed? A weed is a plant whose virtues have never been discovered. (Poet Ralph Waldo Emerson)

Rhetorical questions are also useful for making a point in a non-antagonistic or diplomatic way.

● **Which** estate-agent services warrant the fee?

KEY POINTS
A sentence featuring an indirect question might not be a question,
so careful with those question marks.
Is a question a good way to introduce a topic?

Pronoun (Reciprocal)

A reciprocal pronoun is used to express a mutual action or relationship.

The reciprocal pronouns are *each other* and *one another*.

- When two <u>people</u> are like **each other,** <u>they</u> tend to like **each other.** (Author Tony Robbins)
- <u>Gentlemen</u> don't read **each other's** mail. (US Secretary of War Henry Stimson)
- <u>Laws</u>, like houses, lean on **one another.** (Statesman Edmund Burke)

WHY SHOULD I CARE ABOUT RECIPROCAL PRONOUNS?

There are two common questions related to reciprocal pronouns.

Question 1. How do you write the possessive form of *each other* and *one another*? It's a quick answer. The apostrophe always goes before the s.

- We drink **one another's** healths and spoil our own. (Author Jerome K Jerome)

Even though a reciprocal pronoun refers to two or more things, the possessive form is created by adding 's (as for the possessive form of a singular noun). Some writers feel an urge to place the apostrophe after the s (as for the possessive form of a plural noun). Whatever. The apostrophe goes before the s.

Question 2. What's the difference between *each other* and *one another*? When the antecedent of a reciprocal pronoun is two things, use *each other*. When it's more than two things, use *one another*.

- <u>My dog and cat</u> love **each other.**
- <u>My dog, cat and emu</u> love **one another**.

Under this ruling, the following quotation is wrong:

- I think a couple should complete **one another**, not compete with **one another**. ✘ (Singer Marie Osmond)

It can get complicated because it depends on what the writer had in mind.

- Friends are kind to **one another's** dreams. (There are lots of friends.)
- Friends are kind to **each other's** dreams. (Here, there are two friends.)
- Old and young disbelieve **one another's** truths. (Aphorist Mason Cooley)
  (*Each other* could be justified if you think of two discrete groups, not lots of individuals.)

If you're picked up for writing *each other* instead of *one another*, you might be able to defend yourself by claiming you had two people (or things) in mind. If you're picked up for writing *one another* with an antecedent of two, you're toast. If you're picked up for either, you're dealing with a grammar pedant.

KEY POINT
Write *each other's* and *one another's* (not *each others'* and *one anothers'*).

Restrictive Clause

A restrictive clause is a clause that identifies the word it modifies. A restrictive clause is essential for meaning.

EASY EXAMPLES
In each example, the restrictive clause is bold, and the noun it identifies is underlined.
- The man **who lives next door** has been arrested.
- The apple tree **which produced no apples last year** has loads of blossom.
- Let's find the book **that you recommended.**

Notice how the clauses identify their nouns (i.e. *the man, the apple tree* and *the book*). Without the restrictive clauses, we wouldn't know which man, tree or book we were talking about.

REAL-LIFE EXAMPLES
- It has been my experience that folks **who have no vices** have very few virtues. (President Lincoln)
- The world is a book. Those **who do not travel** read only a page. (Philosopher Saint Augustine)
- I live in that solitude **which is painful in youth but delicious in the years of maturity**. (Albert Einstein)
- A man's character may be learned from the adjectives **which he habitually uses in conversation**. (Writer Mark Twain)
- I love that I have a job **that I love**. (Russian skater Ekaterina Gordeeva)

See also Commas and Relative Pronouns on pages 27 and 221.

WHY SHOULD I CARE ABOUT RESTRICTIVE CLAUSES?
There are four common issues related to restrictive clauses.

Issue 1. Don't put commas around a restrictive clause. Look at the examples above. There's not a comma in sight. Restrictive clauses contrast with non-restrictive clauses. Unlike restrictive clauses, non-restrictive clauses are not essential for meaning. They just provide bonus information. Non-restrictive clauses are so unessential, they can be deleted, put in brackets or – more commonly – offset with commas.

- My cousins **who live in the country** are scared of sheep.
  (The bold text is a restrictive clause. It identifies *my cousins* as the ones from the country, i.e. not some other cousins.)
- My cousins, who live in the country, are scared of sheep.
  (With the commas, it's a non-restrictive clause; i.e. it's bonus information. You'd now infer that all my cousins are scared of sheep, and you'd know, as a

bonus, where they live. We could delete the non-restrictive clause or put it in brackets. If you'd happily put it in brackets or delete it, use commas.)

Writers often ask whether they should put a comma before *who* and *which*. The answer is sometimes yes and sometimes no. It depends whether the *who* or *which* (or any other relative pronoun for that matter) heads a restrictive clause or a non-restrictive clause. Let's imagine we're translating this quotation by French poet Paul Valéry:

- Politics is the art of preventing people from taking part in <u>affairs</u> **which properly concern them.**
- Politics is the art of preventing people from taking part in affairs, which properly concern them.

Should we use that comma or not? Let's remove the bold text to test if it's a non-restrictive clause:

- Politics is the art of preventing people from taking part in affairs.

This makes sense, but it's too broad. Valéry didn't mean all affairs. The clause *which properly concern them* is essential to the meaning. It isn't just bonus information. It's a restrictive clause. The version without the comma is correct.

Issue 2. Brits like *which*, but Americans *don't*. In British English, most restrictive clauses start with *who*, *which* or *that*. Americans, however, don't like using *which* to start a restrictive clause. They way prefer using *that*.

- <u>The apple tree</u> **which produced no apples last year** has loads of blossom.
  (This is acceptable to Brits but not to most Americans.)
- <u>The apple tree</u> **that produced no apples last year** has loads of blossom.
  (This is acceptable to Brits and Americans.)

So, if we were translating our Paul Valéry quotation for an audience that included Americans, we could have gone with the following:

- Politics is the art of preventing people from taking part in <u>affairs</u> **that properly concern them.**

It's worth saying, at this point, that *that* never starts a non-restrictive clause (not in British English or American English). So, you'll never get a comma before an adjective clause that starts with *that*. *That* is strictly for restrictive clauses.

- Almas caviar, that costs over £20,000 per kilo, comes from the Iranian Beluga fish and is the most expensive food in the world. ✘
  (Don't head a non-restrictive clause with *that*. *Which* would have been okay.)

Issue 3. Some people won't like you using *that* for people. As a general rule, *who* is used for people, and *which* and *that* are used for things. However, it's not uncommon to see *that* used with people.

● I think that <u>anybody</u> **that smiles** looks better automatically. (Actress Diane Lane)
● All mankind is divided into three classes: <u>those</u> **that are immovable**, <u>those</u> **that are movable**, and <u>those</u> **that move**. (American founding father Benjamin Franklin)

It would be too harsh to mark these as wrong, but be aware that some of your readers might prefer *who* instead of *that* when referring to people (especially in formal work).

Issue 4. Sometimes, omitting *which* or *that* will give you a more natural-sounding sentence. With a restrictive clause, you can often create a better-sounding sentence by removing the *who*, *that* or *which*.

● <u>The dog</u> **which you fed** is outside.
  (This is a bit contrived. Americans will twitch.)
● <u>The dog</u> **that you fed** is outside.
  (This is still a bit contrived, but all will be happy.)
● <u>The dog</u> **you fed** is outside.
  (This sounds natural.)

The goal is to write a natural-sounding sentence with a clear structure and a clear meaning. Sometimes, this is best achieved with the *that* option, and sometimes it's best achieved with the nothing option. Here's a grammatically sound sentence that highlights why you can't just go with the nothing option every single time.

● The mouse the cat the dog chased chased ate the cheese.
  (Difficult to understand.)
● The mouse that the cat that the dog chased chased ate the cheese.
  (It's still a tough sentence to unpick, but using *that* helps.)

The most common decision you'll have to make is whether to include or omit a *that*. If including the *that* makes your sentence clearer, use it. If it clashes aesthetically with another nearby *that*, think about omitting it.

● Buying food from <u>farmers</u> **that I know** adds <u>that human element</u> **that I love**. (Chef Alex Guarnaschelli)

I prefer this:

● Buying food from farmers **that I know** adds that human element **that I love**.
  (We now have only one *that* in the sentence, instead of three, and – as bit of a bonus – we've avoided the that-for-people issue.)

KEY POINTS
Don't put commas around a restrictive clause (i.e. one that's essential for identification).
Don't start a restrictive clause with *which* if you're writing to Americans. Use *that* or even nothing.

Run-on Sentence

A run-on sentence is a common error caused by merging two sentences without suitable punctuation.

EASY EXAMPLES
- Cannibals don't eat clowns, they taste funny. ✗
- I once went to a toga party dressed as a goat, being dyslexic has drawbacks. ✗
- Lazy is such an ugly word, I prefer to call it selective participation. ✗

These would be correct if the commas were replaced with full stops. When a comma is used incorrectly between the two sentences (which is the main cause of run-on sentences), the error is known as a comma fault or a comma splice.

REAL-LIFE EXAMPLES
The only correct comma in the five examples below is the one after *however* in the last example. All the rest should be replaced with full stops or some other appropriate end mark - see page 236.

- One man in a thousand is a leader of men, the other 999 follow women. ✗ (Groucho Marx)
- Be kind to those that meet you as you rise, you may pass them again as you fall. ✗
- The answers to life's problems aren't at the bottom of a bottle, they're on TV. ✗ (Homer Simpson)
- Egotists are difficult to work with, however, they don't talk about other people. ✗ (The word *however* is a major cause of run-on sentences. When used to bridge two sentences, it should start its sentence or, occasionally, be preceded by a semicolon. *See also* Conjunctive Adverb on page 123.)

WHY SHOULD I CARE ABOUT RUN-ON SENTENCES?
The run-on error is unquestionably the most common grammar mistake made by people with otherwise sound writing skills. It seems that some writers feel a full stop has the same effect as the neuralyzer ('flashy thing') in *Men in Black* (i.e. it makes readers forget everything that preceded it). Don't worry. Your readers' memories will survive your full stop!

Regardless of how closely linked your sentences are, you must choose appropriate punctuation between them. Remember that a sentence is a group of grammatically complete words that expresses a complete thought. A sentence contains a subject and a verb, even if one or the other is implied. Once you've written a sentence, you must end it appropriately. (*See also* Sentence on page 237.)

Often, a run-on error can be fixed with a full stop, but without rewording, there are four other possible fixes, all of which are worth having in your writer's toolbox.

Option 1. Use a semicolon:

- Duty is what one expects from others; it is not what one does oneself. (Oscar Wilde)
  (Using a semicolon gives a smoother transition than a full stop.)

Option 2. Use three dots:

- It's not true that I had nothing on ... I had the radio on. (Marilyn Monroe)
  (Using three dots gives a pause for effect.)

Option 3. Use a colon (if appropriate, which it probably won't be):

- I have made an important discovery: alcohol, taken in sufficient quantities, produces all the effects of intoxication. (Oscar Wilde)
  (If 'sentence' 2 is an expansion of something in 'sentence' 1, you can use a colon. A colon is like an equals sign. Here, *important discovery* equals 'sentence' 2.)

Option 4. Use a dash:

- Please do not shoot the pianist – he is doing his best.
  (A dash looks a bit brash, but it's versatile. It could replace the semicolon, the three dots or the colon in the three examples above.)

You know what a sentence is. Be disciplined with your full stops.

- Age is not a particularly interesting subject. Anyone can get old. All you have to do is live long enough. (Groucho Marx)
- I always pass on good advice. It is the only thing to do with it. It is never of any use to oneself. (Oscar Wilde)
  (There's not a comma in sight. These are both correct.)

KEY POINT

Don't write a sentence, sneak in a comma and then write another sentence. Be disciplined with your full stops.

Sentence

A sentence is a group of words giving a complete thought. A sentence must contain a subject and a verb (although one may be implied). A sentence can convey a statement, a question, an exclamation or a command.

EASY EXAMPLES

There are four types of sentence:

A Declarative Sentence. A declarative sentence conveys a statement and ends with a full stop.

- I have a dog.
- He has every attribute of a dog except loyalty. (US politician Thomas Gore)

An Imperative Sentence. An imperative sentence is a command or a polite request. It ends with an exclamation mark or full stop.

- Fetch the dog!
- When a dog runs at you, whistle for him. (Philosopher Henry Thoreau)

An Interrogative Sentence. An interrogative sentence asks a question and ends with a question mark.

- Does your dog bite?
- Who knew that dog saliva can mend a broken heart? (Author Jennifer Neal)

An Exclamatory Sentence. An exclamatory sentence expresses excitement or emotion and ends with an exclamation mark.

- You bought me a dog!
- In the City, it's dog eat dog. In academia, it's the exact opposite!

In an imperative sentence (e.g. *Run!*) or an interrogative sentence (e.g. *Why?*), the subject or verb is often implied. Incidentally, 'Go' is recognised as the shortest sentence in English. The shortest without an implied subject or verb is 'I am' or 'I go'. ('I'm' and 'I'd' are dismissed for being too unnatural.)

MORE ABOUT SENTENCES

A sentence consists of a main clause and sometimes one or more dependent clauses. It must contain at least one independent clause. (An independent clause (underlined in the examples) is one that can stand alone as a sentence.) There are four sentence structures:

A Simple Sentence. A simple sentence has one independent clause and no dependent clauses (see Clause on page 101).

- I have a dog.

● <u>You can't surprise a man with a dog</u>. (Screenwriter Cindy Chupack)

A Complex Sentence. A complex sentence has an independent clause and at least one dependent clause.
● When I was a young boy, <u>we had a huge dog</u>.
● <u>Diplomacy is the art of saying 'nice doggie'</u> until you can find a rock.
(Actor Will Rogers)

A Compound Sentence. A compound sentence has at least two independent clauses.
● <u>I want a dog</u>, but <u>we've got a cat</u>.
● <u>Cry 'Havoc'</u>, and <u>let slip the dogs of war</u>. (Playwright William Shakespeare)

A Compound-Complex Sentence. A compound-complex sentence has at least two independent clauses and at least one dependent clause.
● When I move house, <u>I'll buy a dog</u>, and <u>I'll buy a cat</u>.
● When a dog bites a man, <u>that is not news</u> because it happens so often, but if a man bites a dog, <u>that is news</u>. (Editor John Bogart)

WHY SHOULD I CARE ABOUT SENTENCE?
There are four key reasons to understand sentence structure and the types of sentence.

Reason 1. Avoid the run-on sentence. By far the most common mistake made by people with otherwise sound writing skills is the run-on sentence (see page 235). Typically, this error is caused by writing a sentence, putting a comma and then writing another sentence.
● Love is so short, forgetting is so long. ✗ (Chilean poet Pablo Neruda)
(The rule for what constitutes a sentence is satisfied twice. This should be two sentences.)

The run-on sentence usually occurs because writers feel a full stop is too much of a speed bump between their closely related sentences. The jolt of a full stop can be smoothed with other punctuation (but not a comma).
● Don't play hide and seek; no one would look for you. ✔
(You can smooth the jolt of a full stop with a semicolon (see page 57).)

● I like a woman with a head on her shoulders – I hate necks. ✔ (Actor Steve Martin)
(You can smooth the jolt of a full stop with a dash (see page 35), but a dash may look a little informal or brash.)

● My friend is a procrastinator…he's afraid of Saturday the 14th. ✔
(You can smooth the jolt of a full stop with an ellipsis, i.e. three dots (see page 38). Using an ellipsis creates a pause for effect.)

Reason 2. Punctuate your sentences correctly. Understanding the four sentence structures helps with punctuating. More specifically, it assists with the following two common decisions:

Decision 1. Deciding whether to use a comma with the dependent clause in a complex sentence. A complex sentence comprises an independent clause (underlined) and at least one dependent clause (bolded). When the dependent clause is at the front and acts like an adverb – typically stating a time (e.g. *When I was six*), a place (e.g. *Where I live*) or a condition (e.g. *If I were you*) – then it is a common practice to offset it with a comma. When such a clause appears at the back, there's usually no comma.

- **When I was six,** I had a wind-up Evil Knievel motorbike. ✔
- I had a wind-up Evil Knievel motorbike **when I was six.** ✔
- **When you're on the internet,** nobody knows you're a dog. ✔
  (Cartoonist Peter Steiner)

Decision 2. Deciding whether to put a comma before a conjunction.
A compound sentence has at least two independent clauses (underlined), which are usually joined with a conjunction (e.g. 'and', 'or', 'but'). A conjunction (bolded) that joins two things is not normally preceded with a comma, but a conjunction that joins two independent clauses in a compound sentence is.

- Lee likes pies **and** cakes. ✔
  (There is no comma before *and*. This is a simple sentence.)
- Lee likes pies, **and** he likes cakes. ✔
  (This time, there is a comma before *and*. This is a compound sentence.)
- Go, **and** never darken my towels again. ✔ (Comedian Groucho Marx)
  (Remember: *Go* is the shortest sentence in English.)

Tip: Look for the subject and verb in the text after your conjunction to confirm the text is an independent clause. If it is, whack a comma in. If it isn't, don't use a comma.

- Non-rabid wolves live away from people **and** have developed a fear of humans. ✔
- Non-rabid wolves live away from people, **and** they have developed a fear of humans. ✔
  (When you add 'they' after the 'and', the second half becomes an independent clause, and a comma is then required.)

Be aware that a compound sentence can have more than two independent clauses.

- Some men are born mediocre, some men achieve mediocrity, **and** some men have mediocrity thrust upon them. ✔ (Novelist Joseph Heller)
  (This is a compound sentence with three independent clauses. The first and second are separated by a comma and no conjunction. This is an occasion when that's allowable.)

'Veni, vidi, vici' [<u>I came</u>, <u>I saw</u>, <u>I conquered</u>.] (Roman statesman Julius Caesar) (I can live with this but not to the extent of giving it a tick. Some grammarians hate the comma splice so much, you will see 'Veni, vidi, vici' translated as 'I came; I saw; I conquered ' and even 'I came, I saw, and I conquered.')

Reason 3. As the subject of an imperative sentence is *you*, you can't use *myself*.

- If you have any questions, email myself or your line manager. ✗
- Please write to myself with any suggestions. ✗

The subject of an imperative sentence is *you*, which is usually implied (i.e. not said or written). This means you cannot use *myself*, which requires the subject to be *I*. Writers often use *myself*, believing it sounds more highbrow. It's wrong. It should be *me*. (*See also* Reflexive Pronoun on page 226.)

Reason 4. Don't use a question mark with a declarative sentence that includes an indirect question.

- She asked **whether I loved her?** ✗

The bolded text is an indirect question (*see* page 149). This is a statement not a question.

KEY POINTS

Don't write a sentence, put a comma and then write another sentence.
With a fronted adverbial, use a comma. Don't use a comma if it's at the back.
Use a comma before a conjunction (e.g. *and*, *or*, *but*) joining two 'sentences'.

Split Infinitive

A split infinitive occurs when a verb in its infinitive form (e.g. to laugh) has an adverb between the to and the verb (e.g. to really laugh).

EASY EXAMPLE

- To really try, to further develop, to secretly watch.

REAL-LIFE EXAMPLES

- To err is human, but **to really foul things up** you need a computer.
  (Biologist Paul Ehrlich)
- We need criminals **to secretly envy** and **to stoutly punish.**
  (Psychiatrist Karl Menninger)

WHY SHOULD I CARE ABOUT SPLIT INFINITIVES?

A split infinitive is often the most succinct, accurate and natural-sounding way to convey your idea. There's bit of an issue though. Without any real justification, some people regard the split infinitive as non-standard English or even a grammar mistake. It's neither. It's perfectly acceptable. But your knowing a split infinitive is acceptable doesn't change those people's understanding. So, the issue we all face is whether to avoid a split infinitive because some of our readers will think it's wrong. I'd say no. But, hey, I like to live on the edge.

You might want to play it safe, in which case, you could try rewording your sentence. If you've ever tried that, you'll know that a sentence reworded to avoid a split infinitive often sounds contrived or gives a different emphasis. If you feel your reworded sentence doesn't scan right, just split the infinitive.

We can't have an entry on split infinitives without talking about *Star Trek*.

- 'Space: the final frontier. These are the voyages of the Starship *Enterprise*. Its five-year mission: To explore strange new worlds. To seek out new life and new civilisations. To boldly go where no man has gone before.'
  (Introductory voice-over from the original series of *Star Trek*)

Ever since its debut in the 1960s, *Star Trek* has been slammed for including a split infinitive in the introductory speech. It is therefore interesting to note that when *Star Trek: The Next Generation* launched in 1987, the updated version of the speech replaced 'Its five-year mission' with 'Its continuing mission' and 'where no man has gone before' with 'where no one has gone before'. The much criticised 'To boldly go' stayed, with good reason. It's fine. Imagine the uproar there would be if they changed it to 'To go boldly'. That's how okay split infinitives are.

KEY POINT

There is no need to actively avoid a split infinitive.

Squinting Modifier

A squinting modifier is a type of misplaced modifier. A squinting modifier makes the meaning of a sentence ambiguous because it is unclear whether it modifies text before it or after it.

EASY EXAMPLES
- Saving lives **often** induces pride. ✗
  (Does *often* apply to *saving lives* or *induces pride*?)
- Getting married **quickly** changes your ways. ✗
  (Does *quickly* apply to *getting married* or *changes your ways*?)

REAL-LIFE EXAMPLES
- She told her nephew **eventually** the dog would have to go back to its owner. ✗
- Public speakers who pause **briefly** refocus their audience. ✗

WHY SHOULD I CARE ABOUT SQUINTING MODIFIERS?
A squinting modifier makes your sentence ambiguous. You can eliminate the ambiguity by changing the position of the squinting modifier or by restructuring the sentence.
- Cycling up hills **quickly** strengthens your quadriceps. ✗
- Cycling up hills strengthens your quadriceps <u>quickly</u>. ✔
- Cycling <u>quickly</u> up hills strengthens your quadriceps. ✔

The intended meaning of the first example would be clear if the sentence were spoken. But, always bear in mind that your readers can't hear that intonation in your voice, so keep your scanner tuned for squinting modifiers. (*See also* Misplaced Modifier on page 162.)

KEY POINT
Fix a squinting modifier by changing its position in the sentence or by restructuring.

Subject

The subject of a sentence is the person or thing being described or doing the action of the verb.

EASY EXAMPLES

Every sentence must have a verb (underlined), and every verb must have a subject (bold).

- **Lee** <u>is</u> chubby.

  (*Lee* is being described. *Lee* is the subject of the verb *is* and the subject of the sentence.)

- **Lee** <u>ate</u> the pie.

  (*Lee* is doing the action. *Lee* is the subject of the verb *ate* and the subject of the sentence.)

MORE EXAMPLES

- **The New York phone book** <u>contained</u> 22 Hitlers before World War II.
- **The world's youngest pope** <u>was</u> 11 years old.
- **All butterflies** <u>taste</u> with their feet.
- **Only one person in two billion** <u>will live</u> to be 116 or older.
- **Digital currency** <u>will be</u> the greatest social network of all. (Entrepreneur Tyler Winklevoss)

The subject of a sentence is a noun (or a pronoun) and all the modifiers that go with it. In the examples above, the 'simple subjects' are *book*, *pope*, *butterflies*, *person* and *currency*. All the other words that have been bolded as part of the 'complete subjects' are modifiers.

A sentence has one main subject, which is the subject of the main verb. However, a sentence can include other subjects that are the subjects of other verbs.

- **Venus** <u>is</u> the only planet **that** <u>rotates</u> clockwise.

  (*Venus* is the main subject, but this sentence also contains another subject and another verb.)

MORE ABOUT SUBJECTS

There are three common terms related to subjects: *simple subject*, *complete subject* and *compound subject*.

Simple subject

- **Pierre** <u>puts</u> a lot of garlic in his food.

  (A simple subject is just one word without any modifiers.)

Complete subject
- **That boy** <u>puts</u> a lot of garlic in his food.
  (*That boy* is an example of a complete subject. It is the simple subject (*boy*) plus all modifiers.)

Compound subject
- **Pierre and Claudette** <u>put</u> a lot of garlic in their food.
  (A compound subject is made up of more than one element.)
- **That new boy from Paris and the tall girl with the long hair** <u>put</u> a lot of garlic in their food.
  (This is two complete subjects, each of which has a simple subject (*boy* and *girl*).)

A complete subject will be a noun phrase or a noun clause (see pages 171 and 172).

Here are the main ways that a subject appears in a sentence: performing an action, being described, being identified and having an action done to it.
- **My dog** <u>bit</u> the postman.
  (The subject performs an action.)
- **My dog** <u>is</u> boisterous.
  (The subject is described. In this case, the verb is a linking verb (see page 160).)
- **My dog** <u>is</u> the one in the middle.
  (The subject is identified (another way of being described). In this case, the verb is a linking verb.)
- **My dog** <u>was taken</u> to the vet.
  (The subject has an action done to it. In this case, the sentence is a passive sentence (see page 63).)

WHY SHOULD I CARE ABOUT SUBJECTS?
There is an excellent reason to care about subjects: subject–verb agreement. Subject-verb agreement means using the right version of the verb to match the subject. That's easier than it sounds. It just means saying 'The dog <u>is</u> happy' and 'The yolk of eggs <u>is</u> yellow' as opposed to 'The dog <u>are</u> happy' ✗ and 'The yolk of eggs <u>are</u> yellow' ✗. Changing a verb to match its subject is called conjugating a verb (or verb conjugation).

- Flies fly, but a fly flies.
  (The plural subject *flies* goes with the plural verb *fly*, and the singular subject *fly* goes with the singular verb *flies*. That's subject–verb agreement.)

Even though native speakers handle verb conjugation effortlessly, it's not uncommon for writers to link a singular subject to a plural verb or vice versa. When this happens, we say there is no subject–verb agreement. It's a grammar mistake. A subject and its verb must agree in number.

Below are the 10 most common issues that cause writers issues with subject–verb agreement.

Issue 1. Modifiers get between the simple subject and its verb and confuse writers. This problem tends to occur with short constructions, typically in a format like 'a list of ideas' or 'a range of factors'. (*See also* Prepositional Phrase on page 209.)
- **A container of nuts and bolts** <u>were</u> found in the cellar. ✗
  (The simple subject is *container*, which is singular.)
- **A range of factors** <u>have</u> been considered. ✗
  (The simple subject is *range*, which is singular.)

Issue 2. Terms like *as well as* do not form a compound subject. Terms like *as well as*, *along with* and *together with* do not compound the subject the way *and* does.
- **Jack and his son** <u>are</u> visiting tomorrow. ✔
  (The word *and* creates a compound subject.)
- **Jack**, together with his son, <u>is</u> visiting tomorrow. ✔
  (The term *together with* does not create a compound subject.)

Issue 3. *Or* and *nor* do not compound the subject. Unlike *and*, the conjunctions *or* and *nor* do not conjoin.
- **Jack or his daughter** <u>is</u> visiting tomorrow. ✔
- **Neither Jack nor his daughter** <u>are</u> visiting tomorrow. ✗
  (This should be *is*, because *nor* does not conjoin, i.e. does not add to the subject's number.)

There's a quirk though.
- **Neither Jack nor his daughters** <u>are</u> visiting tomorrow. ✔
  (This is correct because one of the nouns in the compound subject is plural. There's a little more to this. See Proximity Rule and Logic Rule in Correlative Conjunctions on page 119.)

Issue 4. *Either* and *neither* are singular. When used by themselves (i.e. as pronouns), *either* and *neither* are singular. Writers are often tempted to treat them as plural because they seem to refer to two things.
- Beef or lamb? **Either** <u>is</u> preferable to tofu. ✔
- **Neither of the sisters** <u>is</u> eligible to attend. ✔

Issue 5. Collective nouns can be singular or plural. A collective noun (e.g. *board*, *team*, *jury*) can be singular or plural depending on the sense of the sentence. (*See* Collective Noun on page 176.)
- **The jury** <u>is</u> late returning to the courtroom.
  (When a collective noun is considered as one unit, treat it as singular.)

● **The jury** <u>are</u> all wearing pastel-coloured shirts.
  (When the focus is on the individuals in the group, treat your collective noun as plural.)

Too hard to decide? A good trick is to precede your collective noun with words like 'members of', which forces you to go plural.

● **The members of the jury** <u>are</u> late returning to the courtroom.

Issue 6. Some words that look plural aren't, and some words that are plural in Latin aren't in English. Here are the top four words that cause issues:

Word	Singular or Plural?
agenda	Singular (even though it is the plural of *agendum*)
criteria	Plural (Unlike *data* and *agenda*, criteria has retained its plural status because the singular *criterion* is still in common use.)
data	Singular nowadays (even though it's the plural of *datum*). If you're uncomfortable with going singular or plural, use *dataset*. If you're a statistician or the like and always treat it as plural, hang in there, King Canute.
media	Singular or plural (Treat *media* like a collective noun. See Issue 5.)

Issue 7. The expression *more than one* is singular. Somewhat counter-intuitively (given its meaning), *more than one* is singular.

● **More than one person** <u>was</u> involved in this robbery. ✔
● **More than one swallow** <u>does</u> a summer make, doesn't it? ✔

Issue 8. *None* can be singular or plural. The indefinite pronoun *none* can be singular or plural. However, be aware that treating *none* as plural might irk some of your readers, as many people believe *none* can only be singular.

● **None of the team** <u>is</u> ready. ✔
  (This is the safest option.)
● **None of the team** <u>are</u> ready. ✔
  (This is safe. If your *none* best translates as *not any* as opposed to *not one*.)

If you're facing the 'his/her versus their' issue, then treat everything as plural, including *none*.

● **None of the team** <u>has</u> packed ~~his/her~~ **their** crampons.
  (*His/her* is untidy. Using *has* (singular) and *their* (plural) is acceptable but a bit untidy too.)
● **None of the team** <u>have</u> packed *their* crampons. ✔
  (This is far tidier. Bite the bullet with the plural *none*.)

246

Issue 9. Terms like *half of*, *the majority of*, and *a percentage of* can be singular or plural. Expressions such as *half of*, *a part of*, *a percentage of*, *a proportion of* and *a majority of* are singular when they refer to something singular but plural when they refer to something plural.

- **The majority of my blood** <u>is</u> Asian. (Golfer Tiger Woods)
- **Half of my employees** <u>are</u> women. (Businesswoman Christie Hefner)
- **Seventy per cent of success in life** <u>is</u> showing up. (Film director Woody Allen)

Bear in mind that *number of* is singular when referring to an arithmetical value.

- **The number of women** <u>was</u> sixty-four.

Issue 10. Terms like *all of* and *some of* can be singular or plural. *All*, *any*, *more*, *most* and *some* (types of indefinite pronoun) are singular when they refer to something singular but plural when they refer to something plural.

- **All of Scottish cuisine** <u>is</u> based on a dare. (Actor Mike Myers)
- **Some of my worst mistakes** <u>have</u> been haircuts. (Singer Jim Morrison)

KEY POINT
Don't be distracted by plural modifiers.

Subjunctive Mood

The subjunctive mood is the verb form used to express a hypothetical situation (e.g. *If I were you*) or to express a wish, a demand or a suggestion (e.g. *I demand he be present*). See Mood on page 163.

EASY EXAMPLES

- If it <u>were</u> me, I'd go.
  (As this explores a hypothetical situation, *was* becomes *were*.)
- I wish it <u>were</u> real.
  (As this expresses a wish, *was* becomes *were*.)
- It is imperative that the game <u>begin</u> at once.
  (As this expresses a demand, *begins* becomes *begin*.)
- I propose he <u>work</u> full time.
  (As this expresses a suggestion, *works* becomes *work*.)

MORE ABOUT THE SUBJUNCTIVE MOOD

This table summarises how a verb changes when it's in the subjunctive mood.

Normal form	Normal example	Subjunctive form	Subjunctive example
am, are, is	I am lucky. You are lucky. She is here.	*be*	I demand that I <u>be</u> available. I ask that you <u>be</u> lucky. It's essential that she <u>be</u> here.
has	*She has a chance.*	*have*	I demand she <u>have</u> a chance.
was	I was free. He was happy.	*were*	If I <u>were</u> free, I'd go. I wish he <u>were</u> happy.
prepares, works, sings, etc.	She makes sushi.	*prepare, work, sing, etc*	I propose she <u>make</u> sushi.

REAL-LIFE EXAMPLES OF THE SUBJUNCTIVE MOOD

Here's the subjunctive mood expressing a hypothetical situation.

- If I <u>were</u> in the Beatles, I'd be a good George Harrison. (Musician Noel Gallagher)

The following verbs often attract the subjunctive mood: *to ask, to command, to demand, to insist, to order, to recommend, to suggest* and *to wish*.

- All we **ask** of a president is that he <u>be</u> likeable. We seem to have given up on the Pentagon's corrupt use of our tax dollars. (Author Donella Meadows)

- Saddam Hussein systematically violated every UN resolution that **demanded** he disarm and destroy his chemical and biological weapons. (Politician Henry Waxman)
- I **wish** I were fearless in real life. (Actor Cam Gigandet)
- God forgive you, but I never can. (Queen Elizabeth I)
  (Here, the verb attracting the subjunctive mood is implied. 'I [**wish** that] God forgive you'.)
- First Amendment in the UK? An MP once **suggested** I be put in the Tower of London for slating the royals. (Actress Tracey Ullman)

The following adjectives – especially when used with the word *that* – often attract the subjunctive mood: *crucial*, *essential*, *important*, *imperative* and *necessary*.

- It is **necessary** to the happiness of man that he be faithful to himself.
  (Activist Thomas Paine)
- To keep up, it is **essential** that your firm embrace technology.
  (Digital marketeer Will Humphries)

The subjunctive mood also features in some well-known expressions.

- God bless you. (I wish that *God bless you*.)
- God save the Queen. (I wish that *God save the Queen*.)
- May the Force be with you. (*Star Wars*)

WHY SHOULD I CARE ABOUT THE SUBJUNCTIVE MOOD?

A correctly used subjunctive verb sounds better and 'scores points'. When used in set phrases (e.g. *If I were you*, *God bless you*), the subjunctive mood does not create issues. However, when crafting their own words, some writers feel uncomfortable using the subjunctive mood. Some say it feels archaic, while others are unsure whether they should be using it at all.

Here's some guidance: If you naturally opt for the verb in the subjunctive mood, use it. If you're unsure whether the normal verb or the subjunctive verb sounds best, use the subjunctive one. If you can't bear how the subjunctive one sounds, have the confidence to use the normal verb. We all have different thresholds for what sounds awkward and what sounds right.

KEY POINTS
If you think your subjunctive verb sounds okay,
use it (and enjoy the showing off).
If you think your subjunctive verb sounds awful,
bin it (and enjoy today's leniency)

Tautology

Tautology is the needless repetition of a single concept.

EASY EXAMPLES
- He is a single bachelor. (Bachelors are always single.)
- The vote was totally unanimous. (The word *totally* doesn't add anything.)

REAL-LIFE EXAMPLES
- Many people's commute back and forth to work requires them to spend hours behind the wheel each day.
  (The words *back and forth* don't add anything.)
- That's one of the great advantages of age...you can throw temper tantrums, and nobody minds. (Author James L Burke)
  (The word *temper* doesn't add anything.)

On occasion though, a tautological phrase reads better than the non-tautological version or gives the emphasis sought by the author.
- I asked the question, 'Will I ever perform again?'. (Musician Brian Harvey)
  (*The question* could be removed, but the result would be less empathic.)
- Everyone is the sum total of past experiences. A character doesn't just spring to life at age thirty. (Writer Kelley Armstrong)
  (*Total* and *past* could be removed, but *sum total* and *past experiences* are set terms.)

WHY SHOULD I CARE ABOUT TAUTOLOGY?
Reduce your word count and be sharper. Spotting tautology is useful for eliminating redundant words. Here are some tautological terms that could be shortened safely (i.e. with no loss of meaning):
- ~~Armed~~ gunman   Attach ~~together~~   Warn ~~in advance~~

Remember though. Sometimes, a tautological term will work better for you than the non-tautological version (see above). Also, occasionally, you have to think whether something really is a tautology.

- Present a short summary.

Argument For: As a summary is always short, you don't need the word *short*.
Argument Against: A summary is not always short.

KEY POINT
Remove the redundant words in a tautology. However, if you lose emphasis, desired flow of text or clarity, put them back.

Title Case

Title case is a convention for writing titles.

EASY EXAMPLES
- *The Last of the Mohicans*
- *Snow White and the Seven Dwarfs*
- Newcastle upon Tyne

With title case, the first word is always capitalised. Thereafter, only the 'principal' words are given a capital letter. The principal words are all the words that are not:
- articles (i.e. *a, an, the*) (See page 135.)
- conjunctions (e.g. *and, but, or*) (See page 115.)
- prepositions (e.g. *in, of, on, upon, to, with*) (See page 206.).
  (This includes *to* as part of an infinitive verb, e.g. *to be*.)

Remember that the opening word gets a capital letter, even if it's a non-principal word.
- *And Then Came Love*
- *In the Name of the Father*
- *The Last of the Summer Wine*

WHY SHOULD I CARE ABOUT TITLE CASE?
Understanding title case allows you to write titles using an acceptable (and defendable) convention. It's pretty handy because it removes the need to think about how to write titles. There are four noteworthy issues related to title case.

Issue 1. Giving a two-letter but principal word a capital letter. You will find that two-letter words often look awkward written with a capital letter, but don't worry about that. Stick to the rules.
- I read *How to Be Black* in a day. ✔
  (Despite being short, 'Be' is a principal word here, so give it a capital letter.)

Issue 2. Adhering to official versions that break the rules of title case. Be aware that not everyone follows the rules with title case. You should copy official versions if you know them.
- *The Light Between Oceans* (2016 film)
- *A River Runs Through It* (1976 novel)

In these titles, the prepositions *Between* and *Through* have been given capital letters for aesthetic reasons. Also, be aware that some style guides recommend – purely for aesthetics – giving capital letters to non-principal words with more than three letters.

Title case is useful because it gives you an acceptable (and defendable) convention if you find yourself floundering with a title. Typically, this will be with a document title or a paragraph title in something you're writing yourself, so there won't be an official version to copy.

Issue 3. Using titles as 'compound adjectives'. A title (written in title case) is often used mid-sentence like a compound adjective (i.e. an adjective made up of more than one word).

- Did you get the Interview with a Vampire tickets?
- I love your Thomas the Tank Engine bag.

    (When a title (a type of proper noun) is used like an adjective, it's known as an attributive noun. See page 67.)

The words in a compound adjective are usually joined with hyphens (e.g. *free-range* eggs) to group them, making it clear they're all part of the same adjective. As this grouping effect is achieved with title case, there's no need to use hyphens with a title functioning as an adjective.

Make sure you stop applying title case when you've finished writing your title.

- I love your Thomas the Tank Engine Bag. ✗

    (*Bag* should be *bag*.)

- The Guiding Principles on Business and Human Rights document details how to implement the Protect, Respect and Remedy Framework. ✔

    (Here, the word *document* is not part of the title but *Framework* is.)

Issue 4. Deleting '*The*' if it starts a title used as a compound adjective. When *The* is the first word of a title used as an adjective, logical thinkers might feel the need to use the word the twice.

- The award was won by the *The Last of the Mohicans* director, Michael Mann. ✗

    (This is logically sound, but it's messy. Have the confidence to break logic.)

- The award was won by the *Last of the Mohicans* director, Michael Mann. ✔

    (For the sake of aesthetics (not logic), use *the* once and make it lowercase.)

KEY POINT
When writing a title, capitalise the first word and then just the principal words.

Verbs

A verb is a word that expresses an action or a state of being.

A verb can express a physical action (e.g. to *swim*, to *write*, to *climb*), a mental action (e.g. *to think, to guess, to consider*) or a state of being (e.g. *to be, to exist, to appear*).

EASY EXAMPLES
Verbs expressing physical actions:
- She **sells** pegs and lucky heather.
- A wise man **will make** more opportunities than he **finds**. (Painter Francis Bacon)

Verbs expressing mental actions:
- Peter **guessed** the right number.
- I never **thought** I was wasted, but I probably was. (Rolling Stone Keith Richards)

A small but extremely important group of verbs do not express any activity at all. The most important verb in this group (arguably of all) is the verb *to be*. *To become, to seem* and *to appear* can also express a state of being.
- I **am** only passionately curious. (Theoretical physicist Albert Einstein)
- 'She-Ra' **was** ahead of her time. (Cartoonist Noelle Stevenson)
- All things **are** difficult before they **become** easy. (Persian poet Saadi)

MORE ABOUT VERBS
Verbs can often be further categorised as action verbs, stative verbs, regular verbs and irregular verbs.

An action verb expresses an activity that a person or thing can do.
- Lee **eats** cake.
- If you run from technology, it **will chase** you. (Writer Robert Pirsig)

A stative verb expresses a state (hence the name) rather than an action. It typically relates to a state of being, thought or emotion. Some common stative verbs are *agree, appear, be, believe, belong, feel, hate, know, look, love, own, prefer, realise, recognise, remember, seem, smell, sound, taste* and *understand*.
- I **am** Chevy Chase, and you **are** not. (Actor Chevy Chase)
- Whenever people **agree** with me, I always **feel** I must **be** wrong. (Playwright Oscar Wilde)
- I am always **satisfied** with the best. (Oscar Wilde)

Some stative verbs are also linking verbs (see page 160). A linking verb links their subject to a description. (The most common linking verbs are *appear, be, become, feel, look, seem, smell* and *taste*.)

A regular verb is one that forms its simple past tense and its past participle by adding -ed or -d to the base form of the verb. (NB: There are spelling rules to consider too, e.g. doubling the final consonant for one-syllable verbs that end consonant-vowel-consonant (*stop*, *chat*).)

Regular verb	Simple past tense	Past participle
help	helped	(has) helped
hate	hated	(has) hated
stop	stopped	(has) stopped

An irregular verb is one that does not conform to rules for forming a regular verb.

Irregular verb	Simple past tense	Past participle
tell	told	(has) told
bleed	bled	(has) bled
ring	rang	(has) rung

Verb Tense. The tense of a verb tells us when the verb occurs (i.e. in the past, present or future).

- Past: He **talked** with more claret than clarity. (Writer Susan Ertz)
- Present: A professor **is** someone who **talks** in someone else's sleep. (Poet W H Auden)
- Future: **I will talk**, not on my knees but with prudence. (Founder of Solidarity Lech Walesa)

Verb tense also tells us whether the verb is ongoing or completed. This element of verb tense is called *verb aspect*. There are four aspects:

The simple aspect expresses a fact (e.g. *he saw, he sees, he will see*).

The perfect aspect is used for 'completed' verbs (e.g. *had seen, has seen, will have seen*).

The progressive aspect is used for 'ongoing' verbs (e.g. *was seeing, am seeing, will be seeing*).

The perfect progressive *aspect* marks the end of an 'ongoing' action (e.g. *had been seeing, has been seeing, will have been seeing*).

Verb tense looks a nightmare, doesn't it? It is, and we've only really covered the headings here. There's a bit more in Participles on page 213. Don't worry though. You get this stuff right on auto-pilot. Let's move on.

WHY SHOULD I CARE ABOUT VERBS?

We fill our speech with verbs. For that reason, speech is great. It's clear and structured naturally. Writing, on the other hand, can be boring, predictable and structured abnormally. These bad traits are most often caused by an overuse of nouns. So, a good trick to ensure your writing leans towards verbs and not nouns is to say your sentence aloud and make that the starting point of your sentence structure. This is a good way to get some verbs into your writing and to limit yourself to just enough nouns to get the job done.

Unnatural (overusing nouns)	Natural (deploying a good verb)
I was under the mistaken assumption you had made the payment.	I mistakenly assumed you had paid.
They are in agreement that he was in violation of several regulations.	They agree he violated several regulations.
She will be in attendance to present a demonstration of how the weather will have an effect on our process.	She will attend to demonstrate how the weather will affect our process.

Opting for verbs over nouns will not only make your sentences flow better but also reduce your word count, because you will avoid the articles (e.g. *an*, *the*) and prepositions (e.g. *in*, *on*) required to make nouns work.

There's another refinement. To optimise your sentence flow and to reduce your word count even further, opt for action verbs over linking verbs, which – like nouns – can sound overly formal.

- This rule **is** applicable to both teams.
- The treaty **is** binding for all parties.
  (Both these examples use linking verbs. They're not wrong, but they sound a bit stuffy.)
- This rule **applies** to both teams. ✔
- The treaty **binds** all parties. ✔
  (These use action verbs and sound more natural.)

KEY POINT
Nouns are clunky and eat up your word count. Use more verbs. They're flowing and efficient. 'If your writing reads like writing, then rewrite it.'

Verb, Transitive and Intransitive

A transitive verb is a verb that can take a direct object. The action of a transitive verb is done to someone or something. Most verbs are transitive. An intransitive verb is a verb that does not take a direct object. It is not done to someone or something. It only involves the subject.

EASY EXAMPLES

In each example below, the transitive verb is bold and the direct object (i.e. the thing being acted upon) is underlined.

- Lee **eats** pies.
  (*Eats* is transitive because you can eat something.)
- Lee **loves** mince pies.
  (*Loves* is transitive because you can love something.)
- Lee **bought** dozens of cakes.
  (*Bought* is transitive because you can buy something.)

In each example below, the intransitive verb is bold. An intransitive verb can't have a direct object, so none of the text is underlined.

- He **fainted**.
  (*To faint* is intransitive because you cannot faint something. It cannot take a direct object.)
- A vulture **soared** effortlessly overhead.
  (*To soar* is an intransitive verb. You can't say 'The vulture soared the air.')

REAL-LIFE EXAMPLES

To find the direct object of a transitive verb, find the verb and ask 'what?' or 'whom?'. If this question seems nonsensical, you're probably dealing with an intransitive verb.

- No amount of time can **erase** the memory of a good cat, and no amount of masking tape can ever totally **remove** his fur from your couch.
  (Author Leo Buscaglia)
  (Erase what? *The memory of a good cat.* Remove what? *His fur.*)
- You **can't get** eight cats to pull a sled through snow. (TV producer Jeff Valdez)
  (Can't get what? *Eight cats to pull a sled through snow.*)

Transitive verbs are common. They even appear inside the direct objects of other transitive verbs.

- I **loathe** people who keep dogs. They are cowards who **haven't got** the guts to bite people themselves.
  (Loathe what? *People who keep dogs.* Haven't got what? *The guts to bite people.* If you look at just the two direct objects (i.e. the underlined texts), there's a transitive verb in each one. Keep what? *Dogs.* To bite what? *People.*)

Here are some examples of intransitive verbs.
- **Laugh** and the world **laughs** with you; **snore** and you **sleep** alone.
  (Writer Anthony Burgess)
  (You can't laugh something, snore something or sleep something.)
- If the context **changes**, your greatest strength can **emerge** as a weakness.
  (Cricket commentator Harsha Bhogle)
  (Here, *changes* and *emerge* are intransitive. You can't *emerge* something, but, hang on, you can *change* something (e.g. your socks). So, some verbs can be both transitive and intransitive. Let's put *changes* through the test. *Changes* what? Well, nothing … just changes. It's intransitive.)
- If something **changes** the context, your greatest strength can **emerge** as a weakness.
  (In this amended example, *changes* is now a transitive verb. Changes what? *The context*.)
- Good habits **formed** in youth make all the difference. (Greek philosopher Aristotle)
  (Formed what? Nothing … just formed. Yeah, that's intransitive.)

Here's something to watch out for. The 'what?' test to determine whether a verb is transitive or intransitive doesn't work with linking verbs (e.g. to be, to appear, to seem).
- Laziness **appears** attractive, but work **gives** satisfaction. (Diarist Anne Frank)
  (Appears what? *Attractive*. We have an answer to the 'what?' test, but *to appear* is not a transitive verb. It's an intransitive linking verb (see page 160).)

Here's a list of common verbs that can be transitive or intransitive.

Verb	Transitive and Intransitive Example
to agree	She **agreed** my terms. (transitive) She **agreed**. (intransitive)
to play	She **will play** the hornpipe. (transitive) She **will play** tonight. (intransitive)
to run	I **ran** the show. (transitive) I **ran**. (intransitive)
to eat	Let's **eat** pie. (transitive) Let's **eat**. (intransitive)
to demonstrate	She **demonstrated** her skills. (transitive) She **demonstrated**. (intransitive)
to sit	I **sat** her on my lap. (transitive) I **sat** near the window. (intransitive)
to stand	I **stood** the pole under the sheet. (transitive) I **stood** for hours. (intransitive)

MORE ABOUT TRANSITIVE AND INTRANSITIVE VERBS

You cannot create a passive sentence using an intransitive verb. (In a passive sentence, the action of the verb is performed on the subject. See Active and Passive Sentences on page 63.)

Let's try to create a passive sentence with the intransitive verb *to exist*.
- The megalodon **was existed** about two million years ago. ✗
  (This is nonsense.)

Now, let's try with the transitive verb *to bake*.
- The tart **was baked**. ✔
  (This is fine.)

A transitive verb gets its name from the idea that the action must transition through it to an object in order to complete the meaning.
- Lee **caught** <u>a whelk</u>. ✔
- Lee **caught**. ✗
  (When the action does not transition through the verb to an object, the meaning is incomplete.)

WHY SHOULD I CARE ABOUT TRANSITIVE AND INTRANSITIVE VERBS?

There are two quick points worth making.

Point 1. This is good stuff for learning a foreign language. Understanding the terms *transitive* and *intransitive* is useful for discussing verbs, direct objects and indirect objects when learning foreign languages.

Point 2. Be careful with *to win* and *to learn*. There are a couple of common mistakes associated with the transitivity of verbs to be aware of, but they're pretty basic.
- I won George.

(If you use the verb *to win* transitively, the direct object is your prize. It's not the person you beat. This sentence would be correct if George were a goldfish but not if he were your opponent.)

- He will learn you some manners. ✗

(The transitive verb *to learn* doesn't take an indirect object. You can learn something, but you can't learn someone something in the same way you can teach someone something.)

KEY POINT
'Ha, I won you at chess. That'll learn ya'.'
(Nah, you can't say either of those things.)

Voice

Voice is the term used to describe whether a verb is active or passive. A verb is in the active voice when the subject of the verb is doing the action of the verb. A verb is in the passive voice when the subject of the verb is being acted upon.

EASY EXAMPLES

Here are examples of verbs (bold) in the active voice.

- Lee **ate** the pies.
  (The subject, *Lee*, did the action of the verb.)
- We **play** hopscotch.
  (The subject, *we*, is doing the action of the verb.)
- The sharks **will attack** the cage.
  (The subject, *the sharks*, will do the action of the verb.)

Here are examples of verbs in the passive voice.

- The pie **was eaten** by Lee.
  (The subject, *the pie*, was acted upon.)
- Hopscotch **is played** by us.
  (The subject, *hopscotch*, is acted upon)
- The cage **will be attacked** by the sharks.
  (The subject, *the cage*, will be acted upon.)

REAL-LIFE EXAMPLES

In the examples above, the actions of the verbs (*to eat, to play, to attack*) are obvious physical activities. Remember though that not all verbs describe such obvious activities. This is particularly true for verbs in the active voice.

- I **know** I **have** the body of a weak and feeble woman, but I **have** the heart and stomach of a king, and of a king of England too. (Queen Elizabeth I)
- The voice of Mickey Mouse and the voice of Minnie Mouse **became** husband and wife in real life.
- Only a quarter of the Sahara Desert **is** sandy.

Here are some verbs in the passive voice with less obvious actions.

- At one time, Melbourne **was known** as Batmania.
- Philosophy **was considered** science once. (Satirist P J O'Rourke)

Of note, only a verb that acts on something else, called a *transitive verb* (see page 256), can be written in the passive voice.

- More people **are killed** taking selfies than in shark attacks.
  (*To kill* is a transitive verb; i.e. you can kill something.)

Here's something else to look out for. It is common for verbs in the passive voice to be used after words like *can, cannot, may, might, must* and *should* (called *auxiliary verbs*).

⬤ He who **is** to be a good ruler <u>must</u> **have been ruled**. (Philosopher Aristotle)
 (*Is* is in the active voice. '*Have been ruled*,' which follows *must*, is in the passive voice.)

⬤ Canadians **say** 'sorry' so much that The Apology Act **was passed** in 2009, declaring that an apology <u>cannot</u> **be used** as evidence of admission of guilt.
 ('*Say*' is in the active voice. '*Was passed*' is in the passive voice. '*Be used*', which follows *cannot*, is also in the passive voice.)

WHY SHOULD I CARE ABOUT VOICE?

Writers tend to favour the active voice over the passive voice because it's more succinct, direct, informative, authoritative and engaging. Each of these benefits is explained in more detail in Active and Passive Sentences on page 63.

Even though there are some good reasons to use the passive voice, the bias for the active voice is so strong that proofreaders (real people) and grammar checkers (computer programs) will often try to correct a passive construction to an active one. Before we discuss whether this is right or wrong, there is another issue that needs to be addressed. Proofreaders routinely identify something as passive voice that is, in fact, active voice.

The best way to spot a passive-voice construction is to look for a form of the verb *to be* (e.g. *am, are, is, was, were, has been*) followed by a past participle (i.e. the form of the verb that typically ends in *-ed* or *-en*). (See Participles on page 213.)

Form of the verb *to be*	Past participle	Passive voice
am	licensed	I am licensed to kill.
was	developed	It was developed last year.
has been	seen	He has been seen in France.
will have been	eaten	It will have been eaten by then.

Remember that modal verbs like *can, cannot, could, might* and *should* can also feature (e.g. I cannot be licensed to kill).

Here are examples of things that look like passive voice but aren't.

⬤ I always wanted to be somebody, but now I realise I <u>should have been</u> more specific. (Actress Lily Tomlin)
 (There is no past participle after *have been*.)

⬤ All the mistakes I have ever made *have been* when I <u>have been drunk</u>.
 (Artist Tracey Emin)
 (There is no past participle after *have been*. Here, *drunk* is an adjective (meaning

intoxicated) and not part of the verb chain, even though *drunk* is the past participle of *to drink*. Confused? Think of it like this: the subject of the verb (*I*) is not being acted upon.)

This is passive voice:
● I **have been drunk** under the table by Russian sailors.
  (Here, the subject of the verb (*I*) is being acted upon. 'The Russian sailors drank me under the table' is an active-voice version.)

So, it's quite understandable that some proofreaders confuse the passive voice and the active voice. Here's a fun trick. If you can include the term 'by zombies' after your verb and it still makes sense, then you're dealing with the passive voice. (Thanks to Professor Rebecca Johnson for this tip.)
● The car could have been stolen … by zombies.
  (This makes sense. Therefore, *have been stolen* is in the passive voice.)
● The car could have been illicit … by zombies.
  (This makes no sense. Therefore, *have been illicit* is in the active voice.)

Anyway, now that we can spot the passive voice, we need to decide whether it's something to be avoided. The benefits of active voice are worth having, but so are the benefits of passive voice. The passive voice can be used to avoid blame, and it shows a neutral or objective tone. It is often appropriate when the doer of the verb is obvious, unimportant or unknown. And finally, the passive voice allows you to focus on what's important by bringing it to the front of your sentence. (Each of these benefits is explained in more detail in Active and Passive Sentences on page 63.)

As a native English speaker, you're safe to let your instinct guide you, but as a general rule, you should try to use the active voice unless you specifically want one of the benefits offered by the passive voice.

Here's a great example of a proofreader trying way too hard to avoid the passive voice.
● When the author of *Diabetes for Dummies* (Dr Alan Rubin) wrote, 'The patient was comatose and **was given** thyroid hormone', his editors changed it to 'The patient was comatose and took thyroid hormone'. In response to this edit, Rubin said: 'These are extremely sick patients. They can't take care of themselves. They have to be passive whether Wiley [style guide] likes it or not.'

KEY POINT
Develop a bias for the active voice because active sentences are shorter, more direct, more informative, more authoritative and easier to absorb. Don't be dogmatic about avoiding the passive voice though. Passive sentences are useful for avoiding blame, portraying a neutral tone and focusing on the recipient of an action.

Vowels and Consonants

The letters A, E, I, O and U are called vowels. The other letters in the alphabet are called consonants.

MORE ABOUT VOWELS AND CONSONANTS

● The proper noun *Iouea* (a genus of sea sponge) contains all five vowels and is the shortest word with four syllables.)

● The words *abstemious* and *facetious* contain all five vowels in order.

With seven consonants, *rhythms* is the longest word without any vowels. There are three words with six consonants and no vowels:

● He moved **spryly**. (*Spryly* means in a nimble or agile manner.)

● She is **sylphy**. (*Sylphy* means like a sylph (a slender graceful girl).)

● **Syzygy** cause ellipsis.(*Syzygy* is the straight-line configuration of three celestial bodies.)

Some might argue that these words contain vowels because they include Y, which many classify as a vowel or a semi-vowel. With no vowels (not even a Y), we have **crwth** (a stringed instrument) and **cwtch** (a shed, cuddle or hiding place). But, these both derive from Welsh, which treats W like the U in *cut*.

WHY SHOULD I CARE ABOUT VOWELS & CONSONANTS?

Use 'an' before a vowel sound. The important word here is sound.

● an RTA. ✔   a RTA ✗

('An' is correct because RTA (road traffic accident) starts with a vowel sound (ar), even though the first letter is not a vowel.)

Similarly, use 'a' (not 'an') before a consonant **sound**. Again, note the word **sound**.

● An unidentified man with a unicorn tattoo rented a house an hour ago. ✔

(Notice how *unidentified* attracts 'an' while *unicorn* attracts 'a'. Similarly, notice how *house* attracts 'a' while *hour* attracts 'an'.)

● Becoming a eunuch wasn't a one-off deal – it was a two-off deal. ✔

(*Eunuch* and *one-off* start with vowels but with consonant sounds.)

KEY POINT
Use *an* if the next word starts with a vowel <u>sound</u>.
Use *a* if it doesn't.

Zeugma

Zeugma occurs when a word that refers to two or more other words is appropriate for only one of them or is used in a different sense with each one.

EASY EXAMPLES

Here are some examples of zeugma that are mistakes. In each example, the shared word (bold) is appropriate for just one of the parts it refers to.

- **Wage** neither war nor peace. ✗
  (There's a term *to wage war* but not *to wage peace*.)
- We **watched** the luminescence of the lightning and the thumps of the thunder. ✗
  (*Watch* is appropriate for lightning but not thunder.)

Here are some examples of zeugma used deliberately for literary effect. In each example, the shared word is used in more than one sense.

- The castaways **grew** bamboo, beans and bored.
- His footsteps were as **light** as his fingers.
  (Often, the shared word is a verb, but here it's an adjective.)
- She **took out** a loan for a hitman and then her husband.

REAL-LIFE EXAMPLES

- And all the people **saw** the thundering, and the lightning, and the noise of the trumpet, and the mountain smoking: and when the people saw it, they removed, and stood afar off. ✗ (The Bible, Exodus 20:18)
  (*Saw* is not appropriate for *thundering* or *noise*. Of interest, *saw* is often replaced with *witnessed* or *perceived* in more modern translation sof this verse.)
- They tugged and tore at each other's hair and clothes, punched and scratched each other's nose, and **covered themselves with** dust and glory. ✔
  (Extract from *Tom Sawyer* by Mark Twain)

MORE ABOUT ZEUGMA

Be aware that some dictionaries describe zeugma with a much broader definition, declaring that zeugma is any case of a single word governing two or more other parts of the sentence. Under this broader definition, the following is an example of zeugma:

- Lee **likes** pies, and Mark, scones.

Let's look at the original:

- Lee likes pies, and Mark likes scones.

This example can be described as a parallelism because the structure of the two clauses is the same. As the clauses share the same verb (*likes*), there's an opportunity to remove one of the *likes* without losing the meaning. (This technique is called ellipsis. NB: When using ellipsis, you put a comma where the removed word used to be.)

Syllepsis. Grammarians have been arguing over the distinction between zeugma and syllepsis for decades. Nowadays, it's safe to think of them as interchangeable. (The term syllepsis is much rarer than zeugma – probably because zeugma sounds like a cool alien world and syllepsis sounds like a disease.) Anyway, syllepsis is most commonly seen in the terms 'grammatical syllepsis' and 'semantic syllepsis'.

Grammatical syllepsis is used when the single word is appropriate for only one of words it works with. Remember this example?

● **Wage** neither war nor peace. ✗

Grammatical syllepsis can also occur with ellipsis.

● We like beer; Lee, shandy. ✗
  (The word *like* is only appropriate for *We*. It's not appropriate for *Lee*. 'Lee likes shandy' would be accurate.)

Semantic syllepsis is used when the single word is used in a different sense with each of the words it relates to.

● That wave **sank** my yacht and my dreams.

WHY SHOULD I CARE ABOUT ZEUGMA?

It's worth checking that any word that relates to two or more parts of your sentence is appropriate for all parts, especially when writing long sentences. That's all we need to say about zeugma in the form of grammatical syllepsis. Zeugmas in the form of semantic syllepsis, on the other hand, are far more interesting, because they can entertain, inspire deeper thinking and even shock.

● She **aroused** curiosity and men.
  (Zeugma used to entertain.)

● Lust **conquered** shame; audacity, fear; madness, reason. (Roman philsopher Cicero)
  (Zeugma used to inspire deeper thinking. This is an example of ellipsis in a parallelism. The commas replace the shared word *conquered*. Under the broader definition, it's an example of zeugma. An early translation avoided the zeugma and read 'Lust got the better of shame, audacity subdued fear, and mad passion conquered reason.' However, later translators understood that Cicero sought to inspire deeper thinking.)

● You are free **to execute** your laws, and your citizens, as you see fit.
  (An extract from *Star Trek: The Next Generation*. Zeugma used to shock.)

When your shared word is used literally and figuratively, your sentence will usually read better when the literal element is first.

● I **held** her hand and my tongue.

Putting the literal element second, however, can be useful for creating shock.

● The bank **took** my self-esteem and then my house.

KEY POINTS
Use your grey matter and then zeugma to inspire deeper thinking.
To shock your readers, use zeugma or a cattle prod.

EASILY CONFUSED WORDS

ACCEPT / EXCEPT
Accept (verb) (1) to hold something as true, (2) to receive something willingly, (3) to answer yes (especially to an invitation)
- I <u>accept</u> she may have been tired, but that's still no excuse.
- I <u>accept</u> chaos. I'm not sure whether it accepts me. (Singer Bob Dylan)
- The minister has <u>accepted</u> your invitation.

Except (preposition) (1) apart from, excluding
- Weaselling out of things is important to learn. It's what separates us from the animals ... <u>except</u> the weasel. (Homer Simpson)

Except (conjunction) (1) but, if not the fact that
- Making money would not change me, <u>except</u> I won't answer the door. (Director Abel Ferrara)

Except (verb) (1) to exclude
- You are <u>excepted</u> from the ruling.

ADVICE / ADVISE
Advice (noun) (1) help, a suggestion for a beneficial course of action
- The only thing to do with good <u>advice</u> is to pass it on. It is never of any use to oneself. (Playwright Oscar Wilde)

Advise (verb) (1) to give advice
- One can <u>advise</u> comfortably from a safe port. (Philosopher Soren Kierkegaard)

ADVERSE / AVERSE
Adverse (adjective) (1) hostile, opposing, antagonistic
- To overcome <u>adverse</u> circumstances, you have to learn to overcome your own values and idiosyncrasies. (Businesswoman Anne F Beiler)

Averse (adjective) (1) strongly disinclined, unwilling
- I am not <u>averse</u> to politics, but that does not mean that I am going to join politics. (Politician Rahul Gandhi)

AFFECT / EFFECT
Affect (verb) (1) to transform or to change
- Even if one tree falls down, it wouldn't <u>affect</u> the entire forest. (Politician Chen Shui-bian)

Affect (noun, rare) (1) mood or emotion
- The patient displayed an unusual <u>affect</u> when questioned.

Effect (noun) (1) outcome, consequence, appearance
- Genius is the ability to put into <u>effect</u> what is on your mind. (Writer F Scott Fitzgerald)

Effect (verb) (1) to bring into being
- The new policy will be <u>effected</u> as soon as the paper is signed.

A LOT, ALLOT AND ALOT

A lot (pronoun) (1) the opposite of *a little* (similar to *much* or *many*)

- I don't pay good wages because I have a lot of money; I have <u>a lot</u> of money because I pay good wages. (Inventor Robert Bosch)

A lot (adverb) (1) to a great degree, often, much

- The Hollies had three number-one records after I left. Thanks <u>a lot</u>, guys. (Singer Graham Nash)

Allot (verb) (1) to apportion

- <u>To allot</u> God a secondary place in life was, to me, inconceivable. (Guru Paramahansa Yogananda)

Alot* (noun) (1) a town in India (*apart from this, alot is not a word)

- <u>Alot</u> has a population of over 20,000.

ALLUDE / ELUDE

Allude (verb) (1) to refer to indirectly

- Her letter <u>alludes</u> to a disturbed childhood.

Elude (verb) (1) to avoid, to evade

- William <u>eluded</u> discovery by changing his name to Mark.

AMONG / BETWEEN

Among (preposition) (1) in the midst of a group

- Misfits aren't misfits <u>among</u> other misfits. (Singer Barry Manilow)

Between (preposition) (1) usually used with two (but sometimes more than two) separate and distinct things

- A good -marriage would be <u>between</u> a blind wife and a deaf husband. (Philosopher Michel de Montaigne)

BARE / BEAR

Bare (adjective) (1) naked, exposed or empty

- We are stripped <u>bare</u> by the curse of plenty. (Prime Minister Winston Churchill)

Bear (verb) (1) to carry, (2) to tolerate, (3) to maintain a direction

- The trees that are slow to grow <u>bear</u> the best fruit. (Playwright Molière)
- Humankind cannot <u>bear</u> very much reality. (Poet T S Eliot)
- Drive through the town centre and then <u>bear</u> left towards the tower.

Bear (noun) (1) a large mammal

- I have fished beside brown <u>bears</u> in Alaska and was once charged by a black <u>bear</u>. (Writer Joseph Monninger)

COARSE / COURSE

Coarse (adjective) (1) rough, crude, of low quality

- Idleness is only a <u>coarse</u> name for my infinite capacity for living in the present. (Writer Cyril Connolly)

Course (noun) (1) education delivered in a series of lessons, (2) a direction, (3) a series of events

- Fame is empowering. My mistake was that I thought I would instinctively know how to handle it. But there's no manual, no training <u>course</u>. (Actor Charlie Sheen)
- The world hasn't noticed, but R&B has shifted. It's changing <u>course</u>. (Singer BJ the Chicago Kid)
- Consult: To seek approval for a <u>course</u> of action already decided upon. (Writer Ambrose Bierce)

Course (verb) (1) to move without obstruction, to pursue

- Greek blood <u>courses</u> through me. (Actress Elena Kampouris)

COMPLEMENT / COMPLIMENT

Complement (verb) (1) to enhance

- Your wardrobe should <u>complement</u> your skillset, never detract. (Fashion Journalist Nina Garcia)

Complement (noun) (1) enhancement (2) number or quota

- Constancy is the <u>complement</u> of all other human virtues. (Politician Giuseppe Mazzini)
- I have the normal <u>complement</u> of anxieties, neuroses, psychoses and whatever else. (Director Clive Barker)

Compliment (verb) (1) to give praise

- If you're not the one cooking, stay out of the way and <u>compliment</u> the chef. (Footballer Michael Strahan)

Compliment (noun) (1) an expression of praise

- I can live for two months on a good <u>compliment</u>. (Writer Mark Twain)

DEPENDANT / DEPENDENT

Dependant (noun) (1) a person who relies on another

- I intend my <u>dependants</u> to live with me in the British Consulate grounds.

Dependent (adjective) (1) reliant on

- Success is <u>dependent</u> on effort. (Greek playwright Sophocles)

DISCREET / DISCRETE

Discreet (adjective) (1) respecting secrecy, inconspicuous, diplomatic

- I used to be a lot angrier, but I was quite <u>discreet</u> with it. (Photographer Julian Lennon)

Discrete (adjective) (1) individually distinct, separate

- Innocence could be considered a <u>discrete</u> state of mind. (Writer John Shirley)

EVERY DAY / EVERYDAY

Every day (phrase) (1) each day

- Start <u>every day</u> off with a smile and get it over with. (Comedian W C Fields)

Everyday (adjective) (1) normal, ordinary, usual

- Art washes away from the soul the dust of <u>everyday</u> life. (Artist Pablo Picasso)

FEWER / LESS

Fewer (adjective) (1) use fewer when referring to more than one item

- I know I am getting better at golf because I am hitting <u>fewer</u> spectators. (President Gerald R Ford)

Less (adjective) (1) use less when referring to a single item

- My fat never made me <u>less</u> money. (Singer Dolly Parton)

HISTORIC / HISTORICAL

Historic (adjective) (1) having importance in history

- The guys who walk on Mars are going to be <u>historic</u>. (Astronaut Buzz Aldrin)

Historical (adjective) (1) from the past or relating to history

- The Sixties are now considered a <u>historical</u> period – just like the Roman Empire. (Author Dave Barry)

i.e. / e.g.

i.e. (abbreviation) (1) in other words (from the Latin *id est,* literally 'that is')

- Normal people, <u>i.e.</u> people who aren't actors, are the most bizarre people you can ever come across. (Actor Michael Sheen)

e.g. (abbreviation) (1) for example (from the Latin *exempli gratia,* literally 'for the sake of example')

- Each culture has its own form of staged combat, <u>e.g.</u> Cornish wrestling, karate, kung-fu.

IMPLY / INFER

Imply (verb) (1) to state indirectly

- I don't like when I say 'honestly' – not to <u>imply</u> that I'm otherwise not honest. (Businessman Mark Parker)

Infer (verb) (1) to deduce

- I sometimes allow people to <u>infer</u> that I'm much less successful than I am. (Author Laura Lippman)

INCITE / INSIGHT

Incite (verb) (1) to stimulate action, to rouse, to stir up

- Dreams come true; without that possibility, nature would not <u>incite</u> us to have them. (Author John Updike)

Insight (noun) (1) an understanding of something

- A moment's <u>insight</u> is sometimes worth a life's experience. (Poet Oliver Wendell Holmes Sr)

LAY / LIE

Lay (verb) (1) to place something in a horizontal position, (2) the past tense of *to lie*

- If you <u>lay</u> pre-made and pre-sliced cookie-dough on a sheet and put it in the oven, you're not making homemade cookies.

- I <u>lay</u> in the bathtub thinking how wonderful it would to have a dog like Rin Tin Tin. (Diarist Anne Frank)

Lie (verb) (1) to be in a horizontal position, (2) to say something untrue in order to deceive

- When I feel like exercising I just <u>lie</u> down until the feeling goes away. (Philosopher Robert M Hutchins)
- Men are liars. We'll <u>lie</u> about lying if we have to. I'm an algebra liar. I figure two good lies make a positive. (Actor Tim Allen)

Lie (noun) (1) an intentionally false statement

- Art is a <u>lie</u> that makes us realise truth. (Artist Pablo Picasso)

LICENCE / LICENSE

Licence (noun) (1) a permit from an authority to do, to own, to use or to trade something

- A <u>licence</u> to practise law is not a licence to violate it. (Lawyer Loretta Lynch)

License (verb) (1) to authorise the use, performance or release of something

- You should have to <u>license</u> firearms, so the police can trace it if it's used in a crime. (Politician Michael D Barnes) (NB: Americans use *license* for both noun and verb.)

LOOSE / LOSE

Loose (adjective) [rhymes with noose](1) not tight, (2) free from constraint

- Critics suggested Meghan's gown looked too <u>loose</u> on her slim frame.
- When I open my mouth, all hell breaks <u>loose</u>. (Radio host Ed Schultz)

Lose (verb) [rhymes with snooze] (1) to fail to keep, (2) to fail to win, (3) to fail to make money

- The word 'happy' would <u>lose</u> its meaning if it were not balanced by sadness. (Psychiatrist Carl Jung)
- In football, you win as a group, you <u>lose</u> as a group, and you divide the credit and the blame. (Footballer Gianluigi Buffon)
- If I go solo, I could <u>lose</u> a fortune, but money is not important. (Singer Barry Gibb)

MAY BE / MAYBE

May be (phrase) (1) might be

- To the world you <u>may be</u> one person but to one person you may be the world. (Musician Taylor Hanson)

Maybe (adverb) (1) perhaps, possibly

- <u>Maybe</u> this world is another planet's hell. (Writer Aldous Huxley)

PAST / PASSED

Past (adjective) (1) referring to the time before the present

- A moral being is one who is capable of reflecting on his <u>past</u> actions. (Naturalist Charles Darwin)

Past (noun) (1) the time before the present
- I like the dreams of the future better than the history of the past. (President Thomas Jefferson)

Past (adverb) (1) beyond, having moved from one side of a reference point to the other
- Florence is like a movie set, full of teens with crinkly hair gliding past on Vespas. (Novelist Walter Kirn)

Past (preposition) (1) beyond, movement from one side of a reference point to the other
- If you live to be one hundred, you've got it made. Very few people die past that age. (Comedian George Burns)

Passed (verb) (1) the past tense of the verb *to pass*
- If I studied all my life, I couldn't think up half the number of funny things passed in one session of congress. (Actor Will Rogers)

PERSONAL / PERSONNEL

Personal (adjective) (1) private, individual
- Personality is the original personal property. (Writer Norman O Brown)

Personnel (noun) (1) staff, workforce
- We have the finest military personnel in the world. (Prime Minister Theresa May)

POISONOUS / VENOMOUS

Poisonous (adjective) (1) used to describe something that can cause death or injury if ingested or absorbed
- The poison-dart frog gets a deadly chemical called lipophilic alkaloid from consuming a poisonous food in the rainforest.

Venomous (adjective) (1) used to describe creatures that inject their victims with a toxin
- Around a quarter of all snake species are identified as being venomous.

PRACTICE / PRACTISE

Practice (noun) (1) repeated performance of an activity or skill to acquire or maintain proficiency in it
- An ounce of practice is worth more than tons of preaching. (Activist Mahatma Gandhi)

Practise (verb) (1) to do something regularly in order to acquire, improve or maintain proficiency in it
- The more you practise happiness, the better you get at it. (Director Joe Wright) (NB: Americans use practice for both noun and verb.)

PRINCIPAL / PRINCIPLE

Principal (adjective) (1) main
- The principal act of courage is to endure and withstand dangers rather than to attack them. (Saint Thomas Aquinas)

Principal (noun) (1) head of a department or a school
- You can have great teachers, but if you don't have a good <u>principal</u>, you won't have a good school. (Entrepreneur Eli Broad)

Principle (noun) (1) rule, belief, tenet, theory
- My name in Arabic means 'hope', so I suppose I have to live by that <u>principle</u>. (Actor Aml Ameen)

PROGRAM / PROGRAMME

Program (verb) (1) to electronically create or provide coded instructions for the automatic performance of a task
- My number-one piece of advice: Learn how to <u>program</u>. (Entrepreneur Mark Zuckerberg)

Program (noun) (1) a series of coded software instructions to control the operation of a computer
- I'm looking forward to a computer <u>program</u> winning the world chess championship. (Ethologist Richard Dawkins)

Programme (noun) (1) itinerary, TV or radio show, a collection of work projects
- When you've been on a <u>programme</u> called 'An Idiot Abroad', job offers aren't exactly flying in. (Television presenter Karl Pilkington)

(NB: Americans use *program* for the verb, noun and adjective.)

ROLE / ROLL

Role (noun) (1) an actor's portrayal of a character, (2) a job or function
- I'm not playing a <u>role</u>. I'm being myself, whatever the hell that is. (Actress Bea Arthur)
- She truly epitomised the <u>role</u> of a nurse.

Roll (noun) (1) a list (usually of names), (2) a piece of bread
- Three students missed <u>roll</u> call.
- A Doppelbrötchen comprises two bread <u>rolls</u> pressed together before baking.

Roll (verb) (1) to move by rotating, (2) to move on wheels, (3) to start
- Behind every great man is a woman <u>rolling</u> her eyes. (Actor Jim Carrey)
- Residents cheered from their windows as war tanks <u>rolled</u> past on the empty roads.
- <u>Roll</u> the camera!

SIGHT / SITE / CITE

Sight (noun) (1) vision (2) something that can be seen or is worth seeing.
- The only thing worse than being blind is having <u>sight</u> but no vision. (Author Helen Keller)
- It was a <u>sight</u> surpassing all precedent, and one we never dreamed of seeing. (Egyptologist Howard Carter)

Site (noun) (1) an area or location (usually a piece of land)
- Whenever I pass a building <u>site</u> or see somebody digging a ditch, I always think, 'That's real work.' (Actor Liam Neeson)

Site (verb) (1) to assign a position to
- They will <u>site</u> the new playground by the river.

Cite (verb) (1) to mention or to quote
- By 2007, 85% of Americans <u>cited</u> climate change as an important issue, compared with just 33% in prior years. (Engineer Jeffrey Skoll)

STATIONARY / STATIONERY

Stationary (adjective) (1) not moving
- Mountain-bike riding is much better than riding a <u>stationary</u> bike in the gym. (Tennis player Samantha Stosur)

Stationery (noun) (1) writing or office supplies
- Researchers polled 2,000 office workers and found half of them take pride in having nice <u>stationery</u>.

THEIR / THERE / THEY'RE

Their (possessive determiner) (1) belonging to them
- There are lots of people who mistake <u>their</u> imagination for <u>their</u> memory. (Writer Josh Billings)

There (adverb) (1) in, at or to that place or position
- I saw a mouse! Where? <u>There</u> on the stair! Where on the stair? Right <u>there</u>! A little mouse with clogs on. (Songwriter Myles Rudge)

They're (contraction) (1) contraction of *they are*
- I don't think anyone should write their autobiography until after <u>they're</u> dead. (Producer Samuel Goldwyn)

THEN / THAN

Then (adverb) (1) relates to time
- Get your facts first. <u>Then</u> you can distort them as you please. (Writer Mark Twain)

Than (conjunction) (1) used to introduce a comparison
- Never have more children <u>than</u> you have car windows. (Comedian Erma Bombeck)

TOO / TO

Too (adverb) (1) as well, (2) in excess
- I like making fun of myself a lot. I like being made fun of <u>too</u>. (Comedian John Mulaney)
- I am certain there is <u>too</u> much certainty in the world. (Author Michael Crichton)

To (preposition) (1) expresses motion (physical or metaphorical) in a direction
- Everything is funny, as long as it's happening <u>to</u> somebody else. (Actor Will Rogers)

To (infinitive marker) used to show the infinitive form of a verb
- Tact is the ability <u>to</u> describe others as they see themselves. (President Abraham Lincoln)